South Korean Golden Age Melodrama

Contemporary Approaches
to Film and Television Series

*A complete listing of the books in this series
can be found online at http://wsupress.wayne.edu*

General Editor
Barry Keith Grant
Brock University

Advisory Editors
Patricia B. Erens
School of the Art Institute of Chicago

Lucy Fischer
University of Pittsburgh

Peter Lehman
Arizona State University

Caren J. Deming
University of Arizona

Robert J. Burgoyne
Wayne State University

Tom Gunning
University of Chicago

Anna McCarthy
New York University

Peter X. Feng
University of Delaware

South Korean Golden Age MELODRAMA

Gender, Genre, and National Cinema

Edited by
Kathleen McHugh
and Nancy Abelmann

Wayne State University Press Detroit

Library of Congress Cataloging-in-Publication Data

South Korean golden age melodrama : gender, genre, and national cinema /
edited by Kathleen McHugh and Nancy Abelmann.
p. cm. — (Contemporary approaches to film and television series)
Includes bibliographical references and index.
ISBN 0-8143-3253-6 (pbk. : alk. paper)
1. Motion pictures—Korea (South) 2. Melodrama in motion pictures.
I. McHugh, Kathleen. II. Abelmann, Nancy. III. Series.
PN1993.5.K6S68 2005
791.43'09519—dc22
2004025723

Portions of Nancy Abelmann's essay, "Melodramatic Texts and
Contexts: Women's Lives, Movies, and Men," previously appeared
in *The Melodrama of Mobility: Women, Talk, and Class in
Contemporary South Korea* (University of Hawai'i Press, 2003).
Revised version reprinted here by permission of the publisher.

Kyung Hyun Kim's essay, "Lethal Work: Domestic Space and
Gender Troubles in *Happy End* and *The Housemaid*," previously
appeared in *The Remasculinization of Korean Cinema*
(Duke University Press, 2004). Reprinted here by permission
of the publisher.

Soyoung Kim's essay, "Questions of Woman's Film: *The Maid,
Madame Freedom*, and Women," previously appeared in
Post-Colonial Classics of Korean Cinema (Korean Film Festival
Committee, UCI, 1998). Reprinted here by permission of the
publisher.

ISBN-13: 978-0-8143-3253-5   ISBN-10: 0-8143-3253-6

Contents

Contents

Acknowledgments

In addition to all the contributors to the volume, the editors would like to thank a number of people whose insight and assistance greatly enhanced the realization of this book. A generous Pacific Rim grant from the University of California Office of the President funded a research trip to Seoul in 1998. Professor Hee Moon Cho facilitated our film viewing while we were there and was instrumental in the early phase of this book project. To Hye-young Jo, our deep gratitude for all her help during that research trip. We would like to thank the Korean Film Archives for making beautiful prints of these films available to us. Our Pacific Rim monies also funded an international conference, "From Hollywood to Han: South Korean Melodrama in a Global Context," held at the University of California Riverside Center for Ideas and Society where the ideas shaping this volume were first discussed. We are grateful to all the participants, many of whom are contributors to this volume. For their input and help in making that conference a great success, we would like to thank Professors Hee Moon Cho, Chungmoo Choi, Henry Em, and Chon Noriega as well as Walter Lew. Thanks also to Professor Kyung Hyun Kim for helpful information regarding the availability of the films discussed and his feedback on an early version of the Introduction. As the volume neared completion, Yoonjeong Shim did an outstanding job romanizing the Korean language. Kathleen McHugh would like to extend special thanks to several people. Jinsoo An provided crucial assistance with the planning of the Riverside conference. Together with his wife, Lee Soonjin, he also helped track down images, locate key research details, and secure permissions for the posters gracing the front and back covers. Hye Seung Chung has provided valuable information, ranging from the best places to rent Korean videos in Los Angeles to different types of diacritical marks. Finally, she would like to thank Chon Noriega for his ongoing support of the project from beginning to end. Nancy Abelmann extends her thanks to Ramona Curry, Hye-Seung Kang, Chung-kang Kim, and Jesook Song for their guidance in her continuing journey with Korean film.

Introduction: Gender, Genre, and Nation

NANCY ABELMANN
AND KATHLEEN MCHUGH

A husband and wife are in transit. He has recently quit his job as a police-man, and, with his sizeable severance pay, the two are traveling to the south-eastern coast of South Korea to start a business of their own. In her arms, the wife clutches the pocketbook that holds all of their money, their future. At a bus station, the wife chats with a stranger and only moments later realizes she has lost track of the pocketbook. Husband and wife search for it franti-cally, to no avail. Finally, they continue to the coast and take up peddling shellfish on the beach to feed their family. They barely get by. The husband takes a mistress and abandons the family. The wife is left dissolute and alone.

A South Korean veteran has sustained disabling injuries during the war, which prevent him from earning a livelihood. Although his fiancée still loves him and wishes to marry him, he sends her away, as he considers that he is no longer an appropriate match for her. The fiancée's family is in dire straits— her mother has gone mad; her brother cannot find work; her sister-in-law is ready to give birth. Desperate and having no other prospects, she takes to the streets to earn money as a prostitute for American GIs. Her first night out, she runs, half teasing, half terrified, from a U.S. soldier trying to pick her up. As she dashes across the street, she bumps into someone and knocks him down. It is the war veteran, her ex-fiancé, who has been struggling down the street on his crutches. As they look into each other's eyes, the American GI runs up to her. Devastated, the war veteran realizes what his fiancée has become.

A fatal moment organizes each of these scenarios. In the former, an instant of distraction instigates a life-altering reversal of fortune, sudden and irrevocable. In the latter, an unbelievable coincidence compounds

1

the misery provoked by desperate social circumstances and a woman's equally desperate choice. In all of their particulars, these two scenarios evidence certain qualities of melodrama: dramatic and sudden reversals, remarkable coincidence, pathos, and sensation. In each, precipitous falls—economic, social, and literal—take place within complex causal networks involving gender relations, cultural and economic structures, and the state. In each, this network is both dramatized and veiled by the focus on a calamitous event.

These two narratives are set in postwar South Korea, and though similar in dramatic structure and affective force, they derive from disparate sources and historical moments. The first anecdote is drawn from a 1990s ethnographic account in which an affluent South Korean woman described the fate that befell her sister in the aftermath of the Korean War (1950–53).[1] The second is taken from a classic of South Korean Golden Age melodrama, Yu Hyun-Mok's (Yu Hyŏn-mok) 1961 *The Stray Bullet* (*Obalt'an*), celebrated for its stark realism and artistic achievement. While the first recounts a private familial catastrophe from a female point of view, the second focuses on a masculine crisis that allegorizes the fate of the nation through the figure of a U.S. interloper and his sexual congress with a fallen, "public" woman. In each of these moments, the first an account of lived experience, the second a realistic cinematic fiction, melodramatic narration conveys the force of a specific historical trauma. The essays in this volume focus on South Korean Golden Age melodrama, a vibrant film movement spanning the years from 1955 to 1972, that arose in the traumatic historical circumstances brought about by the Korean War. We approach this film movement with an eye to the convergences suggested by these two gender-inflected anecdotes—between lived experience and cinematic fiction, between melodrama and history.

A Golden Interlude

In the immediate aftermath of the Korean War, the release of two enormously popular South Korean films, *Story of Chunhyang* (*Ch'unhyangjŏn*, 1955) and *Madame Freedom* (*Chayu puin*, 1956), signaled the beginning of what would come to be known as the Golden Age of South Korean cinema. By the end of the 1960s, the increasingly autocratic U.S.-supported dictatorship of Park Chung Hee (Pak Chŏng-hŭi) effected the demise of this efflorescence of cinematic creativity. During the brief period from 1955 to 1972, a number of South Korean directors produced a body of work as historically, aesthetically, and politically significant as that of other well-known national film movements such as Italian Neorealism, French

New Wave, and New German Cinema.[2] Yet unlike these other film movements, South Korean Golden Age film has been largely unknown in the West and is only now becoming available, most forcefully because of the rapid and remarkable emergence of South Korean cinema on a global stage into the twenty-first century.[3] The first impulse motivating this collection of essays, therefore, is to introduce readers to this remarkable body of Golden Age films as the antecedent of the current renaissance. Although critical work on contemporary South Korean cinema and directors is beginning to appear, currently no book-length study of South Korea's Golden Age films exists.[4]

Other considerations shape this collection as well. While a great deal of the work on melodrama in Hollywood has focused on representations of women within the "woman's film" or family melodrama, Western critical understandings of gender and genre cannot be lifted wholesale and imposed on other cinemas. Writing on Chinese political melodrama, Nick Browne advises that we must

> [M]ove toward a more specific account of the constitution, function and interpretation of these forms [that is, genre] as works functioning within the culture in which they originate . . . through an alternative to its familial focus, namely through the juridical. . . . In this way we might treat melodrama as an expression of a mode of injustice whose mise-en-scène is precisely the nexus between public and private life, a mode in which gender as a mark of difference is a limited, mobile term activated by distinctive social powers and historical circumstances.[5]

Browne finds the workings of Chinese political melodrama to suggest important new directions for the study of melodrama both in Asia and in the West. In this book we explore South Korean melodrama's use of gender for its variable articulations of political and cultural forces within a particular national imaginary in a distinct historical moment. In the South Korean films of this period, the crises of the nation manifest themselves in persistent gender and genre trouble. The essays in this volume, individually and taken together, seek to generate a portrait of Golden Age melodrama by combining textual analysis, reception, and historical/cultural context in order to render its historical, aesthetic, and political complexity.

Certain questions immediately arise. Is South Korean Golden Age melodrama truly distinct from Western cinema and its melodramatic tradition and if so, how? Or, was the postwar saturation of U.S. culture in South Korea so pervasive as to render any such assertion suspect? The answer to both questions may be yes. South Korean melodrama certainly does betray some of the generic features of melodrama noted above and exemplified by Hollywood's classical cinema. Peter Brooks, in his famous study of the melodramatic imagination, described a "modern aesthetic" characterized by "the effort to make the 'real' and the 'ordinary' and the 'private life' interesting through heightened dramatic utterance and gesture."[6] If this impulse characterizes melodrama in the West, then South Korean melodrama is somewhat distinct in the alignment or proximity between traumatic lived historical circumstance and melodramatic narrative. While both types of melodrama may well have transformed political, economic, and cultural conflicts into personal narrative, Hollywood's economic focus on regional, national, and international markets resulted in the systematic suppression of historical, political, and local detail in its classical cinema.[7] American studios wanted their product to play well in "all locales" and therefore studiously avoided any potentially provocative historical specificity in their selection of villainous characters or conflict. The result was a cinema that seemed to take place in familiar but unspecified places with plots that were mythic rather than politically or socially realistic or specific—a cinema that played well in South Korea, as it did across the globe.[8]

South Korean Golden Age melodrama suffered from no such compunctions or aspirations, and its consequent historical and social specificity provides a starting point for considering the distinctive features of this genre within its national context. Further, in postwar South Korea, the film industry had no need to *dramatize* private life so as to render it interesting and thereby to allegorize and "resolve" social contradictions. Rather, the South Korean variant of melodrama, with its plot reversals, cataclysmic coincidences, and seismic narrative compressions, seemed uniquely suited to rendering the nation's dramatic history and compressed modernity in the second half of the twentieth century.[9] That life in mid-twentieth-century Korea has been dramatic is lost on few observers of South Korean postwar history. Thus, instead of maintaining generic boundaries between the realistic and the melodramatic, between lived experience and fictional narrative, South Korean cinema construes melodrama as the most efficacious mode of realism. Before detailing the individual essays, we would like to give a broad sense of what was the "lived experience" in twentieth-century South Korea.

A Bitter Legacy

Japanese colonialism (1910–45) subjected Koreans to violence, humiliation, and mass displacements. By 1945, some 20 percent of the population was either abroad or in a Korean province different from that of their birth.[10] In the postcolonial era, the numbers of Koreans who would come to know the world beyond their villages grew even more dramatically: first with the 1948 partition of the country (into North and South); next with the profound dislocations (that is, exile) caused by the Korean War; and finally with rapid and irreversible urban proletarianization of vast numbers of South Korean women and men into the 1970s and beyond.[11]

South Korean history and its radical changes in the twentieth century have again and again inspired one resounding word—compressed.[12] The transformation of Korea from a traditional, primarily agrarian culture at century's beginning, to the modernized, divided, urban state at century's end took place at a dizzying pace. South Korea's experience of dislocation and compression had a particular character—of human misery and devastation. Bruce Cumings describes South Korea of the 1950s as "a terribly depressing place, where extreme privation and degradation touched everyone: Cadres of orphans ran through the streets . . . beggars with every affliction or war injury . . . half-ton trucks full of pathetic women careened onto [U.S.] military bases."[13] In addition to the physical and economic devastation, South Korea also experienced the political humiliation of being passed from one colonial power (Japan) to another (the United States). If immediate postwar Seoul was a city of the walking wounded,[14] so was it also an odd pastiche of a real and symbolic economy of American goods, language, money, and influence, all of which saturated the South Korean landscape, complicating any straightforward sense of national identity.[15]

The multiple ambiguities of postwar South Korea can perhaps best be captured by focusing on one of many key moments whose initial complexity has only been enhanced by subsequent historical developments— a moment at the temporal heart of Golden Age cinema. April 19, 1960, or 4-1-9 as it has come to be known, stands both for the outbreak of student protests against the Syngman Rhee (Yi Sŭng-man) regime (1948–60) as well as for the heavy-handed suppression of those struggles, which left over one hundred dead and nearly 1,000 wounded. Many developments, both positive and negative, led to this uprising. By the late 1950s, the Rhee regime had grown increasingly autocratic, a fact that had become more and more apparent, especially in the light of a stagnating economy.[16] Meanwhile, high school and college attendance had quadrupled between 1948 and 1960,[17] making for an intelligentsia fueled by democratic ideals as well as economic desires. Finally, there was conflict over revisions to tighten the already draconian national security law (that is, the legal arm of anticommunism); and considerable opposition to the prospect of a normalization treaty with Japan.[18]

The April 19, 1960, student uprisings were victorious in the most obvious sense: they toppled the regime. By the end of that April, Rhee took exile in Hawai'i, his refuge an overt indication of who and what (American aid and its graft economy) had been running the country under his aegis. The uprising bore fruit in the brief democratic regime of Chang Myŏn (1960–61), only then to be eviscerated by the military coup of Park Chung Hee on May 16, 1961. Park's regime combined staggering economic growth of world-historical dimensions (South Korea's "economic miracle") with a stunningly autocratic regime whose far-reaching ideological control resulted in unrivaled labor suppression and horrific working conditions.[19]

April 19, 1960, thus emerges as a historical marker that signals both victory and defeat. The date commemorates a successful, if very costly grassroots struggle for political and economic justice, for "Korea's Place in the Sun."[20] Yet, the uprising exacted significant casualties, and the hard-won democratic regime was tragically short-lived. Both the uprising and the Chang Myŏn presidency stand as a precarious interlude between the Rhee and Park presidencies. The popular struggle and democratic achievement of this historical moment do however index a legacy of dissent persisting through and in the aftermath of the colonial period, running through the Park, Chun Doo Hwan (Chŏn Tu-hwan, 1980–87) and subsequent regimes, and into the present.

The films discussed in this volume coalesce around 1960, either grappling with the complexity of this moment, or, in a few instances, evoking this historical time. The compressed, ambiguous, and fundamentally transnational social and political dramas of South Korea's recent history have inspired many of the contributors to contemplate the widespread appeal of particular film modes and aesthetics, especially that of melodrama. Rather than documenting the events of this historical moment, the melodramatic mode adopted in these films apprehends something of their lived impact in the pace, disorienting reversals, and affective excess of their narration. In this way, South Korean cinema infused the conventions of realism, melodrama, and generic classification itself with an ironic overlay based on the audiences' recent experiences.

Taken together, *The Stray Bullet,* celebrated as one of the crowning achievements of the Golden Age, and *Madame Freedom* (1956), a box-office hit, demonstrate this generic complexity and polysemy.

The Stray Bullet, a film that figures prominently in three chapters here (Eunsun Cho, Hye Seung Chung, and Keehyeung Lee), presents perhaps the bleakest, most realistic social portrait of immediate post–Korean War South Korea. The film was based on a 1958 story of the same title that was unsparing in its criticism of the Rhee regime. Subsequently filmed in the democratic Chang Myŏn era, this bleak cinematic portrayal was the result of fleeting artistic freedom.[21] No sooner was the film released, shortly after President Park's military coup, than it was banned.[22] Much as the democratic moment of its production, this film would come to stand for the hopes and struggles of the South Korean people on the eve of the coup. Tellingly, cinematic quality would deteriorate into the late 1960s and was finally eclipsed as the Park regime took its most autocratic shape with the 1972 *Yusin* (or restoration).

In its day, it was not *The Stray Bullet* that captured the popular imagination, but rather box office hits such as *Madame Freedom.* Where the Seoul of *The Stray Bullet* portrays abject suffering, the Seoul found in *Madame Freedom* is that of boutiques, cafés, restaurants, parks, and nightclub/dance halls.[23] If the 4-1-9 student protests were harbingers of fin-de-siècle democracy, no less does *Madame Freedom* speak to South Korea's transnational youth culture in the dawn of the twenty-first century.[24] But neither *Madame Freedom* nor *The Stray Bullet* can be easily categorized or contrasted. As Cho and Chung discuss in this volume, *The Stray Bullet* betrays its "realism"; likewise, *Madame Freedom* encodes, as Kathleen McHugh argues, the crises of its day. Where *The Stray Bullet* places the idea of "Liberation" (*haebang*) (the film's protagonists live in "Liberation Village") in ironic and indelible quotation marks, so does *Madame Freedom* do so for "freedom" (*chayu*). These ironies alter the conventional Manichean binaries of melodrama, and direct the narrative resolutions of this cinema toward more complex social commentary.

The Golden Age, Then and Now

While there is no doubt that South Korean cinematic melodrama derives in part from the example of Hollywood and other national cinemas, the writers in this book attempt to explore how "national specificity" comes to be marked in Golden Age cinema. Thus the individual films discussed don't easily reside within a stable or traditional notion of genre and its function. Rather, in these essays, genre, particularly melodrama, is doing many things, and national specificity emerges precisely in and as its theoretical and historical difficulty. Writing in 1984, Alan Williams called for genre studies to "get out of the United States,"[25] his comment signaling how profoundly the Hollywood cinema and the U.S. imaginary have operated as a tacit limit to academic genre study. In the case of South Korean melodrama, the U.S.'s significant political and cultural involvement and influence necessitate a critical engagement with this cinema that attests to the problems of the colonized national imaginary.

In Golden Age cinema the resulting complexities are "acted out" both through generic hybridity and referential specificity. Melodramatic narratives are rendered in starkly realist styles (*The Stray Bullet; Until the End of My Life* [*I saengmyŏng tahadorok*]); horror conventions are employed by domestic women's film (*The Housemaid* [*Hanyŏ*]); and the style of a woman's dress registers, with catastrophic simplicity, the inability of the nation to lay down its boundaries, to assume its identity free of transnational influence (*Madame Freedom; The Stray Bullet*). Kathleen McHugh's "South Korean Film Melodrama: State, Nation, Woman, and the Transnational Familiar" explores the latter problematic, aligning a discussion of the historical construction of "national cinemas" with the specific instance of the Golden Age. Noting the fundamentally self-conscious quality of this cinema as it attempted to imagine South Korea as both "emergent and divided," McHugh examines how filmic representations of femininity incorporate and dramatize this imagination. Reading the nightclub scene in *Madame Freedom*, McHugh notes that the homosocial and vaguely homoerotic dynamics shaping the relationships among the women in this film erupt in the gaze of Madame Freedom at a female dancer. The visual framing of, and more especially the musical accompaniment to this gaze, register the influence of Hollywood, but also, and more strikingly, of the contemporaneous *cabaretera* or dance hall film in Mexican cinema. Thus the problem posed by Madame Freedom's femininity is inextricably connected to what McHugh terms a "transnational familiar" that the film cannot do away with or resolve.

By contrast, Nancy Abelmann begins from the lived experience of two South Korean women who came of age during the Korean War in her "Melodramatic Texts and Contexts: Women's Lives, Movies, and Men." Using their life narratives, she analyzes the capacity of Golden Age melodrama to engage the moral imagination of a generation of South Korean women whose lives intersect with South Korea's compressed modernity.[26] In an essay that combines ethnographic reception and genre analysis, she argues that for these women, and this era of films, melodrama can be appreciated precisely for its capacity to articulate this imagination. Refusing to distinguish the melodramatic from the real, she suggests instead that this capacity is enlivened because viewers are inspired to take up the question of the distinction between the two for themselves. To demonstrate her point, Abelmann reads the Golden Age melodrama *Neighbor Pak* (*Pak sŏbang*) in conjunction with the personal narratives of the two women.

Taking the notion of imagination in a very different direction, Jin-soo An, in his "Screening the Redemption: Christianity in Korean Melodrama," suggests that for Golden Age cinema, melodrama is a "mode of imagination" consonant with South Korean "popular reasoning." An offer that, within South Korean culture, the Christian promise of salvation is another resonant and related mode of imagining. Christian redemption, he argues, seems "forced" on the surface of key Golden Age films; it jars, appearing as it does just in the moment of the "total disintegration" of these films' "moral economy." He suggests that we might think about South Korea's rapid postwar Christianization along similar lines. Much as he challenges ideas about melodrama, An also describes the "strongly sociological character" of Christian salvation in South Korea for the ways in which it articulates with extant social values as well as political ideologies. Typically, these motifs of Christian redemption are mobilized in ambivalent narrations of imperiled and sometimes fallen femininity.

Crossing genders, Eunsun Cho, in "*The Stray Bullet* and the Crisis of Korean Masculinity," draws our attention to a critically neglected aspect of this canonical Golden Age film—Hollywood's influence on it, notable in the action and film noir elements nested within its otherwise neo-realist mode. Cho describes these generic borrowings and allusions as "cinematic instants" that disrupt the documentary realism of the rest of the film and trouble its easy classification or reading. She offers a provocative analysis of these "instants" of action genres set against the otherwise bleak realism of the film. One such action sequence features a wounded war veteran who abandons the pretense of a "clean life," dreaming to "make it big" with a bank heist. Cho argues that this macho Hollywood moment offers a meta-commentary on South Korean film itself: the bank robbery fails, the action plot dissolves, and the film returns to the gritty world of immediate postwar South Korea. Within this complex narrative, Cho notes that the scopic structure of the film also persistently and symptomatically disallows the masculine gaze. Thus the master's (Hollywood's) filmic mode, visual regime, and generic conventions fail to resolve the crisis of postwar masculinity.

Hye Seung Chung's "Toward a Strategic Korean Cinephilia: A Transnational *Détournement* of Hollywood Melodrama" stages a complex, cross-cultural encounter between the traditions of Hollywood and South Korean melodrama. Noting Hollywood's impact on Golden Age film, she argues that rather than condemning this influence and South Korean audiences' general fascination with Hollywood melodrama as "a symptom of U.S. cultural imperialism," these cross-cultural relationships should be historicized within the postwar context. In her subsequent analysis, Chung notes both the broad contours as well as the textual particulars of South Korean cinephilia. Calculating the relative popularity of an array of Hollywood films from their box-office draw in South Korea, she observes that certain plots ("tragic romances") and stars captivated audiences there. Further, the Hollywood films popular in South Korea differ significantly from those canonized by U.S. film scholars and popular film classics lists alike. Blending reception data with cross-cultural textual analysis, Chung presents a compelling case study of transnational cinematic desire and appropriation.

Beginning with a contrast between Korean war films made in South Korea and those made in the United States, David Scott Diffrient makes a significant scholarly contribution to what has been a neglected genre in Golden Age cinema, the war film. Taking one important example, Sin Sang-ok's *Red Muffler* (*Ppalgan mahura*), he analyzes the text of this film, its director/auteur, and its star, the latter two both very important figures in Golden Age cinema. He finds the film exemplary of the Korean War genre's tendency toward generic blurring and complexity in the meeting it stages between the maternal melodrama and the war film. As Sin Sang-ok, the film's director, and Ch'oe Ŭn-hŭi, its female star, were both renowned for their work in the former genre, their very participation in *Red Muffler* complicated its generic signification. By simultaneously featuring both the war hero pilot and the melodramatic heroine (the widow-turned-prostitute of the pilot's former colleague) in both of its subplots, *Red Muffler* allows for what Diffrient terms a complex "dialogue between the sexes." Further, though the film diverges from the Hollywood war film in directly exposing women to the realities of war, it cites Hollywood and other Western images and icons, thus demonstrating "the remarkable visual literacy" of South Koreans, a legacy of their colonial past and postwar status.

The last three essays in this book relate the melodramas of the Golden Age to contemporary independent and mainstream cinema and television in South Korea. Soyoung Kim's "Questions of Woman's Film: *The Maid, Madame Freedom,* and Women" offers a gendered understanding of "women's film" for South Korean film generally and the Golden Age in particular. She argues that the Golden Age "woman's film" is in fact a 1990s invention. Understanding that those Golden Age films that catered to overwhelmingly female audiences appealed to a particular clientele— "*ajumma* (married women) in rubber shoes with handkerchiefs"—Kim argues that Golden Age cinema blended an appeal to a generic "woman," derived from its use of Hollywood conventions, to more local narrative codings that divided women by kinship roles, class status, and sexuality (for example, chaste widows, promiscuous maids, and such). Tracing this complicated textual address and reception through the example of several films, she finishes her analysis by contrasting contemporary feminist films about the "comfort women" (sex workers mobilized by the Japanese colonial state),[27] with Golden Age melodramas' representations of "Western princesses" (*yanggongju,* sex workers servicing American GIs),[28] underscoring the institutional, infrastructural, and ideological structures that link these two histories.[29]

Turning to contemporary popular cinema, Kyung Hyun Kim focuses on the emergence of a new generation of South Korean filmmakers with the dawn of the twenty-first century, a generation both able and inclined to cite from Golden Age melodrama. He traces how the domestic space in *Happy End* (*Haep'i endŭ,* 1999) updates and renovates the representation of that space in *The Housemaid* (1960). In so doing, he finds the gendered signature of two crisis moments in postcolonial South Korean history: the 4-1-9 Student Revolution (1960) and the IMF Debt Crisis (1997–2001). The claustrophobia of the mise-en-scène and the violence that troubles the domestic in each film, blending conventions of melodrama and horror, reference the respective financial crises of each historical moment, in each case pinning blame on women who work outside the home. If, according to Cho's analysis of Hollywood citation in *The Stray Bullet,* South Koreans must no longer screen recovery with the masters' tools, the historical moment defining *Happy End* presents an ironic juncture: the new dawn of South Korean film takes place just as global neoliberal political, economic, and symbolic economies have colonized South Korea. The timing of South Korea's IMF Debt Crisis (and the largest World Bank bailout in history—a national humiliation to South Koreans) seems uncanny: just as South Korea elected its first truly dissident president in 1997, it had to tend to the socially conservative dictates of the World Bank bailout, many of which seemed to turn the clock backwards in terms of gender equity and social distribution.[30] Kim finds the telling of this national crisis in the uses made by a contemporary film of the tropes of Golden Age melodrama.

Finally, Keehyeung Lee brings the question of genre in the 1990s to television, reading the prime-time serial *Morae sigye* (*Hour Glass*) against the grain of the melodramatic television drama. He argues that this series is generically hybrid, citing as it does the Hong Kong action film, the Hollywood gangster/buddy film, and what he dubs "social melodrama." His analysis indicates the ways that this TV series both unsettles and reinstates elements of classical Golden Age melodrama. Lee asserts that it is precisely the serial's allegiance to melodramatic convention that accounts for its enormous popularity—a remarkable popularity given its bleak focus on the bloody suppression of the 1980 Kwangju Uprising on the eve of the military takeover of Chun Doo Hwan. For its historical focus, *Hour Glass* is indisputably progressive. Lee, however, resists easy celebration; considering the series in the context of South Korea's rapidly expanding media market with its "'halo' of live coverage," he asserts that the series' "social melodrama" is compromised. With an argument about media and temporality that echoes points made by An and Diffrient, Lee concludes that through its manipulation of melodramatic conventions, television is profoundly presentist even as it seems to recuperate the past.

Conclusion

Although the Golden Age of South Korean cinema has no definitive ending, film censorship under Park, the influx of television, and increased market liberalization impoverished the industry. Film freedom, quality, and audience deteriorated in the 1970s, the nadir of South Korean film history. Indeed, as Kyung Hyun Kim observes, "None of the celebrated Golden Age filmmakers had survived the absurdity of the '70s."[31] Most dramatically, Sin Sang-ok, director of several of the films discussed in this volume (*Hell Flower* [*Chiokhwa*], *The Houseguest and My Mother, Red Muffler,* and *Until the End of My Life*), "mysteriously disappeared" to be found later in North Korea where he directed many films; in 1988 he returned to South Korea.[32] True to this story of South Korea's preeminent director, it is no exaggeration to say that Golden Age cinema is itself a product of the so-called division system; the Golden Age was nothing if not deeply political.

At the moment in which we write this introduction, South Korea has only quite recently (2001) declared the IMF Debt Crisis "over." Meanwhile many in South Korea remain unconvinced. For starters, South Korea remains a cold war flash point and neoliberal reforms have compromised much popular progressive vision. With the hindsight of the new century, the mid-1990s emerge as a small but remarkable cultural/political moment, the subsequent potential of the Kim Dae Jung regime (Kim Tae-jung, 1997–2002) curbed by the IMF. It was in the mid-1990s that a new age of film dawned. And as Kyung Hyun Kim argues, it is only later in the decade that an even younger generation of directors, basking in newfound political freedoms and cultural confidence, discovered anew the Golden Age cinema.

That these directors, however, came of artistic age in the midst of yet another national crisis is revealing. Gender, genre, and nation, reminiscent of the Golden Age cinema, are troubled. We predict that South Koreans will continue to rediscover Golden Age cinema and that a vibrant cinematic conversation with these films will enliven contemporary filmmaking. With this volume we too seek a conversation on a national film movement whose expression and context are as timely as they were in their own Golden Age.

Notes

1. See Nancy Abelmann, *The Melodrama of Mobility: Women, Talk, and Class in Contemporary South Korea* (Honolulu: University of Hawai'i Press, 2003).
2. An abundance of research on these film movements exists, including for Italian Neorealism: André Bazin, *What Is Cinema?* vol. 2 (Berkeley: University of California Press, 1971), 1–101; Peter Bondanella, *Italian Cinema: From Neorealism to the Present* (New York: Unger, 1983); Millicent Marcus, *Italian Film in the Light of Neorealism* (Princeton: Princeton University Press, 1986). For French New Wave: Peter Graham, ed., *The New Wave* (Garden City, NY: Doubleday, 1986); Jim Hillier, *Cahiers du Cinéma: 1960–1968, New Wave, New Cinema, Reevaluating Hollywood* (Cambridge: Harvard University Press, 1986); James Monaco, *The New Wave: Truffaut, Godard, Chabrol, Rohmer, Rivette* (Oxford: Oxford University Press, 1976). For New German Cinema: Timothy Corrigan, *New German Film: The Displaced Image* (Austin: University of Texas Press, 1983); Thomas Elsaesser, *New German Cinema* (New Brunswick, NJ: Rutgers University Press, 1989); Eric Rentschler, *West German Film in the Course of Time* (Bedford Hills, NY: Redgrave, 1984).
3. South Korean Golden Age films have been the subject of several high-profile film festivals, most notably Post-Colonial Classics of Korean Cinema held in Irvine, California in 1998.

4. See the very important collection on one of South Korea's most distinguished directors, *Im Kwon Taek: The Making of a Korean National Cinema*, ed. David E. James and Kyung Hyun Kim (Detroit: Wayne State University Press, 2002) and Hyangjin Lee's *Contemporary Korean Cinema: Identity, Culture, Politics* (Manchester: Manchester University Press, 2000).

5. Nick Browne, "Society and Subjectivity: On the Political Economy of Chinese Melodrama," in *New Chinese Cinemas: Forms, Identities, Politics* (Cambridge: Cambridge University Press, 1994), 42–43.

6. Peter Brooks, *The Melodramatic Imagination* (New Haven: Yale University Press, 1976), 14.

7. Robert Ray argues that Classical Hollywood cinema's "thematic conventions rested on a . . . consensus [that] dictated the conversion of all political, social, and economic dilemmas into personal melodramas." See Robert Ray, *A Certain Tendency of the Hollywood Cinema* (Princeton: Princeton University Press, 1985), 57. His thesis is reiterated in a materialist vein in Ruth Vasey's *The World According to Hollywood, 1918–1939* (Madison: University of Wisconsin Press, 1997). Vasey asserts that Hollywood's dominance in the international market after World War I "depended at least in part on its ability to convince its foreign customers that its output was inoffensive and ideologically neutral," 3–4.

8. Vasey, *World According to Hollywood*, 44–45, 115–19.

9. Chang Kyung-Sup, "Compressed Modernity and Its Discontents: South Korean Society in Transition," *Economy and Society* 28, no. 1 (1999): 30–55.

10. See Bruce Cumings, *Divided Korea: United Future?* (Ithaca, NY: Foreign Policy Association, Headline Series, 1995), 25.

11. Hagen Koo, *Korean Workers: The Culture and Politics of Class Formation* (Ithaca, NY: Cornell University Press, 2001). See also Bruce Cumings, *Korea's Place in the Sun: A Modern History* (New York: W. W. Norton, 1997), 301.

12. Chang Kyung-Sup, "Compressed Modernity and Its Discontents"; Cho Hae-Joang, "'You Are Entrapped in an Imaginary Well': The Formation of Subjectivity Within Compressed Development—A Feminist Critique of Modernity and Korean Culture," *Inter-Asia Cultural Studies* 1, no. 1 (2000): 49–69; Koo, *Korean Workers*.

13. Cumings, *Korea's Place in the Sun*, 303.

14. Chong-un Kim, introduction to *Postwar Korean Short Stories: An Anthology*, ed. Chong-un Kim (Honolulu: University of Hawai'i Press, 1983), vii–xxxviii.

15. Cumings, *Korea's Place in the Sun*, 255.

16. John Lie, *Han Unbound: The Political Economy of South Korea* (Stanford: Stanford University Press, 1998), 33.

17. Cumings, *Korea's Place in the Sun*, 339.

18. Ibid., 343; Lie, *Han Unbound*, 36.

19. Koo, *Korean Workers*.

20. Cumings, *Korea's Place in the Sun*.

21. Hyangjin Lee, *Contemporary Korean Cinema*.

22. Young-il Lee, *The History of Korean Cinema: Main Currents of Korean Cin-*

ema, trans. Richard Lynn Greever (Seoul: Motion Picture Promotion Corporation, 1988), 145.

23. Chungmoo Choi suggests that the urbanized mise-en-scène of this film "erases the image of the war-devastated landscape." Chungmoo Choi, "The Magic and Violence of Modernization in Post-Colonial Korea," in *Post-Colonial Classics of Korean Cinema,* ed. Chungmoo Choi (Irvine, CA: Korean Film Festival Committee, UCI, 1998), 6.

24. See Stephen Epstein, "Anarchy in the UK, Solidarity in the ROK: Punk Rock Comes to Korea, *Acta Koreana* 3 (July 2000): 1–34.

25. Alan Williams, "Is a Radical Genre Criticism Possible?" *Quarterly Review of Film Studies* 9, no. 2 (Spring 1984): 121–25.

26. See Abelmann, *Melodrama of Mobility.*

27. See Chunghee Sarah Soh, "From Imperial Gifts to Sex Slaves," *Social Science Japan Journal* 3, no. 1 (2000): 1–33.

28. See Katharine Moon, *Sex among Allies: Military Prostitution in U.S.-Korea Relations* (New York: Columbia University Press, 1997).

29. See John Lie, "The Transformation of Sexual Work in Twentieth Century Korea," *Gender and Society* 9 (1995): 310–27.

30. Jesook Song, "*Shifting Technologies: Neoliberalization of the Welfare State in South Korea, 1997–2001*" (PhD diss., University of Illinois at Urbana-Champaign, 2003); Byung-Kook Kim, "The Politics of Crisis and a Crisis of Politics: The Presidency of Kim Dae-Jung," in *Korea Briefing, 1997–1999: Challenges and Change at the Turn of the Century,* ed. Kongdan Oh (Armonk, NY: M. E. Sharpe, 2000), 35–74.

31. Kyung Hyun Kim, "Korean Cinema and Im Kwon-Taek: An Overview," in *Im Kwon-Taek: The Making of a Korean National Cinema,* ed. D. E. James and K. H. Kim (Detroit: Wayne State University Press, 2002), 32.

32. Ibid.

South Korean Film Melodrama:
State, Nation, Woman, and the Transnational Familiar

KATHLEEN MCHUGH

Nations arise from interactions, whether material or discursive. The nation, as nation-state, says no; it defines its contours by negation, articulating who is not a citizen, what acts are forbidden, where its territory and authority begin and end, what freedoms will be taken away from those who transgress its laws, and what limits will shape the flow of currency, traffic, and communications.[1] Yet the state's negations coincide and overlap with the affirmative interactions that comprise the nation as homeland, interactions that involve knowledge, imagination, memory, and identification. These affirmative interactions shape the citizens' experience of national culture, among other things. But the presumably unique components that make up that experience tend only to become salient, visible, and identifiable in encounters with that which is alien, other to it. For instance, we learn what is "unique" about our own culture when we travel abroad or otherwise encounter different cultural practices; the structure and grammatical particularities of our mother tongue only become evident when we study or learn a second language. As with any other identity, we understand our national identity and who we are as a nation through historically contingent and variable interactions wherein we encounter, identify, and name what we are not.

In this essay, I would like to consider South Korean cinema as an instance of a national cinema from this perspective: as a complex and contradictory entity usually only identified and affirmed in encounters with and negations of that which it is not. These encounters traverse personal, economic, political, aesthetic, intellectual, and international fields and concerns, and include, of course, encounters between film scholars and films. As such, I must first define my own position. I am a U.S.-born and -educated film scholar, trained in a version of world cinema that, marked by the various economic and international exigencies of a specific histor-

17

ical moment (1980s), did not include exposure to Korean cinema. Further, I do not speak, read, or understand the Korean language. Yet rather than being deterred by my ignorance, I would rather propose it as an exemplary component of knowledge production concerning other national cinemas: that the insights generated about Korean cinema or any other national cinema can only derive from error, or better, from what is not familiar to the non-national film scholar, from what s/he does not know.

First Contact

Over dinner several years ago, East Asian anthropologist Nancy Abelmann told me about her work with a group of South Korean women who had come of age right after the Korean War. As they remembered the period, they repeatedly invoked a group of South Korean and American film melodramas that, as she explained to me, "somehow resonated with the quotidian reality and the imagination of these women's youth; with equal verve they recalled the films and the drama of their own lives in those times."[2] While the Korean films the women referenced were contemporaneous, produced and exhibited in the 1950s and 1960s, the Hollywood films dated from the 1930s and 1940s and were just being shown in South Korea for the first time. Thus the ethnography that Abelmann was conducting involved an encounter between Classical Hollywood cinema and the Golden Age of South Korean cinema (1955–72) in the cultural imaginary of these women.[3]

As the Golden Age was precipitated by Korea's liberation from Japanese occupation, it provides both an exemplary and provocative instance of a national cinema for a number of reasons. First, Golden Age South Korean cinema was self-consciously engaged in imagining and narrating South Korea as an emergent and divided nation and one now dominated by a Western power. Second, the claims of the state, in the form of Park Chung Hee's [Pak Chŏng-hŭi] enforcement of censorship laws in 1972, ultimately curtailed, for a time, this national imagining. Third, the divided nation of Korea was embedded in cold war politics, out of which our contemporary sense of the nation emerged. Finally, this historical period was also the one in which film studies, including the study of national cinemas, emerged as a viable scholarly discipline in U.S. universities.

Yet this moment of emergence must be placed in relation to the moment of encounter and reception thirty years later that ultimately generated the essays in this volume. The changing character of the U.S.

academy and its emphasis on interdisciplinary and cultural studies research provided the context wherein a dinner conversation between colleagues and friends in very different disciplines became a viable research project. The University of California's interest in developing ties with Asia and East Asia led to the funding of this project via a Pac Rim grant. This grant and this interest derives from a more pervasive and recent example of what Rey Chow calls "western European and North American fascination with East Asian cinema,"[4] itself perhaps a complex part of or reaction to the contradictory priorities of a millennial moment characterized by globalization, multinational corporations, and the United States' intransigent, unilateral investment in its own imperial brand of nationalism. While the fascination of which Chow speaks is for contemporary Asian cinema, in this volume's fascination with the Golden Age, there is perhaps a nostalgia for the idea of nation and national cinema as resistant, as emergent under conditions of duress, as a perceptible if wholly ephemeral coalescence of two utterly different orders of representation—material and symbolic.

It is fitting then that my first encounter with South Korean cinema had to do with a genre or mode generated from issues of representation and duress. Abelmann described her research to me because of my scholarly work on Classical Hollywood melodrama and domestic labor. As she told me the plots of the Golden Age films, what struck me immediately was their overt attention to women's work and their relationships with money, class, and economic value, a range of concerns generally suppressed by or subsumed within romantic and emotional issues in Classical Hollywood cinema, especially after the institution of the Production Code in 1933. Rather than highlighting connections between the emotional and economic, American melodrama tends to use femininity to mystify class issues.[5] But, as the films themselves amply demonstrated, *working women* women in South Korean melodramas during this period, though abject in the areas of love and romance, nevertheless possess valued economic agency and power—they work, they make money, often enough to save homes, lives, and social status.[6]

Thus I first meaningfully encountered South Korea not as a nation, per se, but via a film genre—melodrama—and my own research priorities: in what I perceived to be a different and comparably stronger construction of femininity in its South Korean variant than in that of the Hollywood cinema with which I was familiar.[7] Several factors contributed to this perception. The first was that, in this body of films, the significance of women's relationships with other women frequently exceeds that of their relationships with men.[8] The second was that the plots of these films often featured women who were more ambitious and economically savvy than their husbands. Finally, the women's economic skills, their labor, and their employment were foregrounded and generally valued in these films rather than being demonized, rendered abject, or adversely compared to emotional and leisure pursuits as women's economic involvement frequently was in Classical Hollywood melodramas.[9] Consequently, the difference in narrative constructions of femininity became a primary, salient component of what I perceived South Korean cinema to be.

The Question of National Cinema

Since the early years of silent cinema, national film industries have existed nearly everywhere. But the economic, industrial, and social conditions that shape critical and theoretical understandings of national cinema began after World War I.[10] The devastation of Europe resulted in Hollywood cinema's rise to international dominance, a position this industry has held ever since. This dominance, though predicated on economics, technology, and issues relating to the state, registers most forcefully in film criticism as an issue of nationalized aesthetics. As one writer on the Hollywood cinema observes:

> By also dominating the international market (which most critics date from 1919 onwards), the American cinema insured that for the vast majority of the audience, both here and abroad, Hollywood's Classic Period films would establish the definition of the medium itself. Henceforth, different ways of making movies would appear as aberrations from some "intrinsic essence of cinema" rather than simply as alternatives to a particular form that had resulted from a unique coincidence of historical accidents—aesthetic, economic, technological, political, cultural, and even geographic.[11]

Early on, these aberrations were assimilated to the cinematic canon primarily as aestheticized or high art alternatives to Hollywood's mass culture norms. Later, the distinctions became politicized.

Significantly, these assimilations have proceeded largely under the aegis of nations:

1. The international avant-gardes of the 1920s, critically and historically categorized as *French* surrealism and impres-

[handwritten in left margin: Hollywood form / the dominant form]

20

sionism, *German* Expressionism, and *Soviet* Montage.

2. The national cinemas and national film movements whose identity as such was facilitated by international film festivals that came to prominence after World War II, a circuit that "invests in and promotes the discovery of new national cinemas."[12]

Yet the award structure of these festivals designated prize-winning films, by definition, as exceptional products of their respective nations, produced by master auteurs: in Japan by Yasujiro Ozu, Kenji Mizoguchi, and Akira Kurosawa; in India by Satyajit Ray; in Mexico, by Luis Buñuel. This structural imbrication of aesthetics and nationalism, while providing very limited international access to a very small number of films from nations other than the United States, nevertheless reified Hollywood's normative and dominant position, while also insuring that the products of other national cinemas would be selected and would circulate as "art" cinema rather than as narratives in direct competition with Hollywood products. Meanwhile, certain film movements, emerging initially in Europe after World War II, designated national contributions to world cinema less securely anchored to specific, exceptional auteurs, but to shared vision, style, and means of production. Examples of these more politically inflected national film groups include, in rough chronological order: Italian Neorealism, French New Wave, Brazilian Cinema Novo, and New German Cinema.

In the 1980s and 1990s, the festival scene came to include pan-African, Latin American, and Asian events. Yet the international festival circuit continued to formulate an equation between access and aesthetics, wherein the economic and industrial apparatuses of the state that provided for or limited access were masked by, even as they shaped, a structurally exceptionalist aesthetics. Film studies since the 1960s has generally accepted this exceptionalist criteria as that which identifies the nation in various national cinemas. Thus the concepts and methodologies articulated by film theorists and historians concerning national cinemas, national film movements, Classical Hollywood cinema, Third World Cinema, political, commercial, and aesthetic cinemas and so on frequently depend upon problematic and unexamined ideas of nations that derive from cold war politics and understandings of national designations from the 1960s: First, Second, and Third World nations.

Many postcolonial critics are now indicating what has been left out of these accounts. Among the omissions are: the lateral relations among

21

non-U.S. film industries—for example, between India and the former Soviet Union, among the cinemas of Latin America, or in the more fraught relationship between the Japanese and Korean film industries; the vibrancy, reach, and power of non-U.S. film industries and their self-articulation within a global context that tends to be suppressed in the Hollywood/other dyad.[13] Finally, film studies has, until recently, tended to ignore the state's role in the formation of national film culture via economic, political, and technological opportunities and constraints.[14]

Within this critical historical scenario, the cinemas of Korea, Germany, and Vietnam pose a unique and substantial challenge to conventional formulations of national cinemas. The reason? Because their cinemas are or were state cinemas within nations whose land, government, and cultural imaginary have been forcibly divided. In each case, the cold war politics that gave rise to contemporary formations of the nation and its manifestations in film and other culture industries also resulted in the division of these nations at the behest of the two camps of the cold war. Thus South Korean cinema, until very recently a cinema whose films were unavailable internationally, constitutes itself within these divisions (of the state and the nation and of the nation with itself) and within global political and aesthetic relations of influence (especially with the United States) that film-studies scholarship and its focus on nationalized aesthetics has been structured to ignore.

In my reception of these films, the symptom of difference that I perceived in (and as) South Korean cinema, that of femininity and, in more general terms, of gender, resonates with the incommensurate division at the heart of South Korean cultural production: the loss of a unified, if fundamentally illusory national identity, for which the negations and constraints of the state are endured. This effect is particularly pronounced in Golden Age films. A brief survey of the major films produced during this period reveals that none feature a strong male protagonist. Rather, a predominant number of films have female protagonists, frequently with children, whose husbands are: absent (*The Houseguest and My Mother/Sarangbang sonnim kwa ŏmŏni; Home Is Where the Heart Is/Maŭm ŭi kohyang; Bitter but Once Again/Miwŏdo tasi hanbŏn*), or impotent (*The Housemaid/Hanyŏ; My Life; The Stray Bullet/Obalt'an*). In those films that do feature a patriarch, he is represented as an endearingly humorous and pathetic anachronism (*The Coachman/Mabu; Mr. Pak/Pak sŏbang; Romance Papa/Romaensŭppappa*).[15] The lack of strong male characters operates as a structuring absence in these films—the

no strong male protags

tragic, empty center that not only wreaks havoc in the lives of women, children, and the social order but also provides the context in which women take up economic agency.[16]

The crisis of national division and the economic and social problems of the postwar years, frequently dealt with explicitly in these narratives, together with the absence of masculine agency, shape the femininity and gender relations within them. In this particular historical moment, Golden Age films articulate a very specific national allegory in melodramatic constructions of femininity. Many critics have made this point.[17] I want to push the issue somewhat further, indicating how the Golden Age construction of femininity and gender borrows from yet alters the Euro-American dynamics of melodrama, while also revealing the illusory character of distinct national cultures and cinemas.

Genre Difference

Although European and American literary and film critics debate whether melodrama is a mode, an imagination, or a genre, all agree that it has had extraordinary reach and power in popular culture in the West. Linda Williams asserts: "[M]elodrama is a peculiarly democratic and American form that seeks dramatic revelation of moral and emotional truths through a dialectic of pathos and action. It is the foundation of the classical Hollywood movie."[18] Williams summarizes the critical tradition on Euro-American melodrama, listing its most salient features: character and action are construed within emotional and moral registers, rather than those of psychology or realism; spectators side with and feel sympathy for virtuous victims who confront forces larger than they are; the narrative is above all constructed to reveal innocence, whether the character possessing that innocence is saved or lost.[19] Peter Brooks argues that melodrama seeks above all to make moral principles clear and accessible to everyone. Coming to prominence in the wake of the Enlightenment and the consequent loss of the sacred, melodrama "represents both the urge toward resacralization and the impossibility of conceiving sacralization other than in personal terms."[20] Thus melodrama articulates the social, economic, and political in the register of the private and the personal. The genre emphasizes moral polarities with clear distinctions between good and evil over nuance, complexity, and subtlety; it fosters affective identification rather than considered analysis. Its narrative focus on clarity and the personal finds spectacular expression in the American cinema's emphasis on continuity and closure. Classic Hollywood's conventional narrative trajectories and resolutions usually leave no doubt or questions about who is the good guy, the bad guy, and what the ending means.

In South Korean melodramas of the Golden Age, many of these conventions are in evidence; however, the emphasis on moral clarity (who is "good" and "innocent" and who is "evil") and on continuity and closure are attenuated in favor of a somewhat different articulation of the melodramatic ethos.[21] This difference hinges on Golden Age cinema's evaluation of leisure and labor, which I will discuss below, and how these values influence the distinction between public and private life. Critics have frequently noted American melodrama's proclivity for converting all political and social problems into personal ones that then are more easily resolved.[22]

By contrast, in Golden Age melodramas, personal frustration becomes the basis for interpersonal identification that is at once familial, social, and political. For example, in Yu Hyŏn-mok's 1961 *The Stray Bullet,* the plight of a group of Korean War veterans, one crippled, all impoverished, opens up a matrix of social and economic connections all adversely affected by the war and its aftermath. In just one of these subplots, a veteran breaks off his engagement to a woman who is part of a formerly North Korean family because he cannot support her. Out of despair and her family's desperate economic need, she becomes a prostitute who services American GIs. Made in the same year, but set in the 1920s, Sin Sang-ok's *The Houseguest and My Mother* aligns the fates of two widows—the protagonist, a well-born woman, and her maid—whose very different class identities dictate whether they can (the maid) or cannot (the well-born woman) remarry. Standards of behavior are thereby articulated apropos of a class structure rather than a moral one. This drama is played out in relation to three generations of women—the protagonist, her daughter, and her mother-in-law—whose kinship duties and structure are depicted as shaping the social world of a certain class of women.

Consistently these films encompass and interrelate injuries and inequities relating to national division, class division, gender division, and property division. Thus Golden Age melodramatic expression documents the formation or destruction of relationships, affinities, and community as a response to shared victimization rather than revealing innocence made manifest within the personal and embodied in exemplary individuals. The causes of this shared victimization range from mothers-in-law and repressive gender codes to the state and the economy, forces that are often at odds with one another and not resolved in pat or moralistic narrative endings. The sense of vulnerability that emerges has much less to do with individual morality and metaphysical clashes that shape the meaning of the material world than it does with an unrelenting emphasis on the fallibility of human social and political systems and their sometimes nefarious effects on human relations and communities. *systems & their human effects*

An understanding of Golden Age South Korean film and its melodramatic applications provides a model for a comparative, transnational approach to national cinema, which includes the machinations of the state in aesthetic considerations. Rather than essentializing an idea of the nation related to national identity, this approach foregrounds sociohistoric and economic context in the analysis of an aesthetic genre. Further, Golden Age cinema's melodramatic ethos testifies to the absence of that which in Euro-American cinemas is an unarticulated backdrop, illusory and mythological: the idea of a unified and autonomous nation.[23]

Gender, Genre, and the Nation: Golden Age Films

In reconceptualizing South Korean melodrama, I would like to have it both ways: first, to consider these narratives as different from Hollywood melodrama in certain distinct ways; and second to suggest the global network of cultural influences within which South Korean cinema imagined itself via femininity in the 1950s and 1960s. If the state says "no" and the nation "yes," I want to explore the ambivalence that necessarily arises in postcolonial self-representations and encounters, an ambivalence registered and represented much more forcefully in South Korean cinema because of its unique position within the cold war and its national fictions. While the postwar South Korean cinema constitutes an exemplary instance of this ambivalence, so does, in a very different way, my own recent encounter with this very cinema. As a product of U.S. education and of U.S. academic film studies, I knew little about Korea, much less Korean cinema, deficits that fueled my sense of the uniqueness and universality of Hollywood melodrama. Thus my entry point to the difference of Korean cinema—what I don't know—interacts with what in South Korean melodrama is marked as other, as not-Korean; this interaction becomes the place where cultural perceptions of identity are formulated.

The canonical films from the Golden Age period include: *The Public Prosecutor and the Teacher* (Yun Tae-ryong, 1948), *Home Is Where the Heart Is* (Yun Yong-gyu, 1948), *Madame Freedom* (Han Hyŏng-mo, 1956), *Hell Flower* (Sin Sang-ok, 1958), *Til the End of My Life* (Sin Sang-ok, 1960), *The Housemaid* (Kim Ki-yŏng, 1960), *Mr. Pak* (1960), *The Coachman* (1961) (both Kang Tae-jin), *The Sea Village* (Kim Su-yong,

1964), *The Houseguest and My Mother* (Sin Sang-ok, 1961), *The Stray
Bullet* (Yu Hyŏn-mok, 1961), *The Mist* (Kim Su-yong, 1967), *Bitter but
Once Again* (Chŏng So-yŏng, 1968), and *Three Singmo Sisters* (Kim
Hwa-rang 1969). These films easily fall into gendered categories—those
that focus on female protagonists and issues (*The Public Prosecutor and
the Teacher, Home Is Where the Heart Is, Madame Freedom, Hell Flower,
The Housemaid,* and *The Houseguest and My Mother*) and those that focus
on male protagonists (*Mr. Pak, The Coachman, The Stray Bullet,* and *The
Mist*). Of these films, those that showed the most pronounced stylistic
and narrative influence of internationally renowned film movements and
auteurs were films concerning male protagonists: *The Coachman, The
Stray Bullet* (Italian Neorealism/De Sica/*Bicycle Thief*), and *The Mist*
(Antonioni, *L'Avventura*). *The Coachman* was also the only film to win a
prize in an international film festival (the Silver Bear at the 1961 Berlin
International Film Festival) during this period.

The films featuring female protagonists were at once more emphatically melodramatic and more stylistically conventional. Film scholar Hee
Moon Cho observes that while films such as *The Stray Bullet* received critical acclaim, they tended to be much less popular than the controversial
Madame Freedom, which "was a huge box-office success" as were other
films geared toward female audiences, such as the more traditional and
"very Korean" *Home Is Where the Heart Is* and *The Houseguest and My
Mother.*[24] This type of breakdown is a typical gendering of high/low art.
What I would like to consider is how the nation, class, property, and gender are configured and interrelated in one of the first and most popular
melodramatic films directed at a female audience in this period. My reading will be based on the two interrelated negations and encounters I
noted at the beginning of this essay: my perception of the difference of
femininity in this film; and that which within the film is designated as not-
Korean.

My reading will also take into account the subject of melodrama in
an international setting. Insofar as I see women in South Korean cinema
as possessing more economic and productive agency and sharing more
profound homosocial bonds with one another than women in Hollywood cinema, South Korean melodrama of this period shares something with the female protagonists of Mexican cinema's Golden Age
(1930s–50s). Mexican melodramatic heroines also are possessed of narrative agency and importance that exceeds that of female protagonists in
Hollywood cinema. Although the examples and narrative paradigms of
Mexican and Korean melodramas are in some ways very different from

each other, they share similarities that distinguish them from the Euro-American model that has defined what melodrama means and how it signifies that meaning.

Madame Freedom: A Femininity to Suit the Nation

South Korean cinema comes "into full existence," writes film theorist So-young Kim, with the extraordinary success of two films, *Ch'unhyangjŏn* (*The Story of Chun-hyang,* Yi Kyu-hwan, 1955) and *Chayu puin* (*Madame Freedom,* Han Hyŏng-mo, 1956). Their box office helped build "a cottage style film industry."[25] Yet the two films could not be more different. While *The Story of Chun-hyang* revived a story from the Yi dynasty that all Koreans would know and that touted traditional Confucian ethics, *Madame Freedom* reflected the period and social upheaval of the postwar era in which it was made.[26] I will consider the latter precisely because it suggests one way in which melodrama negotiates social crises and cultural interactions in Golden Age South Korean cinema.

In some ways a *succes du scandale, Madame Freedom* was taken from the controversial novel of the same name, published the year of the armistice that ended the Korean War and indefinitely partitioned the nation (1953).[27] The film tells the story of a traditional housewife and mother, Sŏn-yŏng, whose professor/husband is cold and withdrawn, interested only in his work. While his occupation grants them a significant degree of social status, his income does not equal that of many of the other women's husbands in Sŏn-yŏng's social cohort. In order to improve their economic situation, Sŏn-yŏng gets a job as a saleswoman in a shop (*P'ari* or Paris) that sells U.S. goods, a job at which she excels. Yet her consequent social exposure results in ruinous financial and sexual dalliances. At film's end, her future and that of her family is uncertain. Her husband, demanding that they separate, has locked her out of the house, an act heightened by the sudden appearance of snow for the first time in the film. When their young son begs him to let her in, the husband relents, and the film ends with the son running outside to embrace his mother, as the husband looks sternly at them from the doorway.

Although this plot summary describes the main action of the film, numerous subplots mirror, nuance, and serve to generalize the tale of *Madame Freedom.* Together with Sŏn-yŏng, several other female characters—Madame Ch'oe and Sŏn-yŏng's social cohort, Miss Pak and the group of secretaries to which she belongs, Sŏn-yŏng's boss's wife and Sŏn-yŏng's niece—represent South Korean femininity across a range of class positions (affluent to working class) and familial positions (married,

Miss Pak and Professor Yi's outdoor tryst, from *Madame Freedom*

single). Each of the main characters confronts morally difficult situations relating to romance. While Madame Ch'oe and Sŏn-yŏng's boss's wife must contend with unfaithful husbands, the other female characters choose different solutions to illicit sexual attractions. The young secretary, Miss Pak, becomes involved first professionally and then romantically with Sŏn-yŏng's husband, Professor Yi, after she approaches him and asks if he will teach her and a group of typists Korean language and grammar lessons every evening. Miss Pak and her group, unlike Sŏn-yŏng, all wear very smart Western suits and have careers.[28] Miss Pak and Professor Yi's trysts take place primarily outdoors, and though they declare their love for each other, they never become physically involved. Sŏn-yŏng, by contrast, comes close to sleeping with two men, her boss and her neighbor, after meeting them in cafés, dance halls, and restaurants.

Meanwhile, Sŏn-yŏng's best friend, Madame Ch'oe, has a husband devoted to his mistress; she encourages Sŏn-yŏng to take dancing lessons, to become financially independent of her husband, to enjoy life more, and to get involved with what becomes a disastrous money-making scheme. Finally, Sŏn-yŏng's niece, also depicted as completely Westernized, is involved with Sŏn-yŏng's neighbor Ch'un-ho, who also seduces Sŏn-yŏng. With these complications, the film relentlessly makes the point that when women leave the domestic sphere, which all the women in this film, and by extension, all Korean women, are depicted as doing, sexual chaos ensues. Yet unlike U.S. cinema's fundamental ambivalence toward women's work and its correlative celebration of leisure, *Madame Freedom* depicts women's sexual independence and vulnerability as inextricable from their much more positively valued financial abilities, status, and concerns, precisely what takes them outside the domestic sphere in the first place!

The motif of women's labor and its appropriate place is introduced very early in the film, following upon the two opening shots, which set up the opposition between the forces of modernity and those of traditional social structures. The film begins with a shot of chaotic urban traffic on a major thoroughfare, followed by one of a still and quaint neighborhood, which then leads to the interior of Professor Yi's home. Sŏn-yŏng kneels on the floor carefully ironing, while her husband sits at a desk working. Bending over his own books, he ignores his son, who asks him for help with his homework, thereby signaling that this is his wife's job. Sŏn-yŏng and her husband then talk about her working outside their home. He thinks it is unseemly for a woman in her position (the wife of a professor), but the next day, as he is leaving the house, he sees her washing their clothes in a tub. Having his wife do the laundry instead of a maid is more unseemly to Professor Yi than having her work for a wage. Class concerns thereby trump traditional gender roles. He tells Sŏn-yŏng she can do whatever she wants.

The film depicts Professor Yi as inadequate to the task of resolving incompatible priorities that have to do with, on the one hand, maintaining a traditional family/gender structure and space, and on the other, sustaining a sufficiently affluent lifestyle in keeping with the symbolic status of his profession. Passive and resigned, he acquiesces to the violation of tradition. Unlike her husband, Sŏn-yŏng's response to their economic troubles depends upon her sense of her own agency: she actively pursues employment and the rewards in status it will afford her family. It is in relation to economic agency and action that the film most noticeably refuses a clear, melodramatic delineation of character. Both Sŏn-yŏng and her

29

Sŏn-yŏng, with an admiring customer, sells Western goods at P'ari, from *Madame Freedom*

husband are depicted as flawed; neither are idealized or demonized. Further, the film extends the significance of the conflicts that will result from these differently gendered responses in its use of setting and mise-en-scène.[29]

From this point in the narrative on, the film orchestrates its melodramatic situations within public and/or commercial urban space: city streets, boutiques, cafés, restaurants, parks, and nightclub/dance halls. The film punctuates this urban milieu with two short sequences that indicate what is getting lost, the traditional home. We see Sŏn-yŏng's son at home alone at ten o'clock at night, his parents each out pursuing their separate careers/romances. All the romances in *Madame Freedom*, illicit and otherwise, are articulated through "professional" relationships—those overtly mediated by economic exchange or professional improvement. Sŏn-yŏng's neighbor gives her dance lessons; her other suitor is her boss. Sŏn-yŏng's niece, who has also been going out with Sŏn-yŏng's neighbor, has temporarily left him so she can go out with an American who can teach her English. Significantly, the quasi-incestuous subplot of aunt and niece competing for the same man depends entirely on the women's public and professional circulation and supercedes the familial hierarchy that would demand the niece honor her aunt.

The film interrelates several sets of oppositions through the figure of its protagonist along three registers: (1) social space (public/private; urban/domestic; work/leisure, professional/familial), (2) gender and family positions (mother/father, husband/wife, married/unmarried woman), and (3) sociohistorical temporalities (traditional/modern). Her eponymic and fundamentally oxymoronic title—Madame Freedom—astutely captures the nature of her crisis and also that facing South Korea. For a Korean woman, the entry into marriage requires her precisely to forego freedom and autonomy and enter into binding relations of duty and hierarchy with her husband and her husband's family. "Madame Freedom" therefore designates a femininity not only inflected by the United States (she is called "Madame" in English several times in the film), but also one that is, within Korean culture, a contradiction in terms.

For this Western viewer and theorist of melodrama, the difference of *Madame Freedom* and its depiction of femininity derives from another set of significations that have to do with women's labor. While the oppositions the film sets into play in some sense reduplicate those of U.S. melodramas, their meanings and value are different. In Hollywood melodrama, the home has been resolutely depicted since the late 1920s as a place of leisure, the domestic labor necessary to maintain that home transformed into affective expressions and imperatives. The U.S. fantasy that everyone can be middle class has depended upon middle-class women whose lifestyle and appearance are leisured; in U.S. melodramas of the classic period, female protagonists are often severely punished for pursuing careers, either in or out of their homes.[30]

In *Madame Freedom*, this is not the case. Professor Yi's household is a place where everyone works; in fact, no leisure or play occurs there, not even with their young son, who is writing or reading at his little desk every time we see him. Sŏn-yŏng's employment in a boutique initially is represented as both necessary and highly valued. Similarly, the film does not critique Miss Pak's employment as a secretary, her smart, tailored suits, which suggest her professionalism, and her desire to learn Korean grammar. In short, neither Sŏn-yŏng nor Miss Pak's *economic productivity* seem to represent a problem.

home = leisure (US)
home = work (SK)

31

Music, Genre, and the Transnational Familiar

What does seem to be problematized via Sŏn-yŏng's employment is the slavish valorization of Western goods, language, and activities, their inflated but ultimately empty value narrativized in the film by Madame Ch'oe's ill-fated get-rich scheme selling Western goods.[31] Madame Freedom "falls" not because she works in the public sphere but because her presence there leads her to investigate social settings and pursue activities devoted to *leisure*. Tellingly, the film imbricates her consequent exposure to sexuality outside the traditional familial structure with more generalized representations of South Korean culture's complicated encounter with the West. All of these themes are fully realized in a lengthy scene that constitutes the turning point of the film. Prior to this scene, Madame Freedom has always worn traditional clothing, and though various men have flirted with her, she has maintained a certain distance and reserve. Finally, she agrees to meet her neighbor/dancing teacher at a nightclub.

The sequence begins with a close-up of a trumpet as it sounds the first note of a big band riff—"Cherry Pink and Apple Blossom White." "Cherry Pink," the most famous song in the world in 1955–56, was written by Cuban composer Pérez Prado, who composed for and acted in the contemporaneous Golden Age Mexican cinema.[32] The band then segues into Prado's song "Mambo," the repetitive lyrics of which the band sings in English. The bar is full of Korean men and women, all, except Madame Freedom and one other woman, in Western clothes. When the riff begins, a Korean Carmen Miranda–style dancer vigorously mambos down a stairway in the middle of the band dressed skimpily in a form-fitting, bare midriff dress covered with fringe. Proscenium shots of her frenzied mambo alternate with long shots of the crowd and close-ups of Madame Freedom staring admiringly at her.

What is initially striking about this scene is how *familiar* it is. The ambiance, the setting, and the blocking of the crowd and the performance shots resemble cinematic scenes from many nightclub and cabaret films in Western cinema. Yet its generic referent seems to derive less from Hollywood than Mexico, as this sequence is more strikingly reminiscent of the Mexican *cabaretera* film than of the Hollywood variant.[33] In one of the exemplars of this Mexican "fallen woman" genre, *Aventurera* (Alberto Gout, 1949), the heroine's fall is instigated in a dance-hall scene in which the musical accompaniment is *also* Prado's "Cherry Pink." Prado did all of the music for this film, which opened and had a successful run in South Korea the year after *Madame Freedom* was released.

Mambo, or the transnational familiar, from *Madame Freedom*

The dancer returns Sŏn-yŏng's admiring gaze, from *Madame Freedom*

Headlined under the Korean title, *Protest of the Flesh,* and featuring star Ninón Sevilla's face in a characteristic snarl, the ad informs viewers that this film sports the same production team and narrative traits of a previous Mexican feature released in South Korea, *Wild Woman Jasgara.* In all likelihood, the earlier feature was *Sensualidad* (Gout, 1950), another *cabaretera* featuring Sevilla.[34] This pronounced connection between Mexican and South Korean cinema is suggestive in several ways.

Scholars have typically noted the influences of Italian Neorealism, French art, and American epic cinema on Golden Age South Korean films. Missing from this account are the visual, generic, and musical influences from Mexico and other Latin American cinemas on South Korean melodramas of this period.[35] Given the panache of the former influences, aesthetic in the case of said Italian and French film movements and economic in the case of Hollywood epics, the exclusion of the Mexican/Latin American influences can be read in terms of the gendered/generic distinctions I have noted above *and* in relation to the aesthetic exceptionalism that has dominated the canonization of certain national cinemas in U.S. and international film studies. The acknowledged challenges to Hollywood in the postwar era came from film movements, auteurs, and films adopting a realist or neorealist aesthetic; Mexican Golden Age cinema with its profoundly musical and melodramatic aesthetic never registered. And yet, in the visual and musical dynamics of this pivotal sequence, the transnational influence of Mexico might be foregrounded over that of Hollywood.

That this axis of influence is predicated on sound as well as image is also very suggestive. The global diffusion of mambo, writes Gustavo Pérez Firmat, could be attributed to its "laconism." He writes:

> Because the mambo began its life only as a type of improvised refrain, when it achieved independence it became a free-standing fragment, a part that has escaped the whole. . . . The words do not help. When they exist, they are minimalist to the point of absurdity. Pérez Prado used lyrics in the manner of scat words. . . . Laconic rather than lyrical, interactive rather than narrative, the mambo does not believe in stories. When music and words meet, the result is often logoclassia, the disarticulation or fragmentation of language. As logoclastic music, the mambo exploits language for its onomatopoetic or phonic qualities, not for its meaning bearing capacity. Words are valued for their sound, not their sense. Since there was no need for translation of lyrics,

diverse nationalities could be reached by the same recordings. The mambo's hybridness remained more "pure" for not having to pick a language.[36]

This verbal laconism was coupled with musical, physical excess; the mambo craze was a dance craze and one accompanied by either the embrace or the fear of its physically frantic, uninhibited style. Pérez Firmat notes: "In the mambo, there is not warming up or cooling down, no foreplay or afterplay. The mambo begins and ends with paroxysm."[37]

The international diffusion of mambo, predicated on both its verbal paucity and physical excess, emulates, in a different register, the structure of melodrama wherein excessive spectacle attends a correlative generic propensity for muteness, for what cannot be said.[38] These kindred generic structures marking mambo and melodrama can be considered in relation to national cinemas and the coming of sound. Ana López observes: "Because the costs of the transition to sound were enormous . . . local investment throughout the world lagged behind that of Hollywood. However, the difficulties of translation did open up a potential window of opportunity for local producers in non-English-speaking markets who suddenly had an easy answer to the question of 'national' differences in the cinema: language and music."[39] Interestingly, in the penultimate scene in *Madame Freedom,* language and music do not mark what is local so much as they stage the mixing of and confrontation among disparate transnational influences. While the mambo enunciates Afro-Cuban, Mexican, and American jazz influences, the repetitive lyrics are voiced in English. Tellingly, the local registers itself elsewhere.

It is in the specular organization of the cabaret sequence that the film distinguishes itself from its antecedents. In *Madame Freedom,* the gaze and its object are emphatically *female.* Sŏn-yŏng's very appreciative look at the dancer is both desiring and identificatory, tinged with eroticism and something between admiration and envy. Although it is perhaps the most noticeable of these looks in the film, a series of them have in fact structured the entire narrative. The first occurs in an early scene when Sŏn-yŏng attends her "wives of famous men" club meeting. A series of point-of-view shots depict Sŏn-yŏng and Madame Ch'oe looking closely at the lavish jewelry and stylish clothing of their fellow club members. This sequence also features a woman singer who sings to and caresses Sŏn-yŏng, later encouraging her to join the dances that she sponsors. In addition to underscoring the material amenities denied to Sŏn-yŏng (as the wife of a high-status but low-paid professor), the club also provides her with the attention and recognition she is not getting at home. The second example of female-to-female gazes occurs at the shop where Sŏn-yŏng works. The shopkeeper's wife watches Sŏn-yŏng closely as Sŏn-yŏng makes a particularly lucrative sale. As Sŏn-yŏng puts the money in the cash drawer, she exchanges an intimate and knowing glance with the shopkeeper's wife, smiling as the other woman winks appreciatively at her. Finally, Sŏn-yŏng and her niece each "spy" on the other's erotic interludes with the dance instructor.

These female-to-female looks are highlighted in the narrative and organize all the spheres of Sŏn-yŏng's life—her family, her female cohort, her work, and her leisure—according to a female point of view. Translated to film, the homosociality of traditional Korean culture gives rise to an alternative specular structure whose threat is finally realized in the nightclub scene. Sŏn-yŏng's look at the dancer, strikingly unmediated by any male gaze, finally precipitates her fall. Immediately following this sequence, Sŏn-yŏng adopts Western clothing and has two disastrous sexual encounters, the first with her neighbor, a tryst interrupted by her son calling out for her, and later on, one with her boss, interrupted by his wife. When she finds Sŏn-yŏng with her husband in a darkened room, the shopkeeper's wife slaps Sŏn-yŏng, who significantly has averted her gaze in shame. This rupture or violation of the female-to-female gaze and homosocial affinities that have structured the film makes way for the final sequence in which, for the first time, the male gaze orients the space and meaning of the mise-en-scène. Although its outcome is left uncertain, Sŏn-yŏng's attempt to return to her familial place occurs under the aegis of her husband's gaze and at the behest of her young son. Both of these characters have been marginal to the narrative, yet they figure here as crucial to what is being narrated. If *Madame Freedom* "imagines the fate of the nation as that of the violated and subjugated woman," father and son are specters of what can no longer or cannot yet be imagined—a distinct nation with tradition, authority, and people intact. Rather than resolve this scenario, either with Sŏn-yŏng banished or reincorporated, the film leaves the moment, the national allegory suspended, haunted by specters.

This irresolution acquires even more significance if we consider the context that precipitates Sŏn-yŏng's transgression. The nightclub scene aligns Sŏn-yŏng's gaze with larger and more generalized issues concerning South Korean culture's encounter with the West. As Sŏn-yŏng looks at the dancer, the band provides accompaniment to this homosocial/erotic moment with bongos and a decidedly Latin beat. The singing and some of the dialogue in this nightclub are in English. More to the point, if Hollywood films of the 1930s and 1940s influence the ambiance, the music, and the dancing, the irony here is that it is a Hollywood itself fascinated with all things "Latin" and specifically derived from Afro-Cuban music. In this manner, the scene opens up a global frame of reference. The nightclub functions as a global chronotope, staging South Korea's encounter with modernity as one that greatly exceeds a dichotomous relation with Europe or the United States per se, albeit implicitly and unnoted by scholars.[40]

The chronotope is a concept articulated in M. M. Bakhtin's "Forms of Time and of the Chronotope in the Novel," in *The Dialogic Imagination*.[41] In "'Lounge Time': Post-War Crises and the Chronotope of *Film Noir*," Vivian Sobchack uses the chronotope to reconceptualize the link between film text and historical context in film noir.[42] Her account of the chronotope of "lounge time" as a threat to domestic space and time resonates with the use of the nightclub sequence in *Madame Freedom*. Yet insofar as Bakhtin's notion of the chronotope attempts to ground representation and discourse historically, in specific, material time and space, the global chronotope is something of a paradox. The referent for the nightclub and lounge time in *Madame Freedom* derives at least as much, if not more, from other transnational cinematic representations than from actual postwar nightclubs in Seoul, which would, in any case, have been populated by American GIs. The chronotope here does not function sociologically so much as allegorically for the influence of U.S. military, economic, and cultural interventions contaminating the coherent imagining of a South Korean nation. However, at the same time, it is important to note that these representations and imaginings are also infused with appropriations from the contemporaneous Mexican cinema and global music, features that expose the Hollywood/national cinema binary for the fiction it is by highlighting the other transnational significations in this scene.

Further, the scene implicates the female gaze and new female freedom in this global chronotope. Unlike Miss Pak, Sŏn-yŏng's donning of Western attire has nothing to do with her productivity and professionalism and everything to do with leisure, dancing, and sexuality. If the film attributes these aberrant and dangerous freedoms to an Americanized West, they enter the female body by way of Latin American music and dance that is itself influenced by African culture. It is here that the nation-state is most ambivalent—inadvertently affirming its porous identity even as it attempts emphatically to isolate what is not-Korean. Yet, significantly, the woman becomes the focus of this irresolvable ambivalence, inhabiting the place of what both is and is not South Korean. Through her, the film plays the domestic against the global, with the nation hiding behind her figure. She takes the fall, her husband and son, marginalized past and virtual future, divided and frozen over her fate. And this arrested, ambiguous moment, insinuated through family, gender, and sex roles, becomes the only possible representation of nation, one that is irresolute, contradictory, and ambivalent, local only within a transnational familiar.

Notes

1. An earlier version of this essay appeared in *Quarterly Review of Film and Video*.
2. Nancy Abelmann, "Melodramatic Memories: Classical Hollywood Cinema meets the Golden Age of Korean Cinema," Pacific Rim Research Proposal, 1997, page 2.
3. My use of the term "cultural imaginary" refers to the social/subjective phenomenon evidenced in Abelmann's study. The women invoked mass media cultural narratives to narrate their own experiences and as a salient part of those experiences. Furthermore, they did so independently of one another, nevertheless referencing the same group of films. The concept of a cultural or national imaginary derives from Benedict Anderson's theorization of nationalism in *Imagined Communities* (1983; New York: Verso, 1991) and has shaped recent work on national cinemas in film studies. For a discussion of Anderson's influence, along with a critique of film theorists' tendency to link Anderson's notion of the imaginary with the Lacanian variant, see Michael Walsh's "National Cinema, National Imaginary," in *Film History* 8, no. 1 (1996): 5–17. While Walsh's review of the literature is helpful, his critique and conclusions are not sufficiently substantiated.
4. Rey Chow, "A Phantom Discipline," *PMLA* 116, no. 5 (October 2001): 1393.
5. I explore this phenomenon in much greater detail in the section "Housekeeping in Hollywood," in *American Domesticity: From How-To Manual to Hollywood Melodrama* (New York: Oxford University Press, 1999), 81–149.
6. Women with economic agency, especially that related to domestic skills, are frequently punished for their success or expertise in Hollywood melodramas of this period. Obvious examples would include: *Imitation of Life* (1933, 1959) and *Mildred Pierce* (1945).
7. When I shared this perception with South Korean women in the United States and Seoul, they quickly qualified my understanding of "strong femininity," stressing the very misogynist and patriarchal character of South Korean culture.
8. See Cho Haejoang's discussion of South Korea as a homosocial culture in "Living with Conflicting Subjectivities: Mother, Motherly Wife, and Sexy Woman in the Transition from Colonial Modern to Post-Modern," in *Under Construction: The Gendering of Modernity, Class, and Consumption in the*

Republic of Korea, ed. Laura Kendall (Honolulu: University of Hawai'i Press, 2002), 165–96.

9. See McHugh, "The Labor of Maternal Melodramas: Converting Angels to Icons," in *American Domesticity,* 130–49.

10. Kristin Thompson, writing on the emergence and significance of the concept of national cinemas ("in the decade after 1915"), limits her comments to the fact that this concept became one of the primary rubrics for writings on film history. "Nation, National Identity and the International Cinema," *Film History* 8, no. 3 (1996): 259–60.

11. Robert Ray, *A Certain Tendency of American Cinema* (Princeton: Princeton University Press, 1985), 26.

12. Julian Stringer, "Traffic in Cinema," in *Regarding Film Festivals* (PhD diss., Indiana University, 2003), 3. See also Bill Nichols, "Discovering Form, Inferring Meaning: New Cinemas and the Film Festival Circuit," *Film Quarterly* 47, no. 3 (Spring 1994): 16–30, and "The International Film Festival and Global Cinema," *East-West Journal* 8, no. 1 (1994).

13. Among many possible examples and in addition to the writers on Korean cinema and film festivals that I have already cited, see Chris Berry, "If China Can Say No, Can China Make Movies? Or Do Movies Make China? Rethinking National Cinema and National Agency," *boundary 2* 25, no. 3 (1998): 129–50; "Race: Chinese Film, and the Politics of Nationalism," *Cinema Journal* 31, no. 2 (1992): 45–58; Nick Browne, Paul G. Pickowicz, Vivian Sobchack, and Esther Yau, eds., *New Chinese Cinema: Forms, Identities, Politics* (Cambridge: Cambridge University Press, 1994); Rey Chow, *Primitive Passions: Visuality, Sexuality, Ethnography, and Contemporary Chinese Cinema* (New York: Columbia University Press, 1995); John King, Ana López, and Manuel Alvarado, eds., *Mediating Two Worlds: Cinematic Encounters in the Americas* (London: BFI, 1993).

14. For some notable exceptions, see Sumita Chakravary, "The Film Industry and the State," in *National Identity in Indian Popular Cinema* (Austin: University of Texas Press, 1993), 19–55; Thomas Elsaesser, "Film Industry— Film Subsidy," in *New German Cinema* (New Brunswick, NJ: Rutgers University Press, 1989); Ian Jarvie, *Hollywood's Overseas Campaign* (Cambridge: Cambridge University Press, 1992); Randal Johnson, "In the Belly of the Ogre: Cinema and State in Latin America," in *Mediating Two Worlds,* ed. King, López, and Alvarado, 204–13; Paul Lenti, "Columbia: State Role in Film Production," in *Mediating Two Worlds,* ed. King, López, and Alvarado, 214–21. E. Ann Kaplan, writing on Chinese cinema, does gesture toward the role of the state, formulating the distinction between national culture and the state as two different kinds of critical discourses that can be applied to the cinematic text: the aesthetic and the political, respectively. But the distinction between cultural imaginary, the citizen's "yes," and the constraints imposed by the government, the state's "no" are limited to the critic's aesthetic and political interpretations of the text. Neither the material context of the state nor the state's impact on the aesthetic makeup of the text are registered. See her "Melodrama/Subjectivity/Ideology: Western Melodrama Theories and Their Relevance to Recent Chinese Cinema," in *Melodrama and Asian*

Cinema, ed. Wimal Dissanayake (Cambridge: Cambridge University Press, 1993), 9–28.

15. Nancy Abelmann makes this point about *The Coachman, Mr. Pak,* and *Romance Papa* in "The Melodrama of Mobility: Film Moments and Film Memories," a paper delivered at the From Hollywood to Han: South Korean Melodrama in a Global Context conference held at the University of California–Riverside, June 25 and 26, 1999.

16. I am grateful to Chon Noriega for this observation.

17. See Soyoung Kim, chapter 7 in this volume, and Chungmoo Choi, "The Magic and Violence of Modernization in Post-Colonial Korean Cinema" in *Post-Colonial Classics of Korean Cinema,* ed. Chungmoo Choi (Irvine, CA: Korean Film Festival Committee, UCI, 1998). Also of interest, though not relating specifically to film or melodrama, are the essays in Elaine H. Kim and Chungmoo Choi, eds., *Dangerous Women: Gender and Korean Nationalism* (New York: Routledge, 1998).

18. Linda Williams, "Melodrama Revisited," in *Refiguring American Film Genres: Theory and History,* ed. Nick Browne (Berkeley: University of California Press, 1998), 42.

19. Ibid.

20. Peter Brooks, *The Melodramatic Imagination* (New Haven: Yale University Press, 1976), 15–16.

21. See Keehyeung Lee's essay in this volume that notes that in television, this distinction is reversed. South Korean serial TV melodrama exhibits more closure from episode to episode than does U.S. serial TV.

22. Ray, *Certain Tendency of American Cinema,* 57.

23. Many film critics and historians are now emphasizing the overlaps and interactions that have existed among supposedly discrete national cinemas. Kristin Thompson describes such interactions within Europe and in relation to the United States in "National or International Films? The European Debate during the 1920s," in *Film History* 8, no. 3 (1996): 281–96. Other scholars have explored this issue in the context of non-Western and postcolonial cinemas, challenging the implicit Eurocentrism of both traditional and revisionist accounts of national cinema. Examples include: Julianne Burton-Carvajal, "*Araya* across Time and Space: Competing Canons of National (Venezuelan) and International Film Histories," and Ana M. López, "Crossing Nations and Genres, Traveling Filmmakers," both in *Visible Nations: Latin American Cinema and Video,* ed. Chon A. Noriega (Minneapolis: University of Minnesota Press, 2000); and Ella Shohat and Robert Stam, *Unthinking Eurocentrism: Multiculturalism and the Media* (New York: Routledge, 1994).

24. The quote is from Isolde Standish, "Korean Cinema and the New Realism: Text and Context," in *Colonialism and Nationalism in Asian Cinema,* ed. Wimal Dissanayake (Bloomington: Indiana University Press, 1994), 70. The information about the other films came from a conversation with Hee Moon Cho.

25. Soyoung Kim, chapter 7 in this volume.

26. Young-il Lee, *The History of Korean Cinema,* trans. Richard Lynn Greever

(Seoul: Motion Picture Production Corporation, 1988), 112.

27. See Chungmoo Choi's illuminating comments on *Madame Freedom* in "Magic and Violence of Modernization in Post-Colonial Korea," in *Post-Colonial Classics of Korean Cinema*, ed. Chungmoo Choi, 6–8.

28. See Chungmoo Choi's discussion of Miss Pak, which concerns the language lessons along with her appearance, her affiliation with an American company, and postcolonial sexual politics in "Magic and Violence of Modernization in Post-Colonial Korea," 8.

29. Chungmoo Choi's "Magic and Violence of Modernization in Post-Colonial Korea" contains a very informative discussion of venues coded as Japanese colonial, traditional Korean, and American in the mise-en-scène of this film, 6–7.

30. McHugh, "Housekeeping in Hollywood," in *American Domesticity*, 81–149.

31. See Soyoung Kim's discussion of this theme in her essay in this volume, chapter 7.

32. Gustavo Pérez Firmat notes, "'Cherry Pink' enjoys the distinction of having stayed on the Billboard charts for twenty-six weeks, a tenure only surpassed by Elvis Presley's 'Don't Be Cruel.'" Prado's "Que rico el mambo," recorded in 1949 after he had left Cuba for Mexico City, "started the mambo craze." See his "A Brief History of Mambo Time," in *Life on the Hyphen: The Cuban-American Way* (Austin: University of Texas Press, 1994), 84–104.

33. On this genre, see Ana M. López, "Tears and Desire: Women and Melodrama in the 'Old' Mexican Cinema," in *Multiple Voices in Feminist Film Criticism*, ed. Diane Carson, Linda Dittmar, and Janice Welsch (Minneapolis: University of Minnesota Press, 1994), 254–70.

34. The ad notes that the production company was Calderon. The Calderon brothers produced a trilogy of films that starred Ninón Sevilla, were directed by Alberto Gout and written by Álvaro Custudio, a film critic and Spanish immigrant: *Aventurera, Sensualidad,* and *No niegro mi pasado* (1951). These films were notable among the *cabaretera* films for their subversive qualities, evidenced most clearly in the ruthless sexuality, virulent and vengeful, exhibited by the characters played with relish by Sevilla. She was celebrated by the surrealists and by the auteur critics for her challenge to all conventional moralities. See Eduardo de la Vega Alfaro, "The Decline of the Golden Age," in *Mexico's Cinema*, ed. Joanne Hershfield and David R. Maciel (Wilmington, DE: Scholarly Resources, 1999), 169, and Ana López, "Tears and Desire," 263.

35. Thanks to Jinsoo An for this summary of critical work by South Korean film scholars.

36. Pérez Firmat, "A Brief History of Mambo Time," 86–88.

37. Ibid., 94.

38. Peter Brooks, *The Melodramatic Imagination* (New Haven: Yale University Press, 1976), 56–57.

39. Ana López, "Facing up to Hollywood," in *Reinventing Film Studies,* ed. Christine Gledhill and Linda Williams (London: Oxford University Press, 2000), 424.

40. M. M. Bakhtin, "Forms of Time and of the Chronotope in the Novel," *The Dialogic Imagination* (Austin: University of Texas Press, 1981), 84–258.
41. Ibid.
42. Vivian Sobchack, "'Lounge Time': Post-War Crises and the Chronotope of *Film Noir*," in *Refiguring American Film Genres,* ed. Nick Browne (Berkeley and Los Angeles: University of California Press, 1998), 129–70.

2

Melodramatic Texts and Contexts: Women's Lives, Movies, and Men

NANCY ABELMANN

This essay considers one Golden Age melodrama and the personal narratives of two fifty-something women who came of age in South Korea in the late 1950s. I interviewed the two women—whom I call The Education Mother and The Moviegoer—at length over several years for a larger oral narrative-based project on women and social mobility in contemporary South Korea.[1]

By Way of a Story

The narrative that follows, which also begins the Introduction to this volume, is The Education Mother's account of the fate of her only sister. I call her The Education Mother because of her tireless efforts on behalf of her children's education.[2] Enveloped in a rich web of interpretive asides and afterthoughts, the story offered much more than a string of events. The Education Mother joins many women of her generation in South Korea in the conviction that their lives are as "dramatic" as those featured in television and film.[3]

At the time the story was told, The Education Mother's younger sister was peddling shellfish on the beaches of South Korea's southeastern coast. Abandoned by her husband early in her marriage, and then part of a marginal economy, this sister inhabited an entirely different world from that of The Education Mother in Seoul, who defined her own "middle-class" identity in terms of the "leeway to live entirely off the interest of stock and real-estate investments" and the "time and money to join a health club and travel with international tours."

At the heart of this story is a melodramatic moment in which her sister's fate turned suddenly—the sort of moment that could easily be accompanied by high-pitched string instrumentation or thunder and lightning in a melodramatic film or soap opera. It happened one day when her sister struck up a conversation with a stranger at a rural bus station. At the time evoked in the story, the sister and her husband were in transit. Her husband had recently quit his job as a policeman, and with his sizable severance pay in hand, they were off to the coast to open a business. Throughout the journey, The Education Mother's sister clutched the pocketbook that held these bills—the promise of their new lives. Chatting with the stranger at the bus station, she somehow lost track of the pocketbook; the bus station thus became the couple's way station to poverty. They continued to the coast and began peddling wares on the fringes of the formal economy. Shortly thereafter the husband took a mistress and eventually abandoned his wife entirely.

The Education Mother mused that by today's standards—and her current middle-class status—the money she would have needed to stem her sister's fate is but a trifling amount. But in those days, The Education Mother's family was enveloped in their own struggles to survive in immediate post–Korean War Seoul.

What I found most intriguing about this story was The Education Mother's reflections on her sister's misfortune—that is, the *way* in which she told the story. No sooner had she led me to the story's climax than she had attributed her sister's woes to her boyish personality (*sŏngkyŏk*), namely her sister's impertinence and impropriety. Snatching her sister's tragedy from the impersonal winds of fate, she delivered it to the workings of personal proclivity. For a moment I was baffled—for all her sister had done was to misplace her purse, or less still to have had it stolen; it struck me as unjust or even unkind to pin the blame for a turn of circumstance on personality. And yet I knew that this was a sister who The Education Mother loved dearly and by whose misfortune she was deeply saddened. But my understanding of these seemingly personal attributions changed as the story of the downward mobility of The Education Mother's sister veered in a different direction.

As The Education Mother continued, she portrayed her sister's personality as not only the *source* of a particular—and in this case devastating—social outcome but also the *product* of a particular family history and social environment. The Education Mother detailed her sister's relationship with their overly ambitious mother, a woman who had been permanently separated from her husband during the division of the country into what became North and South Korea (1945–48). She explained that her sister's "mistaken" marriage to a policeman (in her words, "such a low-class profession") was the result of their mother's "ignorant ambition" that had fixed itself on the policeman's gentrified (*yangban*) origins.

"*Yangban* only in name," The Education Mother continued, as his family coffers were empty and his father had long ago taken up residence with another woman.

While The Education Mother knew how to tolerate her mother's domineering ways—to say "yes" while all along quietly forging her own path—her younger sister grew up at once fighting against, and ironically complying with, her mother's "twisted and ignorant" ambition.

When I reviewed my notes from this rather extraordinary story, I could see that "personality" was not simply a catalog of personal traits or inclinations but rather a discursive site where the workings of a particular family history and even of national histories were at play. When The Education Mother turned from the lost or stolen purse to her sister's personality, it was not to wrest this sad story from the larger course of South Korean social transformations but rather to place it squarely within them—from the national division, to the structure of patriarchy, to the reconfiguration of status hierarchies.

This story captures the melodramatic dimensions of the profound personal dislocations that have accompanied South Korea's rapid postwar social transformation, which incidentally have made for many stories like this one, stories in which small turns of fate spiral into great tragedies or enormous social divides. In her ruminations over her sister's fate, The Education Mother was struggling with nothing less than social justice at its barest bones: whether people get what they deserve. In much the same way that this pocketbook story enlivens a veritable debate on social justice, so does melodrama theory offer an understanding of melodrama as a site of personal and popular discussion.

Signifying Melodrama

"Melodrama" here refers to a complex of theatrical, literary, and cinematic conventions characterized by excess—of affect (the overdrawn, overmarked) and of plot (strange, almost unbelievable twists, coincidences, connections, and chance meetings). Thomas Elsaesser writes that the general use of "melodramatic" describes the "exaggerated rise-and-fall pattern in human actions and emotional responses, a from-the-sublime-to-the-ridiculous movement, a foreshortening of lived time in favor of intensity—all of which produces a graph of much greater fluctuation, a quicker swing from one extreme to the other than is considered natural, realistic or in conformity with literary standards of verisimilitude."[4] Excess also characterizes melodrama's overdrawn characters—moral hero/ines and evil villain/esses.[5] "A particular form of dramatic *mise en scène*," including decor, color, and music, has also been critical to the enactment of excess.[6]

I argue here that a melodramatic sensibility has been pervasive in contemporary South Korea,[7] as it has been in many moments and locales of rapid social transformation. Indeed, many theorists of melodrama assert that the genre rose with the social and class transformations that accompanied the rise of capitalism.[8] Peter Brooks writes about melodrama as both a "mode of expression and representation" and a "means for interpreting and making sense of experience."[9] My use of "melodramatic sensibility" follows his convention, referring not only to the properties of a particular field of texts (including personal narratives) but also to their dialogic context (that is, to the talk that so often surrounds them). Melodramatic texts and narrative conventions are effective in South Korea because they dramatize issues central to rapidly changing societies, and because they draw their audiences into dialogue. We can learn something about the nature of this dialogue by reviewing the contours of some of the scholarly debate on melodrama.

Over the last twenty years, melodramatic novels, films, and television soap operas that were once considered of little cultural or scholarly value have been resuscitated in academic writing. These works are now legitimate texts for inquiry, which reflects the increasing interest in popular culture generally and transformations in theoretical and historical perception. Interestingly, scholars have taken up the touchstones of melodrama's long-standing devaluation to proclaim its very value. This said, neither is contemporary melodrama theory singular nor are the features of the "genre" completely agreed upon.

Scholars of melodrama debate the appropriateness and use of the term for the non-West or for non-Western genres.[10] If some argue that it is imperialistic to transport Western theory to the non-West, others have asked whether it is imperialistic to suggest that melodrama has arrived in the non-West whole-cloth from the West.[11] And again, some argue that it is problematic to abandon Western genre and theory in the examination of non-Western texts.[12] Some scholars focus on non-Western melodramas' distinct features,[13] or argue that the characterization falters because of the historically limited ways in which it has been formulated in the West.[14] These critiques of the cross-cultural use of melodrama suggest necessary cautions: that we cannot assume analogous histories of similar narrative or dramatic forms; that we must consider the limits of theory devoted to the particularities of Western genres; and that we must be wary of universal or pan-historical arguments. Nonetheless, "melodrama" can signal shared properties that are worth thinking about cross-culturally, and, for cross-cultural study, it is important to consider literary and genre developments in their particular historical crucibles. In the case of South Korean melodrama, or *melo-mul* (melo[dramatic] things), we find a local vocabulary and popular sensibility—the delineation of which The Education Mother and her cohort would recognize—that conjures images of excess, tears, and drama in keeping with widespread Western characterization. While Korea has certainly been influenced by the considerable contact with Western melodramatic genres over the twentieth century, also pertinent are premodern literary and dramatic traditions that are easily characterized as melodramatic (for example, *p'ansori*).[15]

At the heart of debates concerning melodrama is the question of realism. Indeed, melodramatic excess can seem unrealistic with every flourish, and it is precisely this lack of realism that has led many to trivialize melodrama.[16] From another vantage point, however, it can be argued that this excess dramatizes the real: namely, that while realistic genres are naturalized or ideologically unmarked,[17] the drama of excess highlights the unreal and by extension the constructedness of the real.[18] In this sense, the affective efficacy of melodramatic unreality derives precisely from its transgressions of reality.

Diverging from the argument that melodrama works by transgressing reality is the position that melodrama can be effective in reflecting "reality"—the melodrama of "real" life, such as that we just met with The Education Mother. Ariel Dorfman makes this argument for Latin American magical realism, suggesting that the North American academy has misunderstood the reality of its representations.[19] The matter of "reality," of course, turns again on the sense of the real and the imaginary (or possible), the here-and-now versus the desired.[20] In this sense, the debates on melodrama negotiate between competing aesthetics in the apperception and narration of the social world: the realm of the possible versus the accommodation to the real.

Integral to contemporary discussion on melodrama is the matter we met in the case of The Education Mother on her sister: namely the relation between the domestic and the social or political. Some scholars argue that melodrama works precisely to collapse the social and political into the domestic: as Elsaesser observes, "the characters are . . . each others' sole referent, there is no outside world to be acted upon."[21] Christine Gledhill asserts, however, that it is wrong to limit the "real" to the "set of socio-economic relations outside the domestic and personal sphere," thereby ignoring the domestic with its "sexual relations . . . fantasy and desire."[22] Gledhill thus refuses to relegate the domestic to a "surrogate level," and instead calls attention to the "'real' social conflicts" of the domestic.[23] Similarly, Peter Brooks argues that melodrama "evokes confrontations and choices that are of heightened importance because in them we put our lives—however trivial and constricted—on the line."[24] These perspectives thus challenge us to question those dichotomies (for example, public [political]/domestic, and personal/social) that obscure the sociopolitical workings of the home and of private lives. The seemingly personal nature of the pocketbook story was in fact entirely social and political.

The debates over melodrama also consider whether characters in melodrama are centers of ("realistic") psychological interiority, or alternatively, social composites or social projections. This discussion is critical because so much of melodrama is structured around good and evil characters. On the one hand, when characters are fashioned with "individual" psychologies, their social fates seem somehow deserved and their good or evil is celebrated or condemned respectively. When, on the other hand, characters are constructed as social composites or projections, their good or evil operate differently. In this latter vein, Elsaesser argues that for Hollywood melodrama, evil "is firmly placed on a social and existential level, away from the arbitrary and finally obtuse logic of private motives and individualized psychology."[25] Brooks notes similarly that melodramatic characters have "no psychology" or "interior depth,"[26] and Gledhill cautions that personalization is not necessarily "a mechanical reflection of the ideology of individualism."[27] Some commentators on Asian melodramatic genres in particular have noted that characters' troubles are framed outside of the self, in "social codes"[28] or beyond human agency entirely.[29] Certainly, in the pocketbook story, the character of the sister is narrated beyond the confines of individual psychology or personality.

Finally, at issue in discussions of melodrama is the extent to which it renders a moral order legible, one of Peter Brooks's central assertions about the genre.[30] Melodrama's metadrama of the affective makes for what Brooks calls the "moral occult"—"the domain of spiritual forces and imperatives that is not clearly visible within reality, but which [is] believe[d] to be operative there, and which demands to be uncovered, registered, articulated."[31] In another idiom, writers on North American soap opera have asked whether melodrama is "open" or "closed." Some have argued that the serialized and open-ended nature of that genre makes for texts that invite audience involvement and reflect the pace and style of women's lives. It has been observed, however, that non-Western soap operas are typically not as open—that although serialized, they tend to complete the narrative, to close off the moral questions and plots.[32] I suggest, however, that melodrama can also be considered "open" when it stimulates and shapes the terms of cultural dialogue.

At issue then is whether to understand melodrama's engagement with moral concerns as fostering a closed Manichean universe or rather as dramatizing, rather than closing, moral debate. It seems that in his later writing, Brooks veers toward a more "open" approach to melodrama's moral universe, offering, for example, that the "moral occult" lays bare "large choices of ways of being."[33] As recounted above, The Education Mother's open engagement with her sister's melodramatic story reveals the sort of discussion (that is, about social justice) that the melodramatic mode can inspire.

In popular discussions of melodramatic texts—discussions that are particularly vibrant among South Korean women—we find echoes of these contests over the contours and meanings of melodrama. To some extent, melodrama successfully engages its consumers precisely because it sets people talking. These issues are of course all the more salient in places and times when the real often seems unreal; when the domestic is easily comprehended as social; when persons are easily taken as social composites; and when the moral universe is unsettled. It is in this sense that I assert that such debate sustains the attention accorded melodrama, or *melo-mul*, and narratives like that of The Education Mother with which I began.

Back to, and Beyond, the Story

The pocketbook in The Education Mother's story works as a melodramatic sign of excess. The Education Mother knew that a listener would be somewhat incredulous at the puissance of the pocketbook; it seems almost unreal that the turn of events in the aftermath of the stolen pocketbook would not have reversed themselves to this day. The reality of the story derives not so much from the plausibility of a woman carrying or losing her entire life's savings, but rather from other social, emotional, and political contingencies that either enabled this melodramatic moment or that transpired because of it. First is the misplaced ambition of her mother, who through her social widowhood, suffered the scars of national division that not only burdened her with responsibilities she was "totally unprepared for," but "distorted" her personality as well. (In the course of my interviews I found frequent, if subtle, commentary on the effects of socially enforced celibacy on young widows.)

49

Second, critical to this story are the fluid and changing contours of class and of the times. The Education Mother's mother—like so many people of her generation—miscalculated by privileging her future son-in-law's *yangban* legacy over his meager prospects and low social standing as a policeman. In my conversations with fifty-something South Korean women, I often heard their praise or disdain for their parents' ability or inability to effectively "read" the changing times. In this vein, The Education Mother faults her mother for being out of sync with the new rules of the game, for her anachronistic decision that set her sister's course. Indeed, Koreans have been straddling multiple status systems for generations; the melodrama of the story of The Education Mother's sister is intimately tied to the personal strategies that people have mobilized amidst the sea changes of social transformation. Although with hindsight it is perhaps easy for The Education Mother to dismiss her mother's ignorant marital choice for her sister, it has in fact not been so easy for people at one or another juncture to know what to do, strategically or ethically. The enormous changes in stratification systems have been neither uniform nor total: premodern status distinctions did not, for example, suddenly or completely lose their social significance or political sway. Rather, the ways in which people calibrate human worth and achievement have been continuously contested.

A third reality entailed in the melodramatic moment featured in the pocketbook story is patriarchy. Patriarchy fashioned the ignorance of The Education Mother's mother (being unschooled), and it was also at work in a *yangban*'s son becoming a policeman, for he was also the son of an abandoned woman. The melodramatic moment is also enlivened by the weighty realities of its aftermath. These include the stark downward mobility experienced by The Education Mother's sister and the further effects of patriarchy (the sister's desertion by her husband for another woman, and her insurmountable economic distance from her natal family).

Echoing another melodrama debate, the style or character of The Education Mother's sister is also at issue in The Education Mother's telling: her boyish personality, her "inability to keep quiet if she disagreed," and her "unwillingness to hide her feelings or engage in pleasantries" "destined" her for a difficult relationship with her mother and a difficult life course. The Education Mother explained that her own femininity had been well suited to the strictures and structures that women in Korea have had to negotiate. She explained that a "woman like my sister would have never survived the early years of my marriage," referring to the early difficulties The Education Mother herself experienced with her husband and mother-in-law. She highlighted her sister's limitations in this way because her own marriage had become, in the final analysis, both a successful and prosperous one. The Education Mother offered not a defense of patriarchy but rather a commentary on the effects of personal proclivity under patriarchy. Her sister's personality—its origins and effects—are neither entirely interior nor personal; it is precisely this tension that makes for The Education Mother's reflexive, dialogic telling of this story.

Finally, in keeping with yet other discussions on melodrama, it is very difficult to identify the villain(esses) or hero(ines) in The Education Mother's story. Each flawed character is an intricate social product. The agent in the purse-snatching story is after all quite irrelevant or absent, and the sister's father-in-law is so remote from the story as to be rather inconsequential. The story is messy, and as such, it serves to open a moral debate.

I turn now to the talk of another fifty-something woman about a Golden Age film that mimics her own and her husband's life. The woman's narration highlights the loss of male subjectivity,[34] which in the melodramatic mode is hard to personalize or vilify because of its profoundly social and historical character. In straddling film and personal narrative in this way, I follow Marc Silberman's suggestion that we read film by oscillating "between the textually inscribed spectator, which tends to undermine historicity in its perpetual present of formal and narrative patterns, and the socioculturally differentiated spectator with a political and institutional identity."[35]

The Moviegoer on *Pak Sŏbang*

I call the woman whose story I now relate The Moviegoer, to capture both her enduring love of film and our shared interest in movies (and television soap operas) that ran the course of much of our talk together. The Moviegoer amazed me with her vivid reminiscences of the films she had watched in her youth and frequently urged me to see Western classics I had missed (to her great surprise), from *Waterloo Bridge* to *Ben Hur*. For The Moviegoer, films recalled the happiest moments of an otherwise difficult youth. At moments when The Moviegoer seemed overwhelmed by the heaviness of her own stories, she interrupted herself to ask me, "Did you see [such-and-such] a movie?" or turned briskly from a moment in her life to the narrative of a film she had seen or a novel she had read.

51

For example, The Moviegoer spoke about Kim Sŭng-ho, the famous actor who played Pak Sŏbang (the father and primary protagonist) in the film of the same name. She described that his image generally, and in *Pak Sŏbang* in particular, was that of a "good father . . . the head of a happy family." "His image," she continued, "isn't that of a man who makes lots of money or has any great masculine appeal, but of a father with an abundance of love—a comfortable father." The Moviegoer was on the way to saying that in spite of having been fond of this sort of actor and role, she herself had never thought to marry a man like that: the "good father" or "comfortable man." Instead, she admitted, the man she chose was a much more "conservative" one. The Moviegoer's remarks on actor Kim Sŭng-ho and *Pak Sŏbang* capture the way in which film memories figure in the lives and narratives of the women I spoke with, not as distinct objects of analysis, but as paths leading elsewhere, en route to other things they had to say.

Other details from The Moviegoer's life are suggestive for thinking about her engagement with *Pak Sŏbang*. Her emphasis on actor Kim's comfortable, loving image—an image that blurs with that of Pak in the movie—provides an important contrast with what she often described precisely as her lack of comfort with her husband, in large part because of his politically conservative manner and goals, and his ambition. Albeit anecdotal, her comments on the matter of "comfort," "conservatism," and "ambition" index critical marital struggles over the course of her own life. Her discussions readily evidenced the tensions concerning men and patriarchy in South Korea, tensions also at the heart of *Pak Sŏbang*. Although The Moviegoer had had a difficult marriage and suffered from her husband's ambition and conservative ways (that is, making her uncomfortable), his life story and current situation made it difficult for her to criticize him. In her conversations about him, she was quick to understand and even sympathize with him as a figure displaced by the course of contemporary South Korean history.

The Moviegoer lives in a medium-sized apartment in a high-rise with a corridor view of Seoul's Han River. Her family is able to own an apartment because her husband purchased it with the severance pay he received from a regional chemical company, where he had spent most of his career working as a chemical technician. In the decades since, he has had several work stints in Iran but now finds it hard to do anything professional in South Korea because he is older and does not have a college degree. After all those years of skilled work, The Moviegoer was distressed that her husband had to do common labor for paltry wages. The

Moviegoer has three children: her eldest daughter who with her husband worked as a social activist educating laborers; a second daughter, a long-time Christian feminist activist, who was at the time "too old to be single" ("I tell her that I've left her marriage up to God") and who was studying to become a minister; and a son who, although an "activist in his heart," had taken a more conventional path, working for a large corporation and having just recently married.

Counting herself in the "lower-middle" or maybe "middle-middle class," she was self-conscious of being a housewife who did not work and also made no investments to raise her family's material standard of living. The Moviegoer was often self-critical, musing about why she never thought to work, or to somehow better her family's circumstances, as so many women of her generation and standing have done. Her regrets in this regard were not, however, so straightforward. In part, she posed this question repeatedly because she knew that such women (the kind who make something out of their own or their husband's money) would have made her husband happier. For her and her husband to live together, she said, "Both of us have had to bear with things (*ch'amta*)": while her husband has desire (*yoksim*) and ambition (*yasim*), she described herself as lacking motivation. Nonetheless, she felt lucky to be married to her honest husband—a hard-working and income-earning man who has given her a "comfortable" (in the other sense of that term) life.

The Moviegoer's narratives on her husband often tacked this way and that: on the one hand, she would proclaim her inabilities in the light of his ambition; while on the other hand, she would muster self-confidence against his conservative mind-set and ways. The Moviegoer, however, was never critical of her husband for long because his dashed hopes and thwarted plans—including her own lack of interest in family finances—demanded her sympathy. This sympathy, the reader will see, is inextricable from the historical specificity of her husband's life over a time of considerable transformation and displacement.

The Moviegoer was keenly aware of herself in contrast with—and as such, seen by—her husband. Although she rarely ventured beyond her apartment and her church, she nurtured her vivid imagination and love of stories through her passion for novels, soap operas, and movies. When The Moviegoer's husband would overhear her effusive storytelling during our discussions, he chided her, "Why are you going on about that?" He claimed to have no interest in stories; indeed he was a man who, The Moviegoer lamented, "could not even stay awake at a movie." For her part, she was not embarrassed about her love of stories; in fact, she once retorted to her husband, "How can you take that away from me? It is all I have!" The Bible, which she spoke of as "the world's best-selling novel," was one of her favorite sources of stories. What did move her husband, she said, was his interest in personal mobility and in the nation's political stability. It was in the context of this contrast that she explained that her lack of ambition (*yasim*) and her rather staid lifestyle were particularly ill suited for him. The Moviegoer knew that her husband was from a poor family, and that he would have liked a prettier, more charming, and, most of all, economically more ambitious wife. Life with her husband was hardly "comfortable" in the way that she imagined it would be with a husband like Pak Sŏbang.

A brief glance at the personal history of The Moviegoer's husband is revealing in the light of The Moviegoer's sense of herself, her marriage, and masculinity. She retreated to the nearby kitchen when her husband and I, in the living room, began to chat about his life. When her husband first left his remote countryside village, he promised himself that he would not return until the day he could fly back in a helicopter—just like the ones he had seen in his childhood when the American military had been stationed nearby. Although that day never arrived, he did manage to finish high school and become a respectable wage-earning technician. None of his achievements, however, ever lived up to his sense of his own promise, and he had many regrets about might-have-been lives that did not come to pass (for example, going to the United States or staying in Seoul and working his way into the government).

The Moviegoer's husband described a decision he made early in his life: to abandon the traditional lettered life of his *sŏnbi* (a poor Confucian scholar) father who was not amounting to anything in the "modern" era and to instead follow the ways of his father's oldest brother. This uncle, although technically at the head of his father's patrilineage, in fact occupied a precarious position. The Moviegoer's husband's father's wife had been unable to bear children and in a measure to secure a son he had borne this uncle with another woman; shortly thereafter, however, the father became dissatisfied with this woman of low standing and brought in a another woman from a *yangban* (gentry) family—the woman who bore The Moviegoer's husband and five subsequent children. Thus The Moviegoer's husband's eldest uncle was technically not even in the family register. Although the uncle (the son of the lower-class woman—who was eventually kicked out of the household) had little scholarly ability or refinement, he managed to travel to Japan during the colonial period and succeed in business there. The Moviegoer was forthright as to her estimation of her husband's sympathies (in favor of the uncle over his own father) when she derided the uncle as "a collaborator with the Japanese."

The Moviegoer's husband's father, having no real occupation himself, other than the preoccupation with classical learning, relied on the earnings of this half-brother (although not even formally recognized as such) for his family's survival. In an act that The Moviegoer's husband praised for its extraordinary generosity, his father decided to have the uncle formally registered as the eldest son of his father, placing him, to his own detriment, at the much-valued helm of the patrilineage. It was this eldest uncle, a man The Moviegoer's husband admitted was a bit of a brute, whom he decided to model himself after. He described his own father, after all, as an anachronistic figure who had amounted to nothing.

The Moviegoer's husband left the village shortly after the end of the colonial period to live in the sumptuous Seoul residence of the uncle so as to procure an education. As it turned out, though, The Moviegoer's husband's education dreams were never fulfilled beyond high school because during the ideologically charged Korean War the sumptuous quarters and social standing of his collaborator uncle were destroyed; with this, The Moviegoer's husband's own world also turned upside down. Thereafter, he followed a local schoolteacher from his home village who had invited him to join a rural ammonia plant. Quiet and more like his own father, the schoolteacher was a far cry from the flashy figure of his uncle. The Moviegoer's husband considered this move to have been the grave mistake of his life for he left Seoul, the heart of South Korean social and political life, where he would, he said, have likely secured an impressive political career. It was an ironic move, back to the countryside and following local lines of authority, hardly the path he had envisioned. Such is The Moviegoer's husband's personal history that figured as the backdrop to his disappointment in his wife—a disappointment that I mostly heard about from her. Her sense was that her husband wished she might have helped him realize the material dreams befitting the course of his much earlier life—a tall order really. Her husband was hardly the happy, comfortable figure of Pak Sŏbang she admired; to the contrary, he was striving, economically interested, and classically masculine.

In the years I was meeting with The Moviegoer, however, her husband's social position had become in fact quite delicate, his early ambition and his self-modeling after his collaborating uncle aside. Indeed, it was the very instability of his social position that made it difficult for The Moviegoer to think about herself definitively in relation to her husband. Alongside The Moviegoer's Christian wall hangings in the living room were two framed, blown-up photographs of the ammonia plant where her husband had worked (a daylight and a nightlight view) in what had been a state-of-the art operation, a cog in the wheel of South Korea's technological development. However, during the early months when I was interviewing The Moviegoer, her husband had sat hunched over a glass-surface coffee table covered with plastic lace with several dictionaries at his side, trying to decipher the English language blueprints of the plant that a Japanese company was going to build in Mongolia. He and several other men with whom he had worked over a decade earlier had been called to go to Mongolia for a half-year or so to help set up this plant. As he painstakingly translated the English and the numbers into registers familiar to him, he made a discovery that kept him muttering to himself in amazement week after week of my visits to his wife: the Japanese were building an ammonia plant at the technological level of the one he had been a part of decades ago—they were knowingly building a dinosaur and a toxic and dangerous one at that. He had been called to service not as the vanguard worker he had once been but as an engineer of anachronism who could make sense of plans that were illegible to the more modern, better trained, Japanese—who would never dream of hardship stints in the likes of Mongolia.

Over the months, his sixties-something cohort one-by-one abandoned the project; their every-several-day gatherings in coffee houses had proved pointless. Limited though he was in English, he fared better with the English than they did. Finally, he was left alone to make his way through the blueprints. Not long after I left, the whole project fell through; even his chance at fossil employment had failed. In the discussion of *Pak Sŏbang* that follows, the reader will meet a robust portrait of similarly anachronistic employment and faltering masculinity. If The Moviegoer's husband seemed to offer nothing of the style of Pak Sŏbang, his contemporary predicament nonetheless echoes that of this Golden Age protagonist.

Through the months we met, The Moviegoer talked repeatedly of the days of her husband's great ambition and of her inability to match it, but checked periodically—a quick jog to the nearby living room from the kitchen table where we sat—to see if her husband had not fallen asleep over the blueprints. If he had, she would remove his glasses and cover him with a colorful afghan. For The Moviegoer, who secretly admired her daughters' activities in the student movement, and who supported their continued political activities, her husband's situation—suffering for want of a college degree, unemployable after a lifetime of hard work—was emblematic of an array of social ills she never tired of detailing. As it became harder and harder for her family to maintain middle-class trappings, she had begun to think that she really had failed her family with her inactivity. This is precisely the sense in which her husband's precarious position made it difficult for her to retain a clear sense of self-confidence for not having participated in the family economy.

In her discussions about her husband, it was very difficult for The Moviegoer to separate her thoughts about him from the challenges of changing times and ways. In this context, the actor Kim Sŭng-ho, and *Pak Sŏbang* (both film and character) offered The Moviegoer a rich foothold for thinking about men and their choices (and destinies) and by extension her own life with such men. A brief reading of this film reveals parallel tensions between the sway and anachronism of patriarchy, as enacted through both her marital experience and Pak Sobang's at-once triumph and defeat, and between nostalgia and a brave new world.

A Melodrama of Social Transformation

The Korean term *chuch'esŏng* translates as the loss of male subjectivity and signifies an important national narrative in South Korea, one with its own historical, gender, generation, and class coordinates.[36] For women like The Moviegoer and The Education Mother, male subjectivity refers to both the personal attributes of the men in their lives *and*, metaphorically, to the nation. A person without *chuch'esŏng* refers loosely, for example, to one with little spine, confidence, or sense of self. In another vein, South Koreans equate *chuch'esŏng* with national subjectivity or sovereignty.

Male loss or dislocation—physical, material, cultural, and social—provides a ready grammar for articulating the costs of colonialism, the Korean War, and rapid social transformation in South Korea. While men did not suffer greater losses (real or symbolic) over the course of contemporary Korean history than did women, the patriarchal and patrilineal character of the country, at least after the war, led to considerable interest in the historical loss and suffering of fathers and husbands, such as that of The Moviegoer in relation to her husband.[37] For the generation of South Koreans that came of age in the 1950s and 1960s (with Golden Age melodramas), the interest in personal, social, and cinematic narratives of this ilk was particularly pronounced because of their vivid experience of the Korean War,[38] the recent memory of colonialism, and the state narratives and projects of national renewal and development.

To complete a consideration of The Moviegoer's engagement with *Pak Sŏbang* (Neighbor Pak), I turn briefly to the film itself, a film that I take as emblematic of Golden Age melodramas of social transformation. *Pak Sŏbang* is one of many Golden Age films that screens the struggles of male subjectivity.[39] Like the life of The Moviegoer's husband, it maintains a creative tension between patriarchy, namely the excesses of male privilege and power, and the dislocation of men on account of radical social transformation. Its staging of patriarchy, alternately comic, melodramatic, and, in certain moments, very "real" and heavy-handed, presents the father figure asserting himself even as he is depicted as being overshadowed by, the mere pawn of, larger social forces. This same structure informed The Moviegoer's conversation insofar as it was hard for her to name and critique patriarchy as such for precisely the same reason: the hand of history, in this narrative complex, mitigates the excesses of patriarchy—however real its local workings might be. Simply put, in the name of larger concerns, women have found it hard to pin blame on the failings of individual men.

Pak Sŏbang features a father who is portrayed as an anachronism: he is a handyman whose specialty is fixing the flues of Korean *ondol* floors, through which hot air passes to heat traditional homes. *"Sŏbang,"* when applied to a middle-aged man, refers both to his familiarity in the neighborhood and to his modest social standing. Until the film's final scenes, Pak is featured in Korean dress, often with a Western hat and black shoes. Although by no means elite, he is well respected in his urban neighborhood (one that acts much like a village) because his children are well mannered, educated (at least through high school), and employed—his second daughter, Myŏng-sŏn, is an office worker at Northwest Airlines, where she is called "Missŭ [Miss] Pak," and his son is a white-collar worker in a prosperous pharmaceutical company.

Most of comedy of the film derives from Pak's relationship with his daughters. In scene after scene, the family scrambles to hide things associated with their romantic exploits from him. Pak's ambivalence about the new culture of dating and romance generates a series of gags whose humor is evoked spatially; in slapstick scenes involving the opening and closing of many doors, the traditional home becomes a labyrinth for the children to evade the disapproving gaze of the "patriarch." The power of this gaze is qualified, however, not only by the slapstick but also by Pak's wife's grumbling under her breath about his constant meddling in their daughters' affairs—"I don't know when he'll grow up"—and her admonishments that he not be so childish. Yet in matters of social ritual, he retains the gravitas of his role. His eldest daughter is at great pains to secure his approval for her marriage plans, as she anxiously queries her mother: "Have you mentioned it yet [to Pak]?" The film's narrative and mise-en-scène thus present us with a patriarchy characterized, in the earlier part of the film, in affectionate comedic antics and gestures. The developmental anachronism the text stages between Pak's position (father) and behavior (as childish) allegorizes the developmental anachronisms he figures for the nation.

Two scenes, one early in the film, one late, parallel each other and indicate the charged and contradictory stakes of this anachronism. In the first, one of Pak's customers, charmed by his provincial manner, invites him in for "Western liquor" and a snack. He comes up from the flooring, wiping his feet and hiding them from the woman, to sit in a chair at the table with her (traditionally, Koreans ate seated on the floor at low tables). The woman chortles, albeit lovingly, at his unfamiliarity with a Western table setting.[40] She then proceeds to report that her maid tells her his family and the successes of his children are the envy of the entire neighborhood. Here and in the comedic scenes mentioned above, Pak's traditional patriarchal role is portrayed endearingly precisely *because* of his anachronistic ways and line of work. His community and his family play along with his domestic and familial authority precisely because his social authority has been displaced.

Yet this portrayal has a dark side as well. In one scene, Pak hits his eldest daughter, an event that the film then comments upon by depicting a captive rat, racing furiously in his wheel to the sounds of high-pitched, hysterical music. Similarly, the sequence with Pak's charmed customer mentioned above is answered later with another, much more sinister visit. Attended by melodramatic hyperbole—a violin crescendo, thunder, and lightning—Pak meets with the villainous aunt of the orphaned young man who would like to marry his second daughter, Myŏng-sŏn. Myŏng-sŏn has earlier begged her father to wear Western clothes for this meeting, but he stubbornly refuses. The aunt, who has recently returned from Hawai'i, where she has immigrated, has summoned him to her sumptuous home because his daughter's intended is her ward. Pak enters the home to the sound of a bulldog barking, foreshadowing the woman to come. The décor is pointedly marked as foreign, from its television set to the prominently placed Japanese-style floral arrangement. The aunt has called him there to inform him that his daughter is not a suitable match for her nephew, given her family's elevated social standing. Before explaining her real motives, though, she goads him, asking if he knows why she has called him. Pak speaks naively of his daughter's charms and of the praise she has garnered in their neighborhood. When the aunt offers Pak tea, she silently ridicules his ignorance as he opens the tea bag into the water. Gone is any neighborhood mitigation of class difference. She tells him outright that he is ignorant and unlearned (*musik*) and that "laborers are meant to marry laborers." At this point the melodramatic storm and its musical accompaniment envelop the scene.

The nakedness of this scene serves as an epiphany for Pak; the humiliation of this encounter—in such stark contrast with the loving coddling of his family and neighborhood—becomes a call to action. He is thrown out of the house, and the longest shot of the film captures him silently leaning against the high walls of the fortress-like house. To the filmic accompaniment of scenes from his past, he walks away, stooped over, reminiscing about the hardships of labor and of the rearing of his children. He goes to his neighborhood bar and sits alone as the furious thunder and lightning rage on.

Meeting his son, Pak immediately asks him what it is that one does with a tea bag and then weeps in the knowledge of his humiliation. He proclaims, "Others say that you are the children of a good family, but you are nothing but the children of a flue-repairman. People look down on you. How will I ever be able to bear the burden of my regret?" He vows to work himself to the bone to send his children to college. His meeting with his son at this moment is similar to another salient thematic arc in this film; its central couple involves neither of Pak's daughters nor his wife, but is rather Pak's relationship with this, his only son (played by major film star Kim Jin-gyu). At many points in the film, the two are portrayed almost as lovers, encircled in greenery, holding hands, in teary raptures, with requisite musical accompaniment. Early on, we hear the father proclaim to his son, in the midst of his consternation about Myŏng-sŏn, "You are the only one I trust."

Pak's son has been asked by his boss at the pharmaceutical company to consider a placement abroad in Thailand. When he broke this news to his father, Pak asked, "Are you the only one they can send? If you leave I have no one else to trust—don't leave!" The son had pleaded, explaining that this was the only way for him to advance, to rise up in the world (*ch'ulse*), but Pak persisted: "What if you die in a plane crash? The neighborhood people all say that you are filial . . . I didn't raise you to go abroad." Now, in the storm of this melodramatic moment, Pak decides that his son must go abroad, that he must allow him to garner the capital of a new era. He tells him, "Go and succeed in Thailand," and walks off to a melodramatic dirge.

With the visit to the vicious aunt, Pak (and the spectator) is made cruelly aware of his displacement—albeit, and importantly, away from the local eye of his family or neighborhood. He retaliates with decisions in step with the times. In this way, he safeguards his ego and makes the patriarchal proclamation that sanctions his son's departure. It is thus the father whose restored ego or subjectivity insures domestic harmony and, in this case, the upward mobility of the next generation.

The film's final scenes are the son's wedding and his immediate departure for Thailand afterward. In these scenes Pak is featured in a Western suit. The wedding is a teary celebration of the son's fealty: the son proclaims his sadness to be leaving, and the father and son leave the festivities for a teary embrace. The son tells Pak to live with hope. As the plane takes off, we see the son crying inside. Pak retreats as the music swells, muttering to himself that the plane better be strong and that his son should return with children. He then walks off down a peaceful tree-lined street of Korea's yesteryear.

This film's melodramatic flourishes and plot structure dramatize South Korea's social transformation and the vicissitudes of personal mobility. The film's tensions—the parallel sway and anachronism of patriarchy, Pak's simultaneous triumph and defeat, and the competition between nostalgia and a brave new world—invite a rich array of commentary and reflection on a changing world.

In this film and many more of this era we find the delicate play of male subjectivity amidst precarious social times and considerable status anxiety.[41] The medium of film is apt here: it allows patriarchy to be staged such that it emerges simultaneously as exaggerated, pitiful (melodramatic), and absurd (comedic), but nonetheless intermittently powerful. Pak is humiliated by his ignorance of a changing world and thus stands for more than his personal predicament. Here we can also recall The Moviegoer: draping an afghan over her husband, pitying his efforts at anachronistic employment, while at once bemoaning her fate to have married a man of such ambition rather than the "comfortable . . . good father" typified by actor Kim Sŭng-ho and by Pak in the film. The ambivalent male gaze of this popular Golden Age movie speaks to prevailing and long-standing ways in which (social and national) displacement have been gendered and narrated in South Korea generally, and particularly for the generation of women featured in this essay.

Often the most melodramatic moments in personal and film narratives—when the sky suddenly trembles in rumbles of thunder (in a film) or a story builds to an emotional climax (in a woman's personal story)—are those that assert the links between the personal and the social. These links are evidenced in the narration of the "loss of male subjectivity" in its melodramatic, and hence dialogic, context. A dialogic approach to this narration mirrors the academic debates on melodrama with which I began. It is precisely because stories of male displacement are inextricable from the social or political context, that patriarchy is necessarily staged and narrated with considerable ambivalence. Melodrama, then, has been a mode well suited to the narration of self and nation over the course of South Korea's tumultuous social transformation. In a similar mode, in their own narratives and in their (film) viewing pleasure, middle-aged South Korean women have often voiced an ambivalent position on the excesses of patriarchy. Golden Age film has been a willing accomplice in this gendered narrative project—one at the heart of the sensibilities of contemporary South Korea.

Notes

1. See Nancy Abelmann, "Narrating Selfhood and Personality in South Korea: Women and Social Mobility," *American Ethnologist* 24, no. 4 (1997): 784–812; Abelmann, "Women's Class Mobility and Identities in South Korea: A Gendered, Transgenerational, Narrative Approach," *Journal of Asian Studies* 56, no. 2 (1997): 398–420; Abelmann, "Women, Mobility, and Desire: Narrating Class and Gender in South Korea," in *Under Construction: The Gendering of Modernity, Class, and Consumption in the Republic of Korea*, ed. Laurel Kendall (Honolulu: University of Hawai'i Press, 2002), 25–53; Abelmann, *The Melodrama of Mobility: Women, Talk, and Class in Contemporary South Korea* (Honolulu: University of Hawai'i Press, 2003).
2. See Abelmann, *Melodrama of Mobility.*
3. Lila Abu-Lughod, "Modern Subjects: Egyptian Melodrama and Postcolonial Difference," in *Questions of Modernity,* ed. Timothy Mitchell (Minneapolis: University of Minnesota Press, 2000), 87–114.
4. Thomas Elsaesser, "Tales of Sound and Fury: Observations on the Family Melodrama," in *Home Is Where the Heart Is: Studies in Melodrama and the Woman's Film,* ed. Christine Gledhill (1972; London: BFI, 1987), 52.
5. Peter Brooks, *The Melodramatic Imagination: Balzac, Henry James, Melodrama, and the Mode of Excess* (1976; New Haven: Yale University Press, 1995), 11–12; Ann E. Kaplan, "Melodrama/Subjectivity/Ideology: Western Melodrama Theories and Their Relevance to Recent Chinese Cinema," in *Melodrama and Asian Cinema,* ed. Wimal Dissanayake (New York: Cambridge University Press, 1993), 10.
6. Elsaesser, "Tales of Sound and Fury," 51. Some have argued that this is particularly pronounced for cinema. See Laura Mulvey, "Melodrama Inside and Outside the Home," in *Visual and Other Pleasures,* ed. Laura Mulvey (Bloomington: Indiana University Press, 1989), 63–80.
7. See also Jinoo An, chapter 3, and Keehyeung Lee, chapter 9, in this volume.

8. Brooks, *Melodramatic Imagination;* Ian Watt, *The Rise of the Novel: Studies in Defoe, Richardson, and Fielding* (Berkeley: University of California Press, 1957).

9. Brooks, *Melodramatic Imagination,* 205.

10. Maureen Turim, "Psyches, Ideologies, and Melodrama: The United States and Japan," in *Melodrama and Asian Cinema,* ed. Dissanayake, 155.

11. Lisa Rofel, "Liberation Nostalgia and a Yearning for Modernity," in *Engendering China: Women, Culture, and the State,* ed. Christina K. Gilmartin et al. (Cambridge: Harvard University Press, 1994). 707.

12. Kaplan, "Melodrama/Subjectivity/Ideology," 26.

13. Dissanayake, ed., *Melodrama and Asian Cinema.*

14. William Rothman, "Overview: What Is American Film Study All About," in *Melodrama and Asian Cinema,* ed. Dissanayake, 269.

15. See Chan E. Park, *Voices from the Straw Mat: Toward an Ethnography of Korean Story Singing* (Honolulu: University of Hawai'i Press, 2003).

16. Elsaesser, "Tales of Sound and Fury," 47.

17. Colin MacCabe, "Theory and Film: Principles of Realism and Pleasure," *Screen* 17, no. 3 (1976): 9–11.

18. Ien Ang, *Watching Dallas* (1982; London: Methuen, 1985), 38; see also Lila Abu-Lughod, "The Objects of Soap Opera: Egyptian Television and the Cultural Politics of Modernity," in *Worlds Apart: Modernity through the Prism of the Local,* ed. Daniel Miller (London, Routledge, 1995), 9; Ien Ang and Jon Stratton, "The End of Civilization as We Know It: Chancy and the Postrealist Soap Opera," in *To Be Continued . . . : Soap Operas around the World,* ed. Robert C. Allen (New York: Routledge, 1995), 126; Dissanayake, *Melodrama and Asian Cinema,* 2; Linda Williams, "Melodrama Revised," in *Refiguring American Film Genres: History and Theory,* ed. Nick Browne (Berkeley: University of California Press, 1998), 53.

19. Ariel Dorfman, "Someone Writes to the Future: Meditations on Hope and Violence in García Márquez," in *Some Write to the Future: Essays on Contemporary Latin American Fiction,* ed. Ariel Dorfman (Durham, NC: Duke University Press, 1991), 201–22.

20. See Arjun Appadurai, "Global Ethnoscapes: Notes for a Transnational Anthropology," in *Recapturing Anthropology,* ed. Richard G. Fox (Santa Fe: School of American Research Press, 1991); Jerome Bruner, *Actual Minds, Possible Worlds* (Cambridge: Harvard University Press, 1986).

21. Elsaesser, "Tales of Sound and Fury," 55–56; see also Mulvey, "Melodrama Inside and Outside the Home."

22. Christine Gledhill, "The Melodramatic Field: An Investigation," in *Home Is Where the Heart Is,* 13; see also Kathleen McHugh, *American Domesticity: From How-To Manual to Hollywood Melodrama* (New York: Oxford University Press, 1999); Gledhill, "South Korean Film Melodrama and the Question of National Cinema," *Quarterly Review of Film and Video* 18, no. 1 (2001); Ning Ma, "Symbolic Representation and Symbolic Violence: Chinese Family Melodrama of the Early 1980s," in *Melodrama and Asian Cinema,* ed. Dissanayake, 33.

23. Gledhill, "Melodramatic Field," 13.

24. Brooks, *Melodramatic Imagination,* ix; see also McHugh, *American Domesticity.*
25. Elsaesser, "Tales of Sound and Fury," 64.
26. Brooks, *Melodramatic Imagination,* 35.
27. Gledhill, "Melodramatic Field," 30.
28. Kaplan, "Melodrama/Subjectivity/Ideology," 24.
29. Mitsuhiro Yoshimoto, "Melodrama, Postmodernism, and Japanese Cinema," in *Melodrama and Asian Cinema,* ed. Dissanayake, 109.
30. Brooks, *Melodramatic Imagination.*
31. Ibid., 20–21.
32. Allen, *To Be Continued,* 18.
33. Brooks, *Melodramatic Imagination,* vii.
34. See also Eunsun Cho, chapter 4, and Kyung Hyun Kim, chapter 8, in this volume.
35. Marc Silberman, *German Cinema: Texts in Context* (Detroit: Wayne State University Press, 1995), xi–xii.
36. See Henry Em, "Yi Sang's 'Wings' Read as an Anti-Colonial Allegory," *Muae* 1 (1995): 105–11; Sheila Miyoshi Jager, "A Vision for the Future; or, Making Family History in Contemporary South Korea," *Positions: East Asia Cultures Critique* 4, no. 1 (1996): 31–58; and Andre Schmid, "Rediscovering Manchuria: Sin Ch'aeho and the Politics of Territorial History in Korea," *Journal of Asian Studies* 56, no. 1 (1997): 26–46, on Korean gendered narratives of nation and history.
37. That narratives of the *chŏngsindae* (comfort women) have become much more public and widespread in South Korea over the last decade and a half indicates a change. See Soyoung Kim, chapter 7 in this volume, on comfort women films in the 1990s. See Dai Sil Kim-Gibson, *Silence Broken: Korean Comfort Women* (Parkersburg, IA: Mid-Prairie, 1999); Chungmoo Choi, ed., "Special Issue: The Comfort Women," *Positions: East Asia Cultures Critique* 5, no. 1 (1997); Chunghee Sarah Soh, "From Imperial Gifts to Sex Slaves," *Social Science Japan Journal* 3, no. 1 (2000): 1–33; see also Sheila Miyoshi Jager, "Women, Resistance, and the Divided Nation: The Romantic Rhetoric of Korean Reunification," *Journal of Asian Studies* 55, no. 1 (1996): 3–21 on female subjectivity in the narration of the division of the peninsula.
38. See David Scott Diffrient, chapter 6 in this volume.
39. For example, *The Stray Bullet, Romance Papa, Until the End of My Life, The Coachman.*
40. See Choi, "Magic and Violence of Modernization" for a discussion of the representation of things Western in South Korean film.
41. See Eunsun Cho, chapter 4, and Hye Seung Chung, chapter 5, in this volume on *The Stray Bullet,* and Jinsoo An, chapter 3 in this volume on *Until the End of My Life;* for a contemporary film see Kyung Hyun Kim, chapter 8 in this volume on *Happy End.*

3

Screening the Redemption:
Christianity in Korean Melodrama

JINSOO AN

In modern Korean literature, the 1913 *sinp'a* work *Changhanmong* (*A Long and Sorrowful Dream*) by Cho Ilche has taken on historical significance as the earliest example of Korean melodrama. *Sinp'a* is Korea's modern melodrama that was imported from Japan (*shimpa* in Japanese) and quickly became a major popular genre in Korea at the turn of the century. Adapted from the famous Japanese *shimpa* drama *Konjikiyasha* by Ozaki Koyo, *Changhanmong* features a turbulent love triangle between a woman and two men who represent opposing social values. Sim Sunae and Yi Suil are in love with each other. Sim's family, however, pressures her to marry a wealthy man, Kim Chungbae. She resists, but then consents to marry Kim, whom she clearly does not love. She comes to regret her decision, feeling great guilt for her betrayal of Yi. Meanwhile, a resentful Yi becomes a greedy moneylender, hoping to take revenge on Sim with his new wealth. As both lovers choose a path counter to their desire, they become the victims of circumstance: namely, money-driven reality. This "antinomy between action [following money] and thought [following love]" illustrates the distinctive feature of *sinp'a* drama.[1] The drama, however, ends happily. Sim becomes insane due to her guilt, but Yi's forgiveness and resumed love resuscitate her at the end. This resolution departs from the original Japanese work, which ends with the female protagonist's suicide. Critics have pointed out *Changhanmong*'s happy ending follows the optimistic worldview of the traditional Korean narrative arts where the good are always rewarded and the bad are punished.[2]

A crucial yet largely overlooked element, however, makes *Changhanmong* a distinctively modern form of Korean melodrama: the theme of Christianity.[3] When Sim and Yi reunite after a long agonizing separation, they explicitly speak of forgiveness and salvation; they are able to resolve misunderstandings, overcome ordeals, and finally bring back their love for each other through Christian virtues.[4] Although the Christian themes are introduced rather abruptly into the narrative, they nevertheless function as the spiritual and ethical mandates around which the drama's fundamental conflict revolves. Thus, contrary to Yu Minyŏng's observations on the negative effects of Christian themes in *Changhanmong,* that is, they displaced the keen naturalist viewpoint of the Japanese work with melodramatic sentiments, I contend these themes play an important function in the moral imagination of Korean people. If *Changhanmong*'s optimism echoes the thematic voice of traditional narrative arts,[5] this was done, I contend, in the dynamic new terms of Christian ideas and practices, which had already become prevalent at the time. Relegating Christian motifs to a minor (or non-) element in the *sinp'a* drama thus misses a critical linkage between melodrama's vernacular way of figuring the meaningful world and the moral universe of Christianity that many Koreans of the era eagerly embraced.[6] Thus I call attention to the overlapping thematic grounds of two modes of imagination: the moral logic of melodrama and the promise of salvation in Christianity, as both emerged at a critical juncture of Korea's modern history. These moral imaginations endowed Koreans with a logical means to cope with tumultuous and traumatic historical experiences.[7] Concurrently, my inquiry considers how this imported religious view formed an odd and ambiguous relationship with the precepts of existing social mores. Understanding the dynamic historical relationship of Christianity and melodrama is a key framework for the examination of cinematic representation of Christian motifs here. In my textual analysis of two key films of the early 1960s, *Until the End of My Life* and *The Houseguest and My Mother,* I pay close attention to the implications of the gendered and hierarchical figuration of religious practices and spiritual salvation. The inquiry subsequently moves to historical questions concerning these gendered images of Christianity when the state demanded substantial reorganization of social relations for its "modernization" project.

Two Modes of Imagination

To understand the close historical relationship between the development of Korean melodrama and the salvific character of Korean Christianity, one must begin with the nation's tumultuous modern history, especially its religious history. Just as drastic social upheavals characterize modern Korean history, significant changes took place in Korea's religious field in the late nineteenth and early twentieth centuries. Confucianism declined rapidly as the nation's dominant ideology. Although Confucianism still commands influence over Korean culture at large, it lost the power and authority that were once vital to the Chosŏn Dynasty (1392–1910). The late nineteenth century witnessed the advent of various religions, both indigenous and Western, that competed to fill the vacuum left by the decline of Confucianism. *Tonghak* ("Eastern Learning"), an indigenous religion founded by Ch'oe Cheu, quickly spread to the farming villages as a new belief system. In *Tonghak,* mankind and The Supreme Being (God) are understood as one and the same. Because the spirit of man is a manifestation of God, serving man, according to its precepts, is also serving God. It combined the ideas and practices of many religions, including Buddhism, Confucianism, Taoism, Shamanism, and even Catholicism ("Western Learning"), the religion against which it established its identity, and gained support predominantly from the oppressed peasantry.[8]

It was, however, Protestantism that showed the most remarkable growth within and influence on Korean society during the late nineteenth and the early twentieth centuries. Several factors have been held to account for this phenomenal success.[9] They include: a precipitous disintegration of Korea's social fabric and nationhood, particularly the demise of the Yi Dynasty and subsequent colonization by the Japanese imperial force; Christianity's lucid vision of salvation; Christianity's conciliatory relationship with Korean nationalism; and the rigorous proselytization program of Revivalism.[10] Protestantism arrived in Korea when the Korean government was in a struggle to defend itself against Japanese aggression. People eagerly embraced the modern educational system and medical facilities that Protestantism brought to Korea, and the religion quickly became associated with modernization and nationalism. The Protestant missionary schools were especially instrumental in arousing Korea's modern national consciousness, as the nation itself faced decline and colonial domination, becoming a protectorate in 1905 and a colony in 1910.[11] For many Koreans, education represented a step toward a patriotic nationalist resistance against Japanese colonial domination. Indeed, many early nationalists were Protestants, and Protestantism grew steadily during the colonial years despite Japanese colonial surveillance and suppression.

After the Korean War, the Syngman Rhee regime (Yi Sŭngman, 1948–60) provided various institutional supports for Christian churches while repressing other religious practices; Protestantism virtually became the national religion.[12] Yet, the most remarkable growth of Korean Protestantism came in the 1960s and 1970s, when membership nearly doubled each decade, and the number of colossal churches increased. If it had previously kindled the resistance and hope for the liberation and sovereignty of the nation-state in early periods, Korean Protestantism now largely complied with the political ideology of the Park regime and was used to demonstrate full support of anticommunism and developmentalism. Industrialization and urbanization created a new urban mass, and the churches blossomed by incorporating this population. Revivalist proselytizers gave passionate sermons in which one's material accumulation was often interpreted as signs of God's blessings. They thereby echoed and paralleled the social ideology of the state's developmentalism. Protestantism's remarkable growth and presence in the urban environment changed the social landscape of the society, and this environment also affected the way Christian ideas and ideals were expressed and understood.

While I value the explanatory power of these contextual accounts on Christianity's success, I also want to emphasize a distinctive mode of engagement through which the new religion came to be seen as an alternative worldview. It was people's common beliefs and worldview, refashioned and retooled in modern times, that perceived and imagined the world as an essentially meaningful and righteous place, even when the world itself was caught in incessant turmoil, crisis, and injustice. In cultural productions, this vernacular order of things appeared in highly affecting and excessive forms. That is, this popular moral imagination found channels of expression in rhetorical excess and affective emotion in cultural forms. I call this phenomenon the "popular reasoning of melodrama." Comprised of residual elements of the past, this popular reasoning encompasses and synthesizes multiple and conflicting ideas to project a seemingly coherent worldview. It refers to the repository of sociocultural values from the past and their volatile transformation and adaptability to modern times. Yet popular reasoning also entails, due to its affective and hyperbolic features, the inherent contradictions and disjunctions at work. It projects unison and continuity on the surface, while formally it undoes its own very process of homogenization through stylistic and rhetorical hyperboles. That is, it implies the transgressive gesture and subversive logic of social codes and boundaries. The dynamics of popular reasoning, its subversive wisdom as well as its conservative character, circumscribe the mode of Korean melodrama's expression and elaboration of the nation's cultural identity.

This term also intimates that Korean people played an active role in formulating a distinctive worldview even while eagerly accepting the new ideas of a foreign religion. In other words, people developed a persistent yet ever-changing mechanism of intelligence, a reasoning process of a particular kind, to cope with difficulties and hardship. This reasoning then informed the dialectical workings of the people's popular philosophy in relation to a hostile environment.[13] Critical inquiries on melodrama thus should discern and describe the contours of this popular reasoning, and interpret its changing ideological implications in history.

I use the term melodrama here to refer to a broad modern mode of representation that dramatizes moral conflicts and spiritual regeneration through rhetorical excess. Instead of a narrow genre, melodrama is, following Julianne Burton-Carvajal's account, "a metageneric category, a way of registering experience, . . . a means of encoding moral and ideological concerns within registers of the aesthetics and the emotional."[14] As Peter Brooks aptly points out, at the center of melodrama lies "the moral occult, the domain of operative *spiritual values* which is both indicated within and masked by the surface of reality."[15] Hyperbolic music, histrionic gesture, and implausible dramatic reversals are all fundamental characteristics of melodrama—"to express all"—which give utterance to feelings that are inaccessible in an ordinary realistic mode.[16] Melodrama thus endeavors to project a transcendental reality by articulating the essential order of things. And, a structure of "dual recognition," which highlights the tension between "how things are and how they should be," works particularly well to enhance its transcendental and spiritual tendency.[17] This bi-focalizing tendency is particularly apt to convey both the rapid changes of social relations and their psychological impact on individuals.

It is important to remember here that Brooks's study of melodrama places this cultural form against the historical backdrop of increasing secularization in the West. He locates the rise of melodrama within the context of bourgeois revolution and its subsequent epistemological impact. The cohesive and explanatory power of sacred myth lost its aura, and ecclesiastical institutions faced the destruction of their authority. Yet there remained a profound need to fill the spiritual and ethical void created by the demise of the old system. Melodrama's hyperdramatization of polarized forces thus represents "the urge toward resacralization and the impossibility of conceiving sacralization in other than personal terms."[18] Similarly, the Korean melodramatic mode is a by-product of history, circumscribed by an erosion of the feudal order and social system. It should be stressed, however, that the nation's tumultuous history was central to the historical formation of Korean melodrama: the precipitous decline of the nation-state, and the equally tempestuous and rapid process of Japan's colonial domination.

The unique historical background of Korean melodrama thus informs a pattern of moral themes different from the Western model. Resacralization in Western melodrama, for instance, restages now-defunct social and cultural values. It has a tendency to evaluate the rapid transformation of social relations by looking back and consulting the old order of things. In contrast, resacralization took a more mediated, qualified, and syncretic form in Korean melodrama. Early melodramatic texts typically dramatize the moral superiority of the old values. Yet turning back to pre-modern values, that is, the Confucian order, was not conducive to clearing up the present crisis. Instead, past values had to be mediated, qualified by, and amalgamated with Western and modern values, often represented by the new religion. Christian values were employed to represent a solution to the social crisis of modern times. They provided the important ground for the same old values to be staged, evaluated, and morally validated (or repudiated) in melodramatic texts.[19] Simultaneously, the character of Christianity itself has been transformed in this dialectical process as it actively engaged in dialogue with the existing moral precepts of Korea.[20] The result of this exchange was dynamic permutations of both the new religion and the indigenous cultural logic. Christianity quickly gained an indigenous character while Christian themes became deeply ingrained in the moral vocabulary of Korean melodrama.

In addition to the thematic significance of the Christian worldview to the development of Korean melodrama, melodramatic reasoning has been crucial to the ecclesiastic practice of Korean Christianity. This is particularly the case when considering proselytization methods and conversion experiences. Revivalism, for instance, has played a major role in the historical development of Korean Christianity.[21] Revivalism, commonly known as Evangelicalism, Fundamentalism, or Pentecostalism, requires not only absolute faith in Christ's redemptive death and resurrection, but also the experience of *"a felt-conviction of rebirth."*[22] In Revivalism, the profound faith comes from one's "born-again" conversion experience, through repentance of sins, acceptance of Jesus Christ as Savior, and the endeavor to live a virtuous life.[23] Faith healing, a sign of a Korean believer's resort to shamanistic rituals, is not an uncommon practice in Korean Protestant churches. Loud and fervent praying, combined with confessions of deep-felt faith, cheerful singing, and praise for the Lord are characteristic features of church services in Korea. In other words, an ordinary Korean becomes a Christian typically through a highly *affective* experience of spiritual regeneration. I stress that the melodramatic imagination is the constitutive fabric of this conversion experience. Melodrama and Revivalism, therefore, form a historical dyad, each giving the other structure, pattern, and color for the mutually enforcing articulation of a similar logic.

Further, there is also a structural and historical connection between the Korean narrative of nation and melodrama's moral imagination. Benedict Anderson's insights on the cultural roots of nationalism are relevant here. For Anderson, the ebbing of religious belief led by rationalist secularism did not alleviate the problems of suffering, fatality, and salvation. Instead, these questions persisted in times of secularization and required a new concept or mode of imagination to resolve symbolically the epistemological crisis that the erosion of the religious authority brought forth. The nation emerged to perform the "secular transformation of fatality into continuity, contingency into meaning," and thereby achieved "profound *emotional* legitimacy."[24] Nationalism was not simply an independent political doctrine but rather a part of larger cultural systems: namely, the religious community and dynastic realm, from which it emerged later.[25]

While Anderson pays close attention to the cultural dynamics that affected the formation of nationalism, the correlation he draws does not fully explain how, or by what mode of representation and address, nationalism is able to project cohesion and meaning onto modern life. I argue that it is the melodramatic mode of representation and its emphasis on spiritual and moral regeneration that filled the gap. As Brooks's aforementioned theory of melodrama suggests, the melodramatic way to perceive and understand the world signals an effort to achieve a proper, if not stable, relation between self-identity and a hostile environment.[26] Melodrama's affective rhetoric and moral economy, both of which generate strong pathos for the suffering yet virtuous protagonist, provide the indispensable conceptual grip to imagine, articulate, and project the nation as a struggling melodramatic hero(ine); the nation as protagonist undergoes hardship and suffering, but his/her destiny is that of prevailing. In the case of Korea, this means a figuration of Korea as the subject of history that overcomes colonial domination and achieves independence and sovereignty. The nation subsequently becomes a virtuous subject in this moral narrative of affect and regeneration.

More specifically, melodramatic representation offers the techniques of temporal figuration that the nation needs to imagine itself as the coherent subject of history. It has already been pointed out that the idea of nation as the ever-renewing and sovereign subject of history has a linear and teleological character.[27] Nations always aspire to achieve, in

71

atavistic fashion, the heritage of the past. Yet, the story of the nation encompasses persistent temporal contradictions, for it paradoxically attempts to liberate itself from the shackles of the past to participate in "the telos of modernity."[28] How does the discourse of nation then resolve this problem of temporality? In my view, one of the ways in which the national discourse manages and overcomes this dilemma is through a melodramatic rendering of time in the modern world.[29] As mentioned earlier, the melodramatic form has a structure of dual recognition: how things are and how things should be.[30] This feature can be conceptualized in temporal terms here. The former designates the irreversible present, that is, the modern environment, often hostile and alien to the protagonist. The latter, on the contrary, connotes the repository of the past values to which the protagonist often has recourse. By mobilizing bi-focal attention to these opposing values, melodrama exposes the fundamental contradiction of these associated temporalities. Melodrama insists on the relevance of the past values, on the one hand, and simultaneously informs viewers of the formidable modern environment that frustrates and threatens the old values, on the other. The narrative obsessively emphasizes the unbridgeable gap between these two conflicting values.

However, melodrama's affective way of conveying a moral worldview mediates these polarizing and contradictory attitudes toward the world. The drama's symbolic resolution eases the aporia of temporal disjuncture by projecting the transcendental impulses of the moral virtues, compounded by affective rhetoric. Its effect is then to illustrate the relevance and continuity of the past and the need to acknowledge the irreversible arrival of modern development. Melodrama's spiritual and transcendental character delivers a mechanism of moral affect that seems to override the dilemma of time. It is through recourse to the melodramatic rehearsal of this temporal dilemma and its affective economy of resolution that the narrative of nation alludes to surmount the rupture of time.[31] This is predicated, therefore, on a tripartite historical relation among political discourse (nationalism), religious practice (Protestantism), and cultural form (melodrama) as they actively share similar thematic and narrative trajectories.

In the modern history of Korea, the moral and transcendental trajectory of melodrama has been instrumental to the conceptual development of Korea's incipient nationalism. Protestantism in particular was instrumental for many Koreans to keep their faith in nationalist resistance and to promote social reform and modern consciousness. It provided a radically alternative worldview, not only to the now-bygone feudal system but also to Japanese colonial discourses, which largely justified Japan's political and institutional violence over Korea. Protestant ideas and ideals provided the conceptual terms for the modernity that nationalists engaged in the discursive struggle against the Japanese model.

Yet embracing Christianity also meant an acceptance of its intro-spective imagination of suffering and redemption. The concept of suffer-ing, to be sure, has long been a part of the cultural vocabularies of Korea. However, the term (*konan* in Korean) acquired new religious connota-tions as Protestantism broadened its cultural influence in Korea. Christian concepts such as sin, repentance, and the dichotomy of good and evil were also used to explicate the relationship between an individual and God. Protestantism taught the masses to understand their present suffer-ing according to the concepts of original sin, spiritual ordeal, and even-tual salvation.[32] Thus, even though Christianity helped many Korean intellectuals to develop a particular mindscape to imagine social regener-ation and nationalist struggle, it simultaneously encouraged the individ-uals turning away from such sociopolitical orientations by figuring social crisis in purely religious and spiritual terms. The cause of human suffer-ing was now interpreted as the result of one's original sin and spiritual alienation. It is thus not too difficult to imagine the problem this reli-gious teaching posed to nationalist discourse, which, by contrast, located social evil in the imperial aggression of Japan. Individual, if not esoteric, practice of the new religion could obfuscate the effort to implement rad-ical political discourse for the nation. Christianity thus produced bifur-cated discursive effects: it offered the imaginative terms for the nation to project an alternative modernity but also conditioned and limited the very potentials of this social imagination with innate spiritual mandates. There was, thus, a persistent aporia in the way Christianity grew and became a dominant religion of the nation.

This persistent dilemma invites us to reconsider a pervasive charac-ter of Korean Protestantism: syncretism. The term typically refers to Protestantism's appropriation and amalgamation of the ideas and prac-tices of the existing folk religions.[33] Yet syncretism, or the cultural process of indigenization, needs to be understood beyond institutional (that is, ecclesiastical) practice and convention. Rather than a mechanical trans-plantation, the discourse of syncretism alludes to a persistent aporia and contradiction as the new religion has actively mediated and promulgated the polarizing but interrelated discourses of modernity and spirituality. In other words, underneath the syncretic character of Korean Protestantism lies the ambiguity of conflicting temporal orientations: the one that is clearly affiliated with the modern and social and the other with the pre-modern and esoteric. By cultivating the vision of an alternative modernity and by selectively adopting an indigenous worldview and practices, Protestantism acquired a syncretic character in Korea. Impulses to modern consciousness and habitual recourse to folk religiosity coexist in contradictory manner. As a discursive process, the notion of syncretism therefore constantly calibrates and equalizes the deep-seated anxiety over the disparity of modernity and tradition. Syncretism then produced highly charged, yet often ambiguous meanings of Christian motifs in cultural representations.

Christian motifs in melodramatic films are then significant because, as signs of syncretism and indigenization, these images are indicative of strategies to represent, manage, and resolve the inherent aporia and ambiguities of the imported religion in a changing social environment. Korean Protestantism voices its character in cinema via melodramatic impersonation and this genre's matrix of familial and interpersonal relations. More importantly, however, the reconfiguration of gender relations persistently functions as the structuring mechanism to deal with the contradictions of these discourses. As I will demonstrate, the dilemma of syncretism is largely organized, represented, and resolved around representations of female protagonists and their actions in postwar South Korean films. Typical is the reestablishment of religious credos, or resacralization, through dramatization of women's survival, transformation, and regeneration. Thus the process of indigenization or syncretism is structurally linked to and made possible by the repositioning of women in different social spheres.

Yet this strategy is not without problems, for highlighting the transformative power of women raises fundamental questions about the existing social matrix that safeguards hierarchical gender relations. Because of the social dimension of gender configurations, the cinematic projection of redemption possesses an ideological character at bottom. Consequently, the ideological effect of such images in relation to the 1960s grand project of nation building, which engineered the arrangement of new gender relations, bears further scrutiny. It is with this awareness of the gendered and ideological nature of Christian images that I now turn to the film texts themselves.

Screening the Redemption

Toward the end of *A Country Bride* (*Ch'onsaeksi*, Pak Yŏnghwan, 1958), there is a scene in which a young woman rushes to church to say her prayers. She has framed her sister-in-law for burglary and infidelity while her brother was away. She has convinced her parents of her sister-in-law's moral failings and made them expel her from their home. The sister-in-law returns to her own family home in grief, only to receive a cold reception from her own brother. Ashamed and shattered, she decides to commit suicide by plunging into the river from a cliff. She is rescued by her husband, who rushes to the scene at the nick of time. He also learns of her innocence and clears the charges against her. Meanwhile, the wicked sister who orchestrated the whole scheme regrets her wrongdoings and runs to a church. She kneels before the church building to make her prayer of forgiveness. Like *Changhanmong*, the film interjects a Christian motif in a very sudden and abrupt manner. In this way, the film strives to achieve a balanced moral economy by attributing strong Christian mores to the seeming irredeemable antagonist. By doing so, the film projects a reconciliation where evil has been largely eliminated. If this narrative strategy—recourse to Christianity—seems obvious and implausible, it nevertheless delivers a sense of understanding, order, salvation, and resolution at the end. This textual effect reminds us of Christianity's formidable moral and spiritual power as the troubled Korean opts to resort, often too easily, for his or her redemption in melodrama. The greater the peril, the mightier the power of religion appears to be, able to eradicate the source of the problem and project the sense of salvation in the film. As the protagonist takes the "easy option" to follow Christianity, then, the film bypasses the moments of critical and contemplative reflections on her wrongdoing. Instead, urgency dominates the character's action as she rushes, literally, to religion to seek forgiveness and salvation. The sudden and charged conversion of the protagonist alludes to the formidable presence of Christianity as the organizing principle of moral mandates in the culture of modern South Korea.

This peculiar moral economy also informs the need for more careful examination of Christianity in filmic discourses; little research has been done on the religion's dynamic relation to the cultural logic of redemption. The filmic motifs that convey the sense of forgiveness and redemption seem too brief and too hastily introduced. Many such representations of Christianity are elemental and one-dimensional in South Korean melodramas of the 1950s and 1960s.[34] Typical is a forced sense of redemption on the surface of the film's narrative.[35] However, the underdeveloped cinematic discourse is not a result of the religion's insignificance to the moral imagination. Rather, it is because the films draw and organize these moral themes largely from the familiar tropes of secular codes. Only when the films' moral economy reaches the point of total disintegration does a dramatic recourse to Christian repentance and salvation occur. Such a narrative strategy then produces and perpetuates fixed and one-dimensional images of Christianity while it also informs the charged and hyperbolic meanings of the new religion to the noncinematic moral vocabulary of the people.

The texts I examine here have these excessive and hyperbolic features. They illustrate the complex way in which Christian ideas are put in cinematic terms of negotiation in relation to changing social relations and moral imaginations. In particular, these works advance new tropes of femininity and masculinity to respond to and engage with the state-led social engineering of the times. Converging on the gendered representation of Christianity in melodrama is thus the volatile relation between the nationalist discourse of the state and the moral imagination of popular reasoning. In order to elaborate this dynamic relation between cinematic discourses of religiosity and related social forces, the films need to be seen foremost in the broader social context of the postwar years and the state-led modernization project of the 1960s.

During the Korean War, over 3 million Koreans died, and tens of thousands of families became separated by the heavily militarized DMZ established between North and South Korea. The years following the Korean War were fraught with social and political turmoil, including the April Revolution of 1960 and the Military Coup in 1961 that established Park Chung Hee (Pak Chŏnghŭi) as a dictator in South Korea. The distinctive social and cultural matrixes that gave rise to the melodramatic cultural expression of this period need to be taken into consideration. In particular, the dynamics of "modernization" in the 1960s is a crucial subtext for understanding South Korean melodrama, for this massive state project fundamentally transformed almost every aspect of South Korean society. And while Park Chung Hee's economic policies were geared toward rapid "industrialization," his social and cultural programs were intent on constructing a particular national subject suitable to this project through various means of control and regulation. The regime widely used the concept of nation (*minjok*) to legitimize its authoritarian politics. Anticommunism and Developmentalism were the bipolar ideologies used by the state to maintain its political hegemony.[36] In addition, the state promulgated ideas and discourses of national identity, tradition, and cultural uniqueness.[37] Within this volatile social context, South Korean melodrama can be viewed as a part of this discursive field; that is, a field of culturally determined meanings where power relations suffuse nation building.

The traumatic experience of the Korean War and the hardships of its aftermath often haunted the frames of South Korean cinema as frequent thematic and visual motifs. These representations emerged around the late 1950s and the early 1960s, circumscribed by political turmoil and socioeconomic crisis. Concurrently, the search for a spiritual center appeared in hyperbolic and desperate gestures in the melodramatic films of this period where social support for the disadvantaged was painfully absent. *Until the End of My Life* (*I saengmyŏng tahadorok*, Sin Sangok, 1960), is a prime example of this cinematic expression. Adopted from a popular radio drama of the same name, the film documents the ordeal of a family struck down by war, poverty, and loss of family members. Set against the backdrop of the Korean War and its aftermath, the film begins with the tragedy of an army captain who becomes critically injured in battle. He survives, but his lower body is paralyzed. His wife subsequently assumes the role of breadwinner for the family, showing the moral and physical strength to lead the family. The drama chronicles the unending hardship suffered by this family, in which the conjugal relationship repeats cycles of abuse and reconciliation. Out of deep frustration over his disability and his jealousy toward his wife at times, the husband abuses her as she struggles to save her family. However, she puts the relationship back on track with her compassion. Their ordeal reaches its nadir, however, when they lose their children consecutively to illness and a traffic accident. Fallen into abysmal despair, the couple then denounces God for abandoning their children and decides to commit suicide together. But they soon change their mind as they realize their mission to look after the war widows, for whom they had just started running an asylum. The film ends with their restored faith in God and their making a commitment to serve those who need their help.

Although the film recounts the unbelievable ordeals suffered by the family, it focuses primarily on the actions and endeavors of the wife. In this regard, the film is undoubtedly a melodramatic text where the woman's changing social position is a persistent thematic concern.[38] Played by the famous actress Ch'oe Ŭnhŭi, the wife's actions in the film echo the social values associated with traditional womanhood in Korea: patience, understanding, and sacrifice for her man and family. When her youngest child dies of pneumonia while the family was seeking refuge in flight from the war, she buries the body of her dead child in a field and returns to what remains of her family. Then she laboriously pulls the cart holding her paralyzed husband and young daughter. This image of a woman, who swallows her grief at the loss of her child and who is now burdened, literally, by the weight of her incompetent husband and her other child, served as a powerful icon for South Korean women in the (post)war years who often had to shoulder difficult responsibilities and tasks alone to insure the survival and maintenance of their families under the most severe circumstances. After the family arrives in Pusan, the wife becomes a street vendor to earn the family's living. She then moves back and forth between the veterans' hospital where her husband stays and the temporary inn where she lodges with her daughter. By selling items on the street, she is able to purchase alcohol for her husband who needs it to alleviate his pain and agony, and to feed her daughter who awaits her in the inn. The wife is the sole laboring body in the family throughout the film.[39]

Yet the film's portrayal of the wife is more complex than these tropes of the woman's traditional obligation and subservience might suggest. Whenever the husband expresses frustrated resentment toward her, she is not silent to his verbal abuse. Instead, she retorts that she is doing her best to improve the situation of their family. The wife becomes increasingly powerful in defining the terms of their conjugal relationship as the film progresses. This, to be sure, is due principally to the husband's total inability to lead the family. The husband, who had thrown himself out on the road to free his wife and child from their obligation to him, screams out when he sees his wife, in search of him, standing on a railroad track as a train approaches. She barely escapes being hit and the couple unites in tears, affirming the inseparable link between them. This scene endorses the man's viewpoint that the wife would not be able to survive without his guidance. However, as she works outside the confines of domestic space (for the traditional domestic sphere is swept away by war situations), she becomes her own advocate, criticizing her husband at times for his lack of understanding about her work. After the husband witnesses her talking with another man, he becomes furious and resentful toward her, erroneously concluding that she is unfaithful. He curses and shouts at her for her betrayal. However, he then quickly begs her in tears not to abandon him, for he now has no one to turn to for help. He earnestly asks her for her compassion, for she is, according to him, a more generous and virtuous person than he. This image of a broken man is quite a striking example of the representation of masculinity in South Korean cinema in that it features its bankrupt condition. More importantly, however, the man appeals to his wife for support in an earnest and pathetic manner instead of using violent means to hide and conceal his injury and disability. Contrary to her endeavor for and faith in the recon-

The veteran's wife, burdened by her incompetent husband and a child, from *Until the End of My Life*

stitution of her husband's leadership, she becomes the dominant figure that sets the terms for the conjugal relationship and family affairs.

It would be a mistake, however, to equate her growing significance as the moral agent of the family economy with power and independence. The film suggests that working outside the home offers temptations to married women to engage in romantic relationships with other men. Thus, even as she becomes the moral and economic agent of the family, her desire for a man outside her marriage is treated very critically. When she starts working as a street vendor, she encounters a young man, Mr. Cho, with whom she develops a friendship and intimate relationship. Mr. Cho is also a street vendor, who lost contact with his sister during the war. He often drinks alcohol to forget his loss, but he soon abandons this habit as he becomes close to the wife. He becomes emotionally attached to her, and asks her permission to call her *nunim*, that is, "sister" in Korean. This bond becomes even stronger as she accepts his offer to move into his place with her daughter. His home gives her a sense of comfort, hope, and joy.

It is in this quasi-domestic space that she comes to terms with the femininity that she had lost after the outbreak of war. She is able to revive her feminine character, feeling connected with the new man. Even though the wife and Mr. Cho occupy different rooms, their intimate nightly conversations transgress the boundary of the wall, facilitating the emotional bond between the two. She tells him she cannot sleep in a new place and then goes to his room. There, she asks for a cigarette and expresses her desire to be drunk and corrupt, free from her obligations and duties. She tells him that she often takes pleasure in self-pity for her situation. Mr. Cho responds by embracing her passionately. This emotionally charged moment is then punctuated by the roar of a train, which signifies the heightened passion of the two characters. However, this sound is soon followed by an imaginary voice, that of her husband, calling out to her to avoid the impending danger. It is a sonic flashback to the previous railway scene, in which the husband had shouted for her to escape the approaching train. Confused and shattered, she shakes her head, runs away from Mr. Cho, and falls on the ground outside, crying. The voice of her husband haunts her, prevents her from fulfilling her need for another man. The sonic flashback is used here to compare her desire to be with a man with the danger of an approaching train. Like the deadly force of the locomotive, a romantic and sexual liaison with a man other than her husband is perceived as a fatally destructive force in the film. Sexual abstinence is the only choice available to her. Yet her bitter tears testify to the oppression of the moral constraints that she is obliged to follow.

The subplot for Yŏngsŏn, the narrative surrounding the lost sister of Mr. Cho, further demonstrates the conservative gender politics of the film by comparing and contrasting the different sexual mores of the two women. When Mr. Cho runs into her by chance on the street, he is joyous to find his long-lost sister. His excitement soon turns into disappointment and agony, for Yŏngsŏn is now a *yanggongju*, a military prostitute serving American soldiers. For Mr. Cho, who holds his family origins in high regard, his sister's profession is especially shameful and degrading. He takes his sister to the veteran's wife to introduce them and to seek the wife's advice. In this scene, brother and sister find no terms of reconciliation. He voices his contempt and bitter disappointment. Yŏngsŏn sobs; for her, it was all a matter of survival. Mr. Cho does not believe her story, pointing out that his *nunim* has not fallen into prostitution despite the hardships she too faced. He compares the protagonist to Yŏngsŏn as a model in overcoming difficulty. Yŏngsŏn now understands why her brother is so upset, but confesses she no longer comprehends the difference between good and bad, nor the reason why she has to shed tears. If the wife's tears in the previous scene signified her sad realization that she has no possibility of fulfilling her desire for a man, Yŏngsŏn's grief testifies to the brutal workings of familial ideology, which allows no compassion for a fallen woman's plight and her need to survive.

In a later scene, Yŏngsŏn commits suicide, poisoning herself. By comparing these two different attitudes toward woman's sexuality and, subsequently, by eliminating the prostituted female body, the film underlines and valorizes the chaste body of a married woman who did not succumb to erotic temptation. It is telling that the relationship between the wife and Mr. Cho dissolves after the death of Yŏngsŏn. In a parting scene, the wife tells Mr. Cho, despite his objections, that the relationship cannot go on anymore. Interestingly, she tells him that she cannot give any reasons for her decision. Implicitly, she decides to accept the burden of her destiny. That the wife accepts and follows the prerogatives of traditional womanhood reverberates with Yŏngsŏn's tragic action. Despite their differences, both women are thus portrayed as victims of circumstances. Concurrently, however, their reluctance, if not refusal, to embrace the mandates of sexual mores and propriety alludes to the very limits of this oppressive gender ideology. It illuminates traces of women's resistant subjectivity, for these women are keenly aware of the oppressiveness of the moral demands. Thus, even though they concede to the obligations, they express in agony and tears that they neither "comprehend" the condemnation nor "explain" the reasons for departure. Their affective gestures thus form a passive mode of critique, unveiling the fundamental contradiction between the demands of traditional morality and the necessity of economic survival that these women are pressured to answer to simultaneously.

The comparison between the wife and Yŏngsŏn invites an examination of war widow and *yanggongju*, two distinctive groups of women in the postwar years that were subjects of constant social debate. The three years of total war made a devastating impact on the society as a whole, and the changes in gender relations were even more obvious and dramatic. The 1950s' social discourse of *ap'ŭre kŏl* (derived from the combination of French word *après-guerre*, and English word "girl") illustrates this social anxiety over the emergence of the so-called new women in the postwar situation.[40] The term *ap'ŭre kŏl*, or *chŏnhup'a*, was originally used to refer to the postwar generation and situation. However, as the French word "guerre" and English word "girl" were compressed into *kŏl*, the term increasingly acquired gendered connotations, signifying the new

81

women of the postwar generation. The most frequent examples of *ap'ŭre köl* were *yanggongju*. Because of their lifestyle, which centered on paid sexual service for American soldiers, *yanggongju* women were seen as the proper woman's Other, who existed outside the boundary of South Korean patriarchal power. Simultaneously, their association with American culture and consumer products distinguished them in the public sphere as the forerunners of a new modern culture, brought by American power and money. The films *Hell Flower* (*Chiokhwa*, Sin Sangok, 1958), and *A Fateful Hand* (*Unmyŏng ŭi son*, Han Hyŏngmo, 1954) feature *yanggongju* as fascinating objects of spectacle, exoticism, sexuality, and social dilemmas.

Although the motif of *yanggongju* was used later by middle-class writers in national literature to mobilize the allegory of the nation,[41] the early cinematic representations, such as *Until the End of My Life* were not strictly in accordance with the didactic nationalist scenario in which the prostituted female body must be eliminated for the sake of the nation.[42] Instead, the postwar films often thematize the impossible contradictions of the community economy by focusing on the problems of *yanggongju* women's sexuality and its moral consequences. Put differently, the films persistently feature the community's need for the material surplus that these women bring from the American military base. As a result, these women perform a vital role in the economy of the poverty-stricken community. The film's moral architecture that eventually punishes these women mystifies the reality of the community economy—that it requires the prostitution of its female members for its survival.[43] Compared to incompetent and emasculated men, the women possess economic power in the films, even though such strength is seen largely in negative fashion, inviting moral condemnation at the end. By amalgamating and critiquing the sexual power and economic autonomy of women, these films echo the contemporaneous view that perceived women's labor outside the domestic sphere as the cause of the moral breakdown of home and society.[44] In *Until the End of My Life,* the brother's judgmental stance on Yŏngsŏn reflects the moral discourse of the time. Yŏngsŏn ends her life in order to expiate the oppressive moral mandates upon which her brother insists.

Her legacy, however, lives on through her inheritance. Yŏngsŏn leaves her inheritance to the protagonist; she wanted her money to be used for the social good. The protagonist accepts Yŏngsŏn's will and later establishes the collective factory-cum-asylum for war widows with the money. That the wife is the sole inheritor of Yŏngsŏn's money informs the film's comparison between the two. They are both "sisters" of Mr. Cho, although the protagonist's relation with Mr. Cho started with friendship and courtship. Both women represent war widows and *yang-gongju*, respectively, who have trouble developing normal relationships with Korean men; the wife's sexuality must be suppressed to fulfill her role of married woman while Yŏngsŏn becomes stigmatized as a prostitute serving foreign men. When the protagonist had to leave her daughter, Sŏnkyŏng, at the inn, to go to work, it is a neighboring *yanggongju* who nannies her. Although war widows and *yanggongju* occupy different sets of social circumstances, they are often seen as twin examples of *ap'ŭre kŏl*, free from men's control and indulging in urban nightlife. The discourse of *ap'ŭre kŏl* could overlook the harsh social reality that connects these two groups, however. Many women simply did not have any means or skills for survival when their husbands died during the war. Veterans' widows received a meager pension, but such benefits would be cut off if they remarry. Some engaged in street vending and other petty labor and some turned to concubinage for survival. Those less fortunate chose prostitution, and war widows often made up a substantial proportion of this profession.[45] The fact that the majority of prostitutes in the 1950s provided services for American soldiers suggests the close link between war widows and *yanggongju* women in the postwar situation.

In this vein, the protagonist's energy to establish a social welfare house for war widows can be seen as an effort to prevent these women from falling down the social ladder, possibly becoming prostitutes. It is also for herself, for she most clearly identifies with the war widows. She is not technically a war widow, yet the wife regards herself as one of them because of her husband's sexual and physical incapacity. Furthermore, she learned from experience that working outside the home poses problems and temptations to her marriage vows. Although she did not lower herself to prostitution for survival, the case of Yŏngsŏn reminded her of what many war widows face under difficult circumstances. By establishing an egalitarian community for socially disadvantaged women, the protagonist fulfills Yŏngsŏn's wishes for regeneration, being a "virtuous" woman. Thus far, the salvation is portrayed in secular terms. Altruism, cooperation, trust, and compassion are the founding fabrics of the collective effort to create a community where every member, that is, war widows, works and shares life together.

This high hope soon receives a devastating blow, however. The couple's remaining child, Sŏnkyŏng, tragically dies in a traffic accident. This event destroys the protagonist's identity as a mother. Although she had become increasingly independent in her relation to her husband, her role as a mother was crucial to her throughout the film. Her adherence to traditional motherhood also enhanced her portrayal as a virtuous figure. The postwar social discourse often valorized the virtuous mother against the morally corrupt *ap'ŭre kŏl* of war widows and *yanggongju*. Further, her daughter Sŏnkyŏng was the last hope of the otherwise very troubled family. Her loss jeopardized the very meaning of the couples' lives, which now consisted solely of service for the needs of the disadvantaged war widows. The couple subsequently falls into agony and despair, denouncing God for bringing incessant misery into their lives.

While the death of Sŏnkyŏng shattered their remaining hope for domestic bliss and growth, the couple's subsequent recovery depicts an equally dramatic conversion to Christianity. Upon hearing of the widows' departure from the welfare house, the wife realizes her mission. She makes a passionate speech to the members to change their minds about abandoning the place. She declares that she is now just like war widows; she has a husband but he has no manly function. In order to live well, she insists, the war widows must live together, helping one another. She becomes fully integrated into the community of war widows in this speech. Even though the film does not feature ecclesiastical motifs of Christianity, Christian ideals define the egalitarian communal life here. And it is through their commitment to maintain this egalitarian community that the couple is able to make their final conversion to Christianity. The wife's passionate speech is an act of repentance as well an appeal to dissuade the members from abandoning the community. This dramatic spiritual conversion signifies the shift of the protagonist's identity: from individual and familial self, existing within blood ties, to the fellowship of Christian community practicing Christian moral virtues to help others. After they lost their only child, the couple subsequently acquired full membership in this community. Salvation in the film thus signifies the complete embrace of Christian communal life. If *Until the End of My Life* is excessive for its melodramatic expression of affect, the trajectory of spiritual salvation equals the film's formal intensity by highlighting the protagonist's profoundly affective experience of ordeal, penitence, rebirth, and conversion.

What does this representation of religiosity tell us about the postwar condition of South Korea? I think the film's rendition of Christian social service is reminiscent of earlier times when Protestantism made great social contributions. The welfare house for the war widows aimed to improve the living conditions of the socially disadvantaged. Yet there is a crucial difference. Whereas the earlier period's social services were part of a nationalist effort to resuscitate the nation from its plight, the film expresses no affiliation with state ideology. As the war-torn landscape and urban settings testify, the political ideology of the state has only brought devastations of war, suffering, and poverty to the people. The critique of the state ideology is more pronounced in the couple's conversation. When the husband celebrates with his friends his medal of honor for his distinguished service for the nation, the wife shows no interest in it. Instead, she resents the award for it will not bring back her husband's health. The husband understands her resentment, but begs her in tears to "pretend" for his joyous event. Without this decoration conferred from the state, he tells his wife, he would be too miserable. The sequence painfully illustrates the very futility of nationalist values that the medal of honor represents. Thus, both husband and wife are keenly aware of its meaninglessness. Contrary to its patriotic opening, a dedication to the war heroes, veterans, and war widows, the film presents a critical popular reasoning, through emotional affect, that indicts the senselessness of the state ideology of the times.

One year after *Until the End of My Life*, Sin Sang-ok made *The Houseguest and My Mother* (*Sarangbang sonnim kwa ŏmŏni*), where Protestantism signifies more conservative moral characters. The film's narrative focuses on a modern love affair between a houseguest and a widow in a provincial town. It begins with the voice-over narration of Okhŭi, the young daughter of the widow, who introduces the family members. The village people call her house "widow house" because two generations and classes of widows (Okhŭi's mother and grandmother, and widowed housemaid) live there together. A young man, who was an acquaintance of Okhŭi's late father, arrives as a houseguest to serve as a schoolteacher in the village. A romantic interest develops between the houseguest and Okhŭi's mother, and innocuous Okhŭi furthers their mutual passion by acting as a messenger between the two. Conflict, however, arises as Okhŭi's widowed mother is caught between the constraints of traditional ethics (remaining widowed for the rest of her life) and her desire for new love. Although the couple passionately loves each other, they cannot realize the fruit of their love due to repressive social mores. The film ends with a haunting image of the widow who silently watches from afar the houseguest's departure on a train. The image of the train here only brings sadness and sorrow for the widow. Such an image echoes the meaning of the train in *Until the End of My Life*, where its roar signified the oppressive gender constraints on the female protagonist. In both

Three widows (left to right): house-maid, mother, and grandmother, from *The Houseguest and My Mother*

cases, the train as an icon of modernity is figured negatively for the female protagonists, by blocking and frustrating their desire for new life.

In examining the gender dynamics and social ethics of the film, it is difficult to overlook its similar emphasis on the widow motif from *Until the End of My Life*. Okhŭi's "widow house" is similar to the welfare house in the former film in that both abodes are for women without men. Whereas the interpersonal relation in the welfare house is that of redefined Christian fellowship and cooperation, the "widow house" in *Houseguest* is a repository of traditional social mores where a matriarchal figure, Okhŭi's grandmother, dictates and regulates the behavioral codes of its members. If the former housing represents the egalitarian notion of a radical family comprised of the horizontal trust among socially disadvantaged women, the latter signifies the vertical relations of familial hierarchy made of blood ties. Although both films feature the lives of women without men, or their failure to have socially sanctioned or fully realized relationships with men, the way this failure is registered and resolved differs radically. While the quasi-familial relationship of war widows promises compensation in lieu of romantic engagement with men in *Until the End of My Life,* such compensation is largely absent in *The Houseguest and My Mother.* Instead, resignation and sorrow fill the heart of the protagonist, who feels compelled to live her life according to the moral precepts of tradition.

How then is Christianity specifically figured in the film? And, more importantly, what cultural function and implications does religion embody in this seemingly conservative universe? In *The Houseguest and My Mother*, Protestantism is figured primarily through the institution of the church and its fully integrated relation to existing social mores. One Sunday, Okhŭi and her mother and grandmother go to the church in the provincial town. The houseguest soon also arrives at the service. Okhŭi sees him and inadvertently makes noise to greet him. Her noise, made during the service, embarrasses her mother and grandmother; she receives their sharp scolding. Okhŭi then returns home alone, feeling abandoned. Okhŭi, whose innocent actions mediated between mother and the houseguest, fails to bridge the communication between the two in the church. Furthermore, she is punished for her inappropriate expression of affection toward the houseguest. This church scene occupies only brief screen time, yet the incident foreshadows the ill-fated nature of the romance between the mother and the houseguest. Without Okhŭi as a messenger, they cannot find room to explore their passion. They are, instead, bound by the two unfriendly spaces of the "widow house" and the church. As an outsider, the houseguest has to abide by the local rules, which do not permit him to interact with the woman he loves.

The church in the film figures as the site of the sacred where every member is expected to follow Christian manners and decorum. It is, however, not separated from the outside world in that it facilitates a strong gender division. For instance, the seating arrangement in the church separates male and female worshippers. Defined in terms of a specific locale, Protestantism in the film thus reproduces the existing gender relations in spatial terms, which do not allow any room, literally, for men and women to interact in a casual manner. If the production of space demands, as Henri Lefebvre points out, the concurrent production of subjectivities that inhabit that space, the mother's confinement to the two segregated spaces predicts her eventual decision, namely to "remain in her place."[46]

However, the film illustrates an alternative type of romantic relationship available to widows. Although Okhŭi's mother is barred from having a love affair with the houseguest, the housemaid, who is also a widow, is able to begin a courtship with the egg vendor. Her sexual relationship with the vendor is largely sanctioned and approved by the narrative, providing a counterpoint to the story of Okhŭi's mother. The housemaid is a different figure in the house. She is free from the conservative familial moral codes because she has virtually no family in relation to whom she has to define herself. A more crucial factor here is her class affiliation, which differs greatly from the middle-class identity of Okhŭi's mother. As a lower-class woman, she is less constrained by existing social mores than middle-class women are. She is, therefore, able to take the initiative to begin a new life with the egg vendor, a man of similar social status. Unlike Okhŭi's mother, who is associated with emotional restraint and the leisure of piano playing (which is an over-determined sign of middle-class identity), the housemaid is portrayed as a character of free expression, boisterousness, laziness, and spontaneity.

There is, yet, another significant factor of difference between two women that also determines the pattern of their behavior: a religious adherence to Christianity. Whereas Okhŭi's mother is a Protestant churchgoer, the housemaid engages in no religious activities. And the film leaves no ambiguity about it. When Okhŭi's family attends the church service on Sunday, the housemaid engages in sexual courtship with the vendor at home. Parallel editing is used to convey the simultaneity of these two contrasting events in different places. This cinematic device thus highlights the conservative social character of Protestantism. On the one hand, the church signifies authority and discipline, discouraging courtship between men and women by stressing conservative social mores. On the other hand, the absence of Christian religiosity leaves room for romance, and eventual marriage, for others. Contrasted with the religion's salvific power for the socially disadvantaged in *Until the End of My Life,* Christianity in *The Houseguest and My Mother* is the religion of the middle class, thoroughly institutionalized with a conservative character. It is fully integrated into and amalgamated with the Confucian social order here. Furthermore, the two belief systems find no point of contention in the film; instead, they establish congruent terms precisely around conservative constructions of proper womanhood. Thus, Christianity reproduces the configuration of gender hierarchy in which the social positioning of woman replicates Confucian demands of subservience. It fails to provide sufficient consolation or support for a young widow like Okhŭi's mother.

Under these repressive circumstances, Okhŭi's mother seeks consolation from a non-Christian cosmology. On her way back home from the church, she hesitantly seeks advice from a male fortune-teller. The fortune-teller reads the palms of her hands and her facial expressions. He then offers a remarkably precise interpretation of her life; she will have a happy life, but it will be a life without a man. She walks off in disappointment and guilt. The sequence illustrates the mother's dependence upon folk religious practices in dealing with the anxiety and uncertainty of her present condition. Instead of sin, guilt, and repentance for salvation, the fortune-teller directly reads her class and social position as well as the

The widow mother consults a fortune-teller, from *The House-guest and My Mother*

responsibilities and restrictions they entail, thereby producing a cogent account of her life. In her case, it is impossible to blend class stability with the pursuit of romance. Thus, fortune-telling works as an alternative cosmology, where the widow could receive a fairly accurate interpretation of her past and future development. Yet the account is too deterministic and conclusive, encouraging a woman to stay in her place and give up her hope for romantic life after all. And, this account, combined with the conservative social mores of Christianity, affects the actions of the female protagonist later on. When asked by her mother-in-law of her decision to choose between being a widow or having a new life, she succumbs to the former option, fulfilling the social demands of being a good mother to her child.

That she seeks out this local practice of fortune-telling suggests the limits of Protestantism in the quotidian life of the village people. When religion does not provide the answer to their present needs, people like Okhŭi's mother turn to a different cosmological framework for an answer. And Okhŭi's mother sees no contradiction in her action. The sequence affords a view of the syncretic, polyvalent, and indigenous spirituality of Korean people. Consulting advice from different cosmologies poses no contradiction to the minds of the people. Instead, it provides the psychological comfort and guidance that an individual fails to receive from Christianity. Such a configuration then informs the peculiar pattern of indigenization of Christianity in Korea.[47] According to Chŏng Chinhong, Korean people historically "accepted" the material, technological culture that Christianity brought along, but resisted and resented its ritual culture. For instance, Korean people quickly embraced the early missionaries' medical technology, but religious doctrine faced brutal suppression and popular resistance because of its adamant refusal to allow the ancestor-honoring ritual (*chesa* in Korean). But, as time went by, the spiritual elements of Christianity were largely subsumed by existing belief systems.[48] Indeed, shamanistic belief is still prevalent in Korean people's theological understanding and practice of Christianity. In *The Houseguest and My Mother,* an alternative cosmology serves the distinctive function of filling the gaps in abstract Christianity. To be sure, there is a difference between Christianity and other modes of folk cosmology. However, instead of contention and opposition, there exists a fluid boundary between Christianity and folk cosmology, each serving the needs of individuals.

Christianity is a minor subject in the world of South Korean melodrama. Nonetheless, the subject renders a dynamic field of contention and negotiation in which competing ideas and ideals of differing worldviews coalesced and dispersed. Central to the historical linkage between South Korean melodrama and its Christian religiosity is the backdrop of the nation's precipitous demise and then equally fervent endeavor to resuscitate the nation-state after colonial domination. In the postwar years, melodramatic films conveyed Christian themes that arose from the crises and contradictions of new social relations. That is, how individuals managed and survived (or failed) the sociopolitical traumas of the period through their Christian faith constitutes the founding narrative of spiritual salvation in many films. This includes the trauma of war devastation on family, the persistence of conservative morality, and the containment of shamanistic worldviews. Salvation thus entails a strongly sociological character. Even though it promises spiritual refuge for the disadvantaged, its doctrine, already melodramatized and indigenized, showed the close affiliation with existing social values, be it Confucian mores or the political ideology of the state.

Central to this narrative figuration of Christian salvation is a rearticulation of femininity according to the very different terms of the new social context. Moral questions about women's actions are almost always about the emphasis on chastity and sexuality. Because Christianity demands these virtues from women, it often formed conciliatory relations with existing social values. In fact, indigenization is made possible in part by an invention of virtuous Christian women whose behavior poses no threat to the conservative gender ideology of the old system. The lucid vision of salvation that the new religion promoted is, after all, in the eyes of the beholder. It precipitated a new imagination within which to project the new moral order and salvation; yet the terms of spiritual elevation are deeply rooted in the constant cultural engineering of gender. Seen from this viewpoint, the cinematic configuration of Christian religiosity is, after all, a part of vast cultural productions aimed at implementing the idea of nation through a calculated redistribution of symbolic values to women. Concurrently, however, the melodramatic elaboration of women's suffering alludes to the space where oppressed female protagonists have opinions and feelings that contradict the dominant moral precepts structuring the films. The pathos of these suffering protagonists thus invites a reading of popular reasoning that may, in fact, express defiant gestures for female personal redemption and well-being. There should be, then, a continuous effort to describe, discern, and articulate the subversive implications of these gestures in melodramatic texts.

Notes

I wish to thank Timothy S. Lee for his insightful suggestions to an early draft of this essay. I am also grateful for the guidance and encouragement I have received from Kathleen McHugh and Nancy Abelmann; their thoughtful suggestions forced me to clarify some crucial points. Generous fellowship grants from the Fulbright Program and the Korean Foundation provided most of the funding for my research.

1. The antinomy reverberates the binary sentiments of *kiri* and *ninjo* in Japanese tragedy. The former refers to honorable duty or obligation while the latter signifies the warm human feelings such as mercy and love. According to theater historian Kang Yŏnghŭi, the antinomy between thought and action is one of the most distinctive character traits in Korean *sinp'a* drama. Namely, characters often act in ways that contradict their desires, leading to greater misunderstanding and tribulation. It also reflects the split subjectivity of the characters. See Kang Yŏnghŭi, "A Study of the *Sinp'a* Mode during the Colonial Period (Ilche kangjŏmgi *sinp'a* yangsik e taehan yŏn'gu)," in *Yŏnghwahak ch'ongnon* (Seoul: Wŏnbanggak, 1990), 568–75.

2. Ibid., 575.

3. Yu Minyŏng mentions, in passing, the element of Christianity in *Changhanmong* when he discusses its difference from the original Japanese work. Similarly, Ch'oe Hyŏngmi's study on *Changhanmong* does not take this theme seriously. See Yu Minyŏng, *Han'guk kŭndae yŏn'gŭksa* (*A History of Modern Korean Drama*) (Seoul: Tan'guk taehakkyo ch'ulp'anbu, 1996), 245. Ch'oe Hyŏngmi, "*Kŭmsaegyach'a* wa *Changhanmong* ŭi pigyo yŏn'gu (The Comparative Study on *Konjikiyasha* and *Changhanmong*)," (master's thesis, Tan'guk taehakkyo, 1991), 50.

4. I want to note that it is Yi, the male protagonist, who plays the lead in this

morality drama. It is his endeavor to forgive and take care of then-insane Sim that brings the miracle after all.

5. As Yi Miwŏn notes, the repertoire of *sinp'a* includes traditional novels, such as *Changhwa Hongnyŏnjŏn, Sassi Namjŏnggi,* as well as *p'ansori* works, e.g., *Simch'ŏngjŏn.* Furthermore, *sinp'a* works typically feature motifs of familial conflict common in traditional novels. Exemplary motifs include conflicts between wives and concubines, enmity between women and their mothers-in-law and among step-siblings. More importantly, Yi argues that the success of *sinp'a* has less to do with the novelty of the form; rather, it owes its popularity to "(the effective recycling of) already familiar motifs of traditional novels, combined with the contemporaneous *kaehwa sasang* (the discourse on modern consciousness and 'civilization,' prevalent in the late nineteenth and early twentieth century) and theater art." Yi Miwŏn, *Han'guk kŭndaegŭk yŏn'gu (Study on Modern Korean Theater)* (Seoul: Hyŏndae mihaksa, 1994), 93.

6. Some critics remain dismissive of this cultural and historical function of *sinp'a* melodrama for the Korean people's moral imagination. Ch'oe Wŏnsik's elitist approach is a prime example. Writing from the nationalist standpoint, Ch'oe perceives *Changhanmong* as a failed adaptation that diverted the people from realizing Korea's social reality, namely the demise of the nation. For Ch'oe, *Changhanmong* belongs to a literature of "consolation (*wian* in Korean)": an escapist text of the masses. See Ch'oe Wŏnsik, "*Changhanmong* kwa wian ŭrosŏŭi munhak (*Changhanmong* and Literature as Consolation)," in *Han'guk kŭndae taejungsosŏl pipyŏngnon (Study on Modern Korean Popular Novels)* (Seoul: T'aehaksa, 1997).

7. I want to note that the connection between early melodrama and Christian themes was not limited to the theater arts alone. A new literary genre, *sinsosŏl* ("new novel"), emerged in the first decade of the twentieth century and similarly featured Christian themes. Like *sinp'a* drama, *sinsosŏl* was a transitional novel form, bridging the traditional narratives and modern novel. Many *sinsosŏl* works emphasized the promotion of social reform, which often overlapped with the progressive ideas of Christianity. For an explanation of *sinsosŏl* and Christianity, see Ch'oe Chaesŏn, "Han'guk hyŏndae sosŏl ŭi kidokkyo sasang yŏn'gu (A Study on Christianity in Korean Modern Novels)" (PhD diss., Sookmyung Women's University, 1999), 25–28. Kim Kyŏngwan, *Kodae sosŏl kwa kaehwagi sosŏl ŭi kidokkyojŏk ŭimi (Protestant Meanings in Novels of Pre-Modern and the Open-Door Periods)* (Seoul: Wŏrin, 2000).

8. Because of its millenarian vision and egalitarian social ideas, *Tonghak* quickly came under the government's suspicion and was brutally suppressed. The increasing tension between the government and the *Tonghak* believers led to the uprising of a peasant army in 1894, by which time *Tonghak* had become a radical social movement. Many have understood this peasant uprising as "an incipient form of modern nationalism," which might have realized its revolutionary social reform had the foreign interventions, i.e., the Chinese and Japanese armies, not exerted its aggression to end the struggle. See Carter J. Eckert and others, *Korea Old and New: A History* (Seoul: Ilchogak, 1990), 221.

9. I am greatly indebted to Timothy S. Lee in my understanding of the history and characters of Korean Protestantism. I draw this summary of Korea's religious landscape from his doctoral dissertation, "Born-Again in Korea: The Rise and Character of Revivalism in (South) Korea, 1885–1988" (PhD diss., University of Chicago, 1996).

10. Ibid., 8–9.

11. American missionaries established modern private schools and engaged in medical work. At these new schools, young Koreans learned Western liberal ideas through a curriculum that emphasized Western knowledge and thoughts. Ewha Girls' School (later Ewha Woman's University), established by American missionaries in 1886, was Korea's first educational institution for women. For an understanding of the early history of Protestant missionaries in Korea, see Everett Nichols Hunt Jr., *Protestant Pioneers in Korea* (Maryknoll, NY: Oris Books, 1980).

12. Kang Inch'ŏl, *Han'guk kidokkyohoe wa kukka, simin, sahoe, 1945–1960* (*Korean Church, Nation, and Civil Society, 1945–1960*) (Seoul: Han'guk kidokkyo yŏksa yŏn'guso, 1996), 162.

13. Antonio Gramsci's concept of common sense as folklore was helpful to formulate my ideas on popular reasoning of melodrama. According to Gramsci, people possess numerous conceptions of the world that are often contradictory, yet still constitute a coherent whole. The common sense is "the conception of the world which is uncritically absorbed by the various social and cultural environments in which the moral individuality of the average man is developed. Common sense is not a single unique conception, identical in time and space. It is the 'folklore' of philosophy, and, like folklore, it takes countless different forms. Its most fundamental characteristic is that it is a conception which, even in the brain of one individual, is fragmentary, incoherent and inconsequential, in conformity with the social and cultural position of those masses whose philosophy it is." Gramsci's idea on common sense encompasses all sociocultural discourses in general; I use the term "popular reasoning," to discuss specifically the cultural logic of melodrama and its relation to the dominant (state) ideology of the time. See Antonio Gramsci, "Observations and Critical Notes on an Attempt at a 'Popular Manual of Sociology,'" in *An Antonio Gramsci Reader: Selected Writings, 1916–1935,* ed. David Forgacs (New York: New York University Press, 2000), 343.

14. Julianne Burton-Carvajal, "Mexican Melodrama of Patriarchy: Specificity of a Transcultural Form," in *Framing Latin American Cinema: Contemporary Critical Perspectives,* ed. Ann Marie Stock (Minneapolis: University of Minnesota Press, 1997), 190.

15. Peter Brooks, *The Melodramatic Imagination: Balzac, Henry James, Melodrama, and the Mode of Excess* (New York: Columbia University Press, 1985), 5. (Emphasis mine.)

16. Ibid., 4.

17. I take the term "dual recognition" from Linda Williams's study of melodrama. This concept echoes Kang's term "antinomy of action and thought" in her aforementioned study of Korean melodrama. See Linda Williams,

"Melodrama Revised," in *Refiguring American Film Genres: History and Theory,* ed. Nick Browne (Berkeley: University of California Press, 1998), 48.

18. Brooks, *Melodramatic Imagination,* 16.

19. The total embracement of Christian worldview was particularly strong during the "opening door" period (i.e., the years preceding Korea's annexation to Japan in 1910). Christianity was seen and embraced as the fundamental framework with which to preserve the Korean nation and people, not only by the militant nationalists but also by the intellectuals who had faith in the project of radical "enlightenment," (i.e., modernization). See Ko Misuk, "Kŭndae kyemonggi, kŭ saengsŏng kwa pyŏni ŭi konggan e taehan myŏkkaji tansang (Modern Enlightenment Period: Some Thoughts on the Formation and Permutation of Its Space)," *Minjok munhaksa yŏn'gu* 14 (1999): 115.

20. According to Don Baker, Christianity has acquired the Korean identity through a process of unconscious and conscious inculcation. Not only has Christianity become Koreanized through this process, he notes, but also transformed other traditional religions as they encountered this new religion. See his "Christianity 'Koreanized,'" in *Nationalism and the Construction of Korean Identity,* ed. Hyung Il Pai and Timothy R. Tangherlini (Berkeley: University of California Press, 1998).

21. Timothy S. Lee goes so far as to assert that Revivalism has not merely been a central feature of Korean Protestantism, but "(Korean) Protestantism is predominantly Revivalism." See his "Born-Again in Korea," 11.

22. Ibid. (Emphasis mine.)

23. Ibid.

24. Benedict Anderson, *Imagined Communities: Reflections on the Origin and Spread of Nationalism* (London: Verso, 1983), 11 and 4. (Emphasis mine.)

25. Ibid., 12.

26. Here I am exploring the overlapping cultural logic in the theory of nationalism (Benedict Anderson) and the theory of melodrama (Peter Brooks). Central to these two seemingly disparate studies is the similar historical backdrop, i.e., the decline of religious cosmology and the subsequent need to forge a vernacular way to imagine the world continuous, meaningful, and virtuous.

27. Prasenjit Duara, *Rescuing History from the Nation: Questioning Narratives of Modern China* (Chicago: University of Chicago Press, 1995), 4.

28. According to Duara, the question of "atavism of the nation and its telos of modernity" is one of the most persistent dilemmas in nationalist histories. Ibid., 28.

29. Although I fully agree with the constructed and contingent nature of nation, I am hesitant to attribute the trajectory of its moral and spiritual narrative solely to the mode of Enlightenment logic. I contend that the melodramatic reasoning and its cultural expression need to be taken into the consideration. The cultural form of melodrama, to be sure, is a modern phenomenon. However, the popular reasoning embedded in the form informs reworking and relevance of the old values, refashioned in modern times, to project the meaning and vision to the present. Thus, the narrative of nation is marked by both the Enlightenment mode of thinking and the cultural residuals of

the past, represented by the melodramatic reasoning. And, the relationship between the two needs to be understood in conciliatory and mutually enforcing terms rather than exclusive ones.

30. This peculiar feature was, according to Christine Gledhill and Peter Brooks, a cultural response to the crisis of bourgeois epistemology in the West. Christine Gledhill, "The Melodramatic Field: An Investigation," in *Home Is Where the Heart Is: Studies in Melodrama and the Woman's Films,* ed. Christine Gledhill (London: BFI, 1988), 45. Cited in Williams, "Melodrama Revised," 48.

31. I would like to further add that this binary structure of melodrama can be reconsidered in spatial terms for anticolonial nationalism. In particular, melodramatic dichotomy of environment vs. self-identity echoes the social domain of anticolonial nationalism, which Partha Chatterjee divides into two parts— the material and the spiritual. The former signals the domain of economy, statecraft, science, and technology, while the latter is that which bears the "essence" of cultural identity. According to Chatterjee, anticolonial nationalism in Asia and Africa differs fundamentally from the European model in that it already established the domain of sovereignty well before it engaged in political struggle against the imperial domination. The moral mandates that melodrama persistently articulate through affective means registers, in my view, the effort to cultivate "modern" national culture that has not totally been swamped by Western values and influences. See Partha Chatterjee, *The Nation and Its Fragments: Colonial and Postcolonial Histories* (Princeton: Princeton University Press, 1993), 6.

32. Ko, "Kŭndae kyemonggi, kŭ saengsŏng kwa pyŏni ŭi konggan e taehan myŏkkaji tansang (Modern Enlightenment Period: Some Thoughts on the Formation and Permutation of Its Space)," 116.

33. The issue of *"t'och'akhwa"* (indigenization) spawned an extensive debate on the study of Korean Christianity. See the collection of excellent essays in *Han'guk ŭi munhwa wa sinhak (Korean Culture and Theory)*, ed. Kidokkyo sasang p'yŏnjippu (Seoul: Taehan kidokkyosŏhoe, 1992).

34. A few examples of rudimentary treatment of Christian motifs include *That Woman's Life (Kŭyŏja ŭi ilsaeng,* Kim Han'il, 1957), *Zelkova Tree Hill (Nŭt'inamu innŭn ŏndŏk,* Ch'oe Hun, 1958), *A Bell House (Chonggak,* Yang Chunam, 1958), *A Snowy Night (Nun naerinŭn pam,* Ha Hansu, 1968).

35. On the contrary, a body of films called *"chonggyo yŏnghwa"* (Religious Films) features the religious themes explicitly. These didactic texts were produced in few occasions in Korean film history for the evangelical purpose. The study on this genre is very underdeveloped, however. Yi Hyoin questions the very validity of this generic category that is commonly used in the *Annual Korean Film Catalogue.* He points out that the lack of consistent production undermines the categorical term itself. Although I understand his reservation to employ the generic term for this group of films, I think the term itself can be productively used to open a critical debate. In particular, I want to point out that the religious films developed a production mode and exhibition pattern starkly different from those of mainstream commercial films. These films were often made by producers and actors who themselves were devout pros-

elytizers, and the films were shown primarily for the church members. Thus, instead of profit making, the religious films were designed for evangelical purpose. The specificity of this marginal filmmaking practice deserves greater attention. See Yi Hyoin, "Han'gŭk yŏnghwa ŭi pullyu e taehayŏ (On Classification of Korean Cinema)," *Yŏnghwa ŏnŏ* 15 (1995): 178. I do want to point out, however, that these religious films employed the strong melodramatic structure to emphasize the re-birth moments of spiritual regeneration.

36. Gi-Wook Shin, "Nation, History, and Politics: South Korea," in *Nationalism and the Construction of Korean Identity,* ed. Hyung Il Pai and Timothy R. Tangherlini (Berkeley: University of California Press, 1998).

37. For analysis of the Park regime's construction of nationalist history and "invention" of tradition, see Seungsook Moon, "Begetting the Nation: The Androcentric Discourse of National History and Tradition in South Korea," in *Dangerous Women: Gender and Korean Nationalism,* ed. Elaine H. Kim and Chungmoo Choi (New York: Routledge, 1998), 33–66, and Chŏn Ch'aeho, "Minjokjuŭi wa yŏksa ŭi iyong (Nationalism and the Use of History)," *Sahoegwahak yŏn'gu* 7 (1998): 83–106.

38. Many film scholars and theorists have examined the significance of women's issues in melodrama. See, for example, the collection of essays in *Home Is Where the Heart Is,* ed. Gledhill.

39. Please see Kathleen McHugh's essay, chapter 1 in this volume, for examination of women's labor in South Korean melodrama.

40. See Sŏnjŏng Yŏ, "Arŭmdaun angny ŭi sidae: Yanggongju wa ap'ŭre kŏl (Times for Beautiful Femme Fatale: *Yanggongju* and Apres-Guerre)," in *Yŏsŏng yŏnghwain sajŏn (Encyclopedia of Korean Women in Film)*, ed. Chu Chinsuk, Chang Mihŭi, and Pyŏn Chaeran (Seoul: Sodo, 2001), 28–29.

41. Hyun Sook Kim, "Yanggongju as an Allegory of the Nation: The Representation of Working-Class Women in Popular and Radical Texts," in *Dangerous Women,* ed. Kim and Choi, 175–201.

42. Yŏ notes, "Compared to the representation of the 1960s' femme fatale [referred to here as *yanggongju*], who repented and begged for mercy of the nation, the images of these women in the 1950s were more *beautiful,* for they had lived their lives for themselves and reject[ed] the shameful subservience." (Translation mine; emphasis original.) See her "Arŭmdaun angny ŭi sidae," 28. Two notable examples of such 1950s films are *A Fateful Hand* (*Unmyŏng ŭi son,* Han Hyŏngmo, 1954) and *Hell Flower* (*Chiokhwa,* Sin Sangok, 1958).

43. In *Hell Flower,* the female protagonist *yanggongju,* Sonya, is in control over the livelihood of her life, so much so that she is careless about her husband's promise for a more luxurious life. Men, meanwhile, are not economically viable; their livelihood is structurally dependent upon these women. When they concoct a criminal plan to smuggle and steal the goods from an American military base, they have to rely on the inside information and coordination that *yanggongju* women provide. Even though Sonya is portrayed as a femme fatale, she is not condemned for her profession of serving foreign men. Instead, it is her sexual interest in another South Korean man, i.e., her brother-in-law, and subsequent betrayal of her husband that causes her downfall.

44. Yi Kŏnhyŏk, "Ton kwa kajŏng saenghwal kwa sarang (Money, Domestic Life, and Love)," *Yŏsŏnggye* (April 1956): 60–62. Cited in Yi Imha, "Han'gukchŏnjaeng i yŏsŏngsaenghwal e mich'in yŏnghyang: 1950 nyŏndae chŏnjaeng mimangin ŭi sam ŭl chungsim ŭro (Effects of Korean War on Women's Lives: On the Lives of 1950s War Widows)," *Yŏksa yŏn'gu* 8 (2000): 32–33.

45. I draw the social reality of war widows from Yi Imha's study. See her "Han'gukchŏnjaeng i yŏsŏngsaenghwal e mich'in yŏnghyang: 1950 nyŏndae chŏnjaeng mimangin ŭi sam ŭl chungsim ŭro."

46. Henri Lefebvre, *The Production of Space,* trans. Donald Nicholson-Smith (Oxford: Blackwell, 1991).

47. Harvey Cox, *Fire from Heaven: The Rise of Pentecostal Spirituality and the Reshaping of Religion in the Twenty-First Century* (Reading, MA: Addison-Wesley, 1995), 221; Boo-Woong Yoo, *Korean Pentecostalism: Its History and Theology* (Frankfurt: Verlag Peter Lang, 1988), 72.

48. Chŏng Chinhong, "Han'guk minsok munhwa ŭi chŏngsinjŏk kiwŏn (The Spiritual Origins of Korean Folk Culture)," in *Han'guk ŭi munhwa wa sinhak,* 77.

4

The Stray Bullet
and the Crisis of Korean Masculinity

EUNSUN CHO

"Let's go!"[1] This phrase is uttered over and over again by the mad, bedridden mother of the family portrayed in *The Stray Bullet* (*Obalt'an,* Yu Hyŏn-mok, 1961).[2] Her words form a leitmotif that resonates throughout the film, emphatically evoking the hopelessness of the family, their poverty, and their life without a future, a fate they futilely try to escape.[3] The old woman's frightening voice conjures up not only the hopelessness of the family but also the dismal reality of South Korea after the Korean War. *The Stray Bullet* tells the story of a family that has fled from North Korea and now lives in a shantytown for war refugees. The name of the village—"Liberation Village" (*Haebangch'on*)—signifies that the people living there have been liberated from oppressive communist North Korea; it thereby alludes both to the division of nation that literally afflicts the family and also to South Korea's cold war system that names these exiles, called *sirhyangmin* or *wŏllammin,* the quintessential victims of communism. The film's ironic depiction of this "liberation" suggests that the family's history and plight mirror the complexity and ambiguity of postwar South Korean life as a whole.[4]

In *The Stray Bullet,* the life of the family/nation is portrayed as agonizing and nightmarish. The historical traumas Korea has suffered register dramatically in the film's depiction of gender relations. The power and authority assigned to South Korean men by the patriarchal social order are seriously undermined by national traumas, and, as a result, their masculinity is brought to crisis. The crisis of male subjectivity inevitably involves the trauma and sexuality of South Korean women as well. In *The Stray Bullet,* troubled masculinity and its relation to female sexuality are visualized vis-à-vis the film's particular scopic arrangement between the male gaze and the female body. This scopic regime differs in certain ways from that theorized in relation to Classical Hollywood film. In Laura

Mulvey's canonical essay, men are the agents of action and the bearers or subjects of the gaze, while women are to-be-looked-at and the passive objects of narrative sadism.[5] Importantly, in *The Stray Bullet*, the male characters are not positioned clearly or unequivocally as subjects of the gaze.[6] I will illuminate this altered scopic regime by analyzing the relationships between the eldest son in this family, Ch'ŏr-ho, and his sister, Myŏng-suk, and also between Myŏng-suk and her fiancé, Kyŏng-sik.

Yet the motif of troubled masculinity plays itself out not only on a scopic axis but also in terms of genres. One of the film's subplots, which involves the younger brother Yŏng-ho robbing a bank, mimics the stylistic and narrative elements of the Hollywood genres of film noir and the gangster film. This subplot provides one example of South Korean national cinema imitating Hollywood film language. This moment, which we could read as the colonized subject's mimicry of the colonizer's male image, formally reiterates the theme of impaired masculinity prevalent in many film narratives during the postwar period. My analysis of this mimicry in *The Stray Bullet* challenges the prevailing reading of the film as a quintessentially realist text antithetical to the "cheap" melodramas of the 1960s, a reading which has been established in the histories and critical formulations of South Korean cinema so far.[7] Instead of understanding the film in this way, I carefully look at the instances of male crisis presented through the scopic mode and through tropes of mimicry, a critical process that reveals the text as fractured. It breaks the promises of realism, notwithstanding its seemingly realistic quality. Disclosing such breaks and ruptures in the representational mode of *The Stray Bullet*, I will shed light on how these breaks embody and also speak to the troubles of gender and genre in South Korean cinema.

Masculinity in Crisis and Scopophobic Symptoms

The Stray Bullet portrays the hopeless life of a desperate family. The eldest son, Ch'ŏr-ho, who works in an accounting office, cannot afford to have his rotten teeth pulled. The younger son, Yŏng-ho, a veteran, is still unemployed two years after the war; he dreams of "making it big" and ends up a bank robber. Ch'ŏr-ho's wife dies during the delivery of their second child, and his sister, Myŏng-suk, becomes a military prostitute.[8] Against the grim reality of the family's lives, the mad, bedridden mother's voice echoes like a curse.

This portrayal of a "dysfunctional" family allegorizes postwar South Korea and the life of Korean people in their devastated land. The family's "aimless and restless" life is like the stray bullet Ch'ŏr-ho's refers to near the end of film when he says, "I might be God's stray bullet." Similarly, South Korea's failure to imagine or cinematically image itself coherently as a nation and a unified homeland for its people aligns the country with the stray bullet of the title as well. While a nation is defined as a cultural system that provides meanings for its people and their reality and thus, as Benedict Anderson maintains, functions to "[transform] fatality to continuity, contingency to meaning," the nation shown in this film is not sufficiently coherent, not sufficiently free of foreign bodies and influences, to articulate a continuity, "to turn chance to destiny."[9] *The Stray Bullet* thus dramatizes the fragmented and divisive national imaginings of the colonized and/or postcolonial nation.[10]

Such an imaginary divisiveness both indexes and produces masculinity in crisis—and femininity as both the actual victim and the symbolic symptom of that crisis.[11] Anderson argues that the "deep horizontal comradeship" by which "the imagined community" is made possible is characterized by a gender-specific form of "fraternity."[12] If national imaginings have seized upon patriarchy as one of the most crucial social formations, a damaged patriarchal authority at a certain moment can significantly alter the character of these imaginings. George L. Mosse also argues in *Nationalism and Sexuality* that "nationalism had a special affinity for male society and, together with the concept of respectability, legitimized the dominance of men over women."[13] The impossibility of a belief in the nation as a place of collective belonging is thus interconnected with the broken imaginary comradeship of brotherhood and a disabled patriarchal function that no longer promises unconditional male dominance. In such a compromised fraternal nation, the discursive violence of a damaged, male-centered nationalism metaphorizes the nation as feminine, thereby rendering female subjectivity contingent and wholly repressed.[14]

In her book *Male Subjectivity at the Margins,* Kaja Silverman explains the link between crises of masculinity and historical trauma in the psychoanalytic sense. Certain historical events, she argues, bring a "psychoanalytically specific disruption with ramifications extending far beyond the individual psyche." This disruption can effect a temporary withdrawal from what she terms "dominant fictions," that is, collective beliefs or assumptions in social formations. A dominant fiction operates as an "ideological system through which the normative subject lives its imaginary relation to the Symbolic order."[15] Moreover, such a fiction "neutralizes the contradictions which organize the social formation by fostering collective identifications and desires, identifications and desires which have a

range of effects, but which are first and foremost constitutive of sexual difference." When a historical trauma threatens the dominant fiction, the
male subject can no longer sustain his relationship to it, a phenomena that
alters the basis of the power distribution informing gender identity. In this
way the normative male subject can no longer fully identify with his
socially sanctioned position—his patriarchal authority.[16]

In *The Stray Bullet,* the disempowered male position is explicitly
represented through images of men's damaged bodies, from Ch'ŏr-ho's
rotten teeth to the mutilated bodies of war veterans.[17] For example, Yŏng-
ho has a bullet wound in his side and Kyŏng-sik, Myŏng-suk's fiancée,
lost a leg in the war. One of Yŏng-ho's veteran friends also lost one of his
arms and has a prosthetic hook instead.[18] The film begins with a sequence
in which Yŏng-ho and his war veteran friends are drinking, out on the
town. In a bar, they fight with the waiter over the window that one of
them has broken, and they march, singing a war song, naming each other
"captain," or "corporal" as if they were still in the army. Their behavior
expresses exaggerated, yet frustrated, masculinity. Their wounded and
amputated bodies present visible evidence of their lack of power, that is,
their maimed masculinity.

The relationship between Kyŏng-sik and Myŏng-suk demonstrates
this lack in terms of gender dynamics. Before the war, they were engaged,
but when Kyŏng-sik returns without one of his legs, he refuses to marry
her. He is so discouraged by his amputated leg that he doesn't think himself worthy of her. When he avoids her, she follows him and begs him to
marry her. This reversed courtship inverts their gender positions: the
male is situated in the position usually occupied by the female in cinema.
Such a gender-role reversal, along with the image of physically disabled
male bodies—an image that renders *men's* bodies objects of the gaze—
visually depicts castrated cinematic masculinity within very specific historical circumstances.

The Stray Bullet also plays out the disempowered male position vis-
à-vis the conventions of men looking at women's bodies, thereby rendering its construction of masculinity within a historically specific scopic
regime. The Korean War and the divided nation after the war are, of
course, the historical events that most threatened the masculinity of South
Korean men at the time. In order to depict the connection between the
divided nation and its maimed citizens, the film localizes this trauma in
the scopic relationship it constructs between women's bodies and men's
visual perceptions of those bodies. By doing so, the film profoundly and
concretely renders the causal relations linking the subjectivity of South

Korean men, the historical traumas of Korea, and the consequent gender formations structuring the experience of those traumas. In this way, the film constructs historically determined gender relations that are visually represented through the specific power dynamics of the film's scopic structure.

The paradigmatic example of this structure is the scene in which Ch'ŏr-ho discovers Myŏng-suk with an American GI. Ch'ŏr-ho is riding a bus that stops at a traffic signal. Looking out the window, he spots his sister sitting next to an American soldier in a jeep. Wearing Western attire and sunglasses, a sharp and noticeable contrast to the traditional Korean garb she was wearing when she begged Kyŏng-sik to marry her, she is ostentatiously flirting with the soldier. Two other men on the bus, also observing the scene, converse sarcastically about Myŏng-suk:

> "A good business, huh? It doesn't even need capital."
> "But, can she get married?"
> "If she has a problem getting married, she will pass herself off as a college girl or an office girl. Who knows?"
> "I bet she will turn into a virgin, ha ha ha!"

Overhearing their dialogue, Ch'ŏr-ho turns around and walks away. Three different gazes distinguish the male subjects who take Myŏng-suk as their object in this scene: the erotic gaze of the American soldier; the derisive gaze of the two men on the bus; and the shamed gaze of Ch'ŏr-ho. The first perhaps exemplifies the scopic organization between male subject and female body delineated by Mulvey in "Visual Pleasure and Narrative Cinema"; that is, the male gaze orients the female body as object of his desire. The second gaze, which is from the voyeuristic position of her countrymen (Myŏng-suk is not aware of being looked at), is judgmental: the two onlookers condemn the woman for selling her body to American soldiers and also derisively speculate that she will later pass herself off as a "good" girl and get married.

The third, Ch'ŏr-ho's gaze, has special status in this scene as his look encompasses and yet is shaped by the other two—that is, he sees and understands the looks of the American soldier and of his countrymen at his sister. His gaze therefore incorporates a familial, a national, and a transnational perspective. Significantly his understanding of these other gazes compounds his shame; and in reaction, he turns away so he cannot see. In so doing, he obstructs other people's view of the scene. When he walks away, turning his back on Myŏng-suk, he blocks her from the view of the other people on the bus. As he then moves down the aisle, the camera follows him, thus also depriving the film's audience of their voyeuristic view of his sister. In this way, Ch'ŏr-ho obstructs the entire traffic of looking in this scene that mediates the female body by the voyeuristic male look, the voyeuristic gaze of the audience and, most of all, his own gaze.[19] By interfering with the circulation of gazes, he manages not to see and not to let his sister be seen. Here, he is not the subject who exerts the privilege of looking. Rather, he strives to avoid the gaze.

At first glimpse, the positions of male and female in the sequence seem to conform to the classical arrangement in Western film as described by Western film theory. That is, the men in the bus appear to be agents of the gaze, while Myŏnk-suk, the woman, is exhibited as the passive object of their gaze. The visual transaction between Ch'ŏr-ho and Myŏng-suk, however, presents a completely different arrangement. When he witnesses his sister made object by the erotic gaze of an American soldier and the demeaning gaze of her countrymen, he turns his back, thus averting his gaze from the disturbing sight. Denied the enactment of scopic power, his act of turning away negates the presence of her scandalous body. By pretending not to see her, the object to be looked at, he forsakes himself as the "bearer of the look."[20] He forsakes himself as the subject of the look because the look brings with it the painful encounter with the reality that he is a helpless colonized man who can do nothing about his sister's prostituting to the colonizer due to his family's poverty. The shame and disgrace that Myŏng-suk's body carries, therefore, are his own as well. The only positions available to the South Korean men in this scenario are that of shamed brother or judgmental countrymen, which further underscores the exclusion of these men from the erotic dynamics of the scopic field, a field dominated by the U.S. GIs. Ch'ŏr-ho, who perceives the female body as an object of uneasiness and fear, is unable to enjoy the pleasure of looking as the male subject is supposed to. Instead of visual pleasure, he suffers from an anxiety of looking at the female body. His scopic relation to the female body illuminatingly discloses a symptom of visual phobia. He becomes a "scopophobic" subject rather than a scopophilic one.

Ch'ŏr-ho deals with his scopophobia, as aforementioned, by avoiding looking at the troubled female body. To him this avoidance functions as a way of disavowing the anxiety-evoking vision of the female body. His manner of disavowal is, however, significantly different from the ones discussed in Western film theory such as voyeurism and fetishism. While a male subject, as argued in Western film theory, disavows the castration anxiety provoked by a female body vis-à-vis the mobilization of voyeuristic and fetishistic modes of vision, the male subject presented in *The Stray Bullet* does not have recourse to such devices. Instead of controlling the female body through voyeuristic punishment or fetishistic idealization, Ch'ŏr-ho can only turn away from the sight evocative of his anxiety, an act that erases sexual difference from a specific visual field—that determined by a familial or national perspective. Eroticism and sexual difference, the film suggests, can only be imaged and narratively configured within a transnational scopic field.

The film revisits another version of this scenario in the coincidental encounter between Kyŏng-sik and Myŏng-suk as she is hustling an American soldier on the street. This perturbing encounter shocks and shames the war veteran, a shame visually generalized and exacerbated by the fact that it takes place in front of the Chosŏn Hotel, which was occupied and exclusively used by U.S. military personnel at the time. Tellingly, after this incident, Kyŏng-sik completely disappears from the narrative and screen as well—he is excised from the scopic regime. Neither Ch'ŏr-ho nor Kyŏng-sik can punish Myŏng-suk's "degraded" sexuality as voyeurs usually do in Hollywood films—in contrast, she is the only one among the main characters of the film who survives without being completely lost. The male character's traumatized subjectivity impedes the construction of masculinity that enacts the power of looking and satisfies the desire of pleasurable looking. This impediment in looking renders them phobic subjects who avoid the scopic annihilation of their masculinity by averting their gaze or disappearing from the visual field altogether. As a corollary, South Korean women's sexuality becomes invisible to any other figuration than that of colonized sexual body. The scopic arrangement in *The Stray Bullet* translates a historically determined national crisis into the visual and narrative rhetoric of the classical feature film, the history marking this rhetoric in an altered configuration of the gaze. Scopophobia, the visual symptom of this crisis, demonstrates the topology of the South Korean male's psyche.

Generic Play in *The Stray Bullet*

Scopophobia shapes the visual field as well. In the scene on the bus, the scopophobic symptom is doubled through its self-referential mise-en-scène. The bus window through which Ch'ŏr-ho looks at his sister resembles the frame of a film or the screen on which a film is projected. It articulates a parallel between Ch'ŏr-ho's vision and the vision of South Korean

105

cinema. That the bus stops for the traffic signal at the moment he catches sight of Myŏng-suk, and that the window/frame/screen is arrested when he turns away suggests the fact that the scopic anxiety portrayed is not just that of the male characters alone. This frozen frame registers the refusal to see Myŏng-suk enacted by the medium of the film itself. The medium of film, we might say, tries to evade capturing her. The scopophobic symptom that troubles the male subject is inscribed in the cinematic apparatus at this historical moment as well. *The Stray Bullet,* in this sense, might not be as "realistic" as has been believed. The "realistic aesthetics" of the film, I argue, are permeated by this scopophobic vision. This film, placed at the pinnacle of cinematic realism in Korea, is, to be profoundly ironic, driven by the will not to see reality.[21]

Thus, the symptom of scopophobia is manifested in the cinematography of the film. Its images are mostly rendered in long shot and with an extreme depth of field, so that the characters often become unrecognizable, small and overwhelmed within the mise-en-scène. The human images are visualized such that they don't appear as spectacle or intimidate the spectator as being "larger than life." In these ways, the cinematography of the film avoids spectacularization; it foregoes pleasure-driven visuals. Even though such a de-spectacularized visualization can be easily categorized as realistic, and, in fact, contributes to the real-life representation of devastated, dismal postwar South Korea and this family struggling within it, what seems to drive the realist tendency in this film is the will of the scopophobic subject not to see.

This tendency is countermanded by another made manifest in the film and connected with male trauma: that of an exaggerated and reactive acting out in fantasy scenarios, an aspect of performance that also tempers the realist aesthetic of this film. As Ch'ŏr-ho's character presents the colonized male's masculinity in crisis, the character of his younger brother, Yŏng-ho, also displays damaged masculinity, yet in a very different way. While Ch'ŏr-ho suffers from scopic anxiety generated by historical and familial crises, these same crises position Yŏng-ho as an object of the gaze, which, according to Mulvey's theory, is reserved for women. In the beginning of the film, the camera positions his and the maimed bodies of his veteran friends as objects of the viewer's gaze. Although the "realistic" cinematography generally de-spectacularizes the body, their bodies, with hooked arm and lame legs, become a spectacle.[22]

One episode that focuses on Yŏng-ho's wound illustrates the male body as spectacle in an emphatic way. In the episode, Mi-ri, Yŏng-ho's (girl)friend brings him to a film studio so that he can have an audition.

When he comes for the audition, she says to the assistant director, "He's a war veteran; got the wound the character has. From personality to wound he's exactly the same as the character. Isn't he perfect for the part?" Then, the assistant director says to Yŏng-ho, "I'm glad to hear that you are like the character. If you don't mind, can you show me your wound?" Yŏng-ho, upset at their words, yells at them, "Change the script! Switch the character to one without arms and legs. Won't your movie sell better then? So what you need is not me, but my wound? I didn't get it in a kid's game!"

In the sequence, Yŏng-ho's statement seems to criticize the inhumanity of money-obsessed commercial filmmaking. Through his character, the director of *The Stray Bullet* criticizes those commercial films that use a veteran's wounded body as a box-office draw. At a deeper level, however, what actually enrages Yŏng-ho is, I argue, that he is positioned as an object to be looked at and that his wound, a mark of his impaired masculinity, is spectacularized on the screen. His character therefore serves as a critique of the medium of cinema itself, for, at this moment in South Korea, the cinema is a vision machine that exhibits and exploits wounded masculinity. In this incident, we again see an instance where vision provokes significant anxiety and anger because it threatens to expose male lack—and places the male subject in the feminine scopic position.

The subsequent plotline involving Yŏng-ho chronicles his response to this threat to his masculinity. Talking big, he brings together his veteran friends and gets a jeep and a gun. He brags to his friends that "tomorrow will be the best day of our lives," and he proceeds to rob a bank.[23] His dream of "making it big" by committing a robbery reveals his strategy to compensate for his deprived male power. By successfully transgressing the law, he wishes to set himself up as an outlaw hero who can transcend the limitations imposed by society, the economy, and his body. As an outlaw, he is not to be pitied but feared.

Of particular interest is not only the drama he deploys but also the ways in which this drama is represented. At the narrative level, Yŏng-ho assumes the role of a boss of gangsters. In the film's depiction of the robbery it is not only the character who undergoes a transformation, becoming a gangster for a moment. Rather, the film itself undergoes a generic transformation, assuming the stylistic characteristics of the gangster film or film noir in very specific instants throughout the rest of Yŏng-ho's story. The sequence depicting Yŏng-ho's robbery, for example, progresses at quite a fast pace, complete with a chase scene and a shoot-out. The dark, dramatic background music, typical of film noir, signals an impending catastrophe. The visual and sonic quality of the sequence poses a distinct contrast to that part of the film devoted to Ch'ŏr-ho's plot. While the rest of the film mainly draws upon "realistic" film language to portray the heavy, depressing, and slow vision of the world stuck in torpor, Yŏng-ho's robbery sequence displays a noticeably Hollywood-style action and mood. The robbery sequence, therefore, interrupts the film's "realistic" aesthetic with another cinematic aesthetic.

The representation of Yŏng-ho's relationship with women furthers the noir elements in the Yŏng-ho plot. There are two women Yŏng-ho feels attached to: one is Mi-ri, the actress who sets up an audition for him at the film studio; the other is Sŏr-hŭi, a nurse at the military base where Yŏng-ho was hospitalized during the war. Yŏng-ho happens to meet Sŏr-hŭi again on the street and gets close to her. In an episode where Yŏng-ho visits her at night, she mistakes him for her bothersome neighbor, and threatens him with a pistol. When he stays with her that night, they smoke together, lighting one cigarette with the other. In these two instances, she takes up the props of the femme fatale from film noir, carrying a pistol and smoking a cigarette. Mi-ri also fosters Yŏng-ho's transformation into the noir figure. In fact, their scenes together foreshadow his transformation. For instance, in the sequence where Yŏng-ho visits her at the studio before committing the robbery, he kisses her passionately behind the staircase, thus conveying the sense of an encounter between two doomed lovers who will soon face a calamity. Mobilizing the tropes of a twisted fate and impossible dreams, visually suggested by the vertical drop of the staircase and emotionally by the gasping, impassioned kiss, the sequence effectively adapts and exhibits these noir elements, creating a highly stylized generic instant within the "life-like" realism of the rest of the film.

Yŏng-ho's temporary transformation into a noir hero goes far to signify that his actions are an attempt to recover his damaged masculinity. The cinematic configuration of the action, however, reveals that the representation of this attempt at empowerment is mediated through the West—the Hollywood genre of film noir, a genre that interestingly speaks to America's own postwar malaise. Yŏng-ho's dream of empowerment is articulated as a desire to be an outlaw noir hero and a lover of the femme fatale. The Yŏng-ho plot is, therefore, the representation of the fantasy of a South Korean man who dreams of regaining his lost masculinity by identifying himself with a male figure modeled on Hollywood iconography.

This failure of the imagination illuminates a crucial aspect of the psyche of the colonized male. The colonized male who is feminized and disempowered by the colonizer fantasizes his empowerment through mimicry of the image of the colonizer, believing that he can recuperate his masculinity through imitation. Through this imitation, he attempts to compensate for his impaired authority and to sustain his belief in the power that has been granted to him by patriarchal society. What his imaginary transaction with the Hollywood iconography uncovers is the painful irony in which he is caught: to maintain the "dominant fiction" organized by gender difference he seizes upon the colonizer's male image. His survival, therefore, rests upon the colonizer's iconography even as the colonizer's presence undermines his masculinity. This is the dilemma that the colonized male, haunted by the presence of the colonizer, faces.

Although the imitation of Hollywood iconography displayed via Yŏng-ho's characterization and the film's stylization provides an instance of what Homi Bhabha would call "cultural hybridity," it doesn't seem to allow, as he argues, the space for the colonized subject to enact opposition to colonial domination.[24] Through the cultural hybridization and its functioning of "double narrative movement," he claims, the pedagogy of the dominant is undermined and rewritten by the performativity of the dominated.[25] The mimicry that is, according to Bhabha, a crucial part of such a double inscription, has a menacing power that comes from "its double vision which in disclosing the ambivalence of colonial discourse also disrupts its authority."[26] Mimicry does so by "revers[ing] in part the colonial appropriation by now producing a partial vision of the colonizer's presence; a gaze of otherness."[27] In other words, the mimicry that doubly registers similarity and difference, and thus generates a colonized subject that is "almost the same but not quite" as the colonizer, illuminates the incommensurable difference between the two. The incommensurable difference, then, functioning as the returning gaze of the colonized, reflects back the colonizer's own "otherness," which significantly destabilizes the colonial authority.

Yŏng-ho's mimicry, however, does not offer the momentum that returns the otherness of the colonizer—the otherness of colonial iconography of Hollywood. Rather than revealing the colonizer as the other, the difference disclosed through his mimicry reinforces the perception of his position of being othered. Yŏng-ho's final statement to Ch'ŏr-ho, who visits him at the police station after he has been arrested, implies his eventual acknowledgment of such a position, that is, his inferiority as the colonized subject: "I just wanna get hanged so that this kind of thing may never happen again. Hope a lot of people come see it." Here he asserts his position as an object exposed to the public gaze, which suggests his awareness of being caught in the gaze of the colonizer, a captivation internalized in his psyche in the form of the panoptic gaze.[28] Contra Bhabha, his mimicry returns his gaze to himself, intensifying his self-consciousness that he is, after all, a mere object to be looked at by the all-knowing gaze of the colonizer inscribed in the structure of colonial relation and also in the screen of his self-image.

Yŏng-ho's desire to mimic the image of the colonizer, which ends up exacerbating his acknowledgment of his disempowered position, offers multilayered meanings on the overall situation of South Korean cinema and the filmmaking of the director himself. Even though Yŏng-ho fears the medium of cinema and criticizes the commercial filmmaking that spectacularizes his vulnerability, what he does to be relieved from his fear is to insert himself into the other fantasy component that Mulvey finds at the heart of commercial filmmaking. That is, instead of being the object of the gaze, he forcefully takes up the position of the autonomous agent of the action. Since this role is performed by Ch'oe Mu-ryong, one of the biggest male stars of the 1960s in South Korea, the implication extends to the significance of male iconography in the South Korean cinema as a whole. This iconography of strong and glamorous masculinity, which was built up by the actor through such films as *Marines Who Never Return* (*Toraoji annŭn haebyŏng*, Yi Man-hŭi, 1963), *Red Muffler* (*Ppalgan mahura*, Sin Sang-ok, 1964), and *South and North* (*Nam kwa Puk*, Kim Ki-dŏk, 1965), works to compete with and mimic the heroes of the colonizer's cinema. In other words, to make up for the threat to his attractiveness and luster posed by Hollywood male stars, the South Korean male icon borrows the aura of Hollywood.

The fact that Yŏng-ho prepares for the crime in the film theater, Tansŏngsa, has interesting implications in terms of the correspondence between Yŏng-ho's plot and South Korean cinema. Tansŏngsa was South Korea's first full-scale, modern film theater that screened the first Korean kino-dramas, *Righteous Revenge* (*Ŭirijŏk kut'o*[*tu*], Kim To-san, 1919) and *Arirang* (Na Un-kyu, 1925). These films are generally regarded as the foundations of realist filmmaking in Korea, and at the same time as a pinnacle of cinematic forms of nationalist resistance.[29] *The Stray Bullet* makes an ironic comment on the historical significance of this theater as a central place for Korean nationalist spirit by mobilizing it as a place for a turning point, where the film's style transforms from realism to the expressionist flourishes of film noir. Through the transition Yŏng-ho is transferred into the "space" of Hollywood film, at the same time that the film itself (and, by implication, South Korean national cinema) is reconstructed according to generic idioms of the colonizer's cinema. Altering the historical memory of the theater, the film employs the theater as a symbolic vehicle that refers to the South Korean male and cinema caught in the mimicry of the colonizer's imagery.

Yŏng-ho's plot, including the theater sequence, can be read as a self-reflexive remark on Korean national cinema.[30] Situated in the historical condition of neocolonialism, South Korean cinema has had to compete with and imitate the dominant film language of Hollywood cinema. Through the story of Yŏng-ho, the director aligns the situation of South Korean men, that of South Korean cinema and, indeed, his own situation as a film director. We hear the director's skepticism about his own filmmaking: he wanted to create a film to represent the "real" life of the nation, but what he has done instead is to mimic the colonizer's version of postwar crises. Yŏng-ho, who dreams of a "real" life, criticizes his brother Ch'ŏr-ho's life by saying that it is like a "10-cent toy peep show for kids." In reality, this statement makes his own life a peep show and, finally, reflects back onto the director himself; he confesses his own powerlessness in filmmaking via Yŏng-ho's story.

The Yŏng-ho story is about how the colonized male subject (and national cinema) dissimulates his powerless position, how he reconfigures himself to cover his injured masculinity. While Ch'ŏr-ho avoids the unpleasant encounter with his demasculinized position by not looking, Yŏng-ho attempts to put forth an unimpaired masculine image through his identification with and mimicry of Hollywood heroes. Like Ch'ŏr-ho's, Yŏng-ho's attempt at adopting the iconography of Hollywood's heroes is a way of integrating himself into normative masculinity as it is defined by patriarchal social codes, thus sustaining the principle of gender difference that organizes the imagined community. It is as such a feeble, self-conflicted disavowal of his lack and of the breakdown of his imagined community.

Impossible Visions

The story of male disavowal played out in *The Stray Bullet* is, after all, that of failed disavowal. The defensive modes the two male characters desperately cling to turn out to be useless and their vulnerabilities are finally laid bare. Yŏng-ho's failed attempt to transform himself into a powerful male image ends with his arrest. As his final statement to Ch'ŏr-ho suggests, he cannot escape the feminized position as an object to be looked at. At narrative's end, the only agency left to him is that of becoming a spectacle by way of his own actions and his own desire, a Pyrrhic victory at best.

Ch'ŏr-ho, who struggles throughout to carry on his masculine subjectivity within the boundaries of tradition and the law, in the end also succumbs to complete chaos. His capitulation is triggered by two incidents: the arrest of Yŏng-ho and the death of his wife. These two traumas exceed the limits of Ch'ŏr-ho's strength and destroy his efforts to hang on to his position as head of the family. Yŏng-ho's arrest for the crime is a blow to Ch'ŏr-ho, who, in Yŏng-ho's words, cannot even afford a monthly bus pass or to have his rotten teeth pulled, but nevertheless tries to maintain certain ethics such as diligence and integrity. His brother's illegal action signifies that the moral code necessary to keep family life legitimate or, in its extended sense, to sustain nationhood, has utterly broken down. The death of his wife during her delivery is another fatal blow to Ch'ŏr-ho. With her death the patriarchal family he is supposed to keep alive is irrecoverably crippled and damaged. The crippled family is a metaphor for the divided nation after the Korean War, thus signifying that the national identity and male subjectivity that sustain and define it are, likewise, divided and diminished. The last image of Ch'ŏr-ho, who passes out in a taxicab murmuring, "I really don't know where to go . . . I know I have to go somewhere now. . . . Let's go," vividly captures the collapse of his subjectivity and national identity. The eldest brother, the man of the family, here echoes the words of his mother with which the film began. Whereas she sought to return to the home from which she had been displaced by national division, his words have no referent as he has no possible home or destination.

Notes

1. This line is translated both as "Let's go!" and "Let's get out of here!"
2. The film is based on a short story with the same title by Yi Pŏm-sŏn. The short story is translated into English by Marshall R. Pihl and Vreni Merriam, *Korea Journal* (1976).
3. Kyung Hyun Kim also reads the phrase as emblematic of the trauma of family and nation, which interestingly he uses as a point of departure for the discussion of Korean road movies. The immobile mother's desperate chant, he argues, shares the symptom of Korean men on the road who fear that their homeland might have been permanently lost. See the chapter "Nowhere to Run: Disenfranchised Men on the Road in *The Man with Three Coffins, Sopyonje,* and *Out to the World*" in his *The Remasculinization of Korean Cinema* (Durham, NC: Duke University Press, 2004).
4. There was in fact a liberation village located behind the U.S. military base in Seoul. Chungmoo Choi describes its significance in terms of cold war ideology in "The Magic and Violence of Modernization in Post-Colonial Korea"

in *Post-Colonial Classics of Korean Cinema,* ed. Chungmoo Choi (Irvine, CA: Korean Film Festival Committee, UCI, 1998). *The Stray Bullet* was produced during the first republic and released immediately before the 5.16 (May 16) coup (1961). But soon after its release, it was censored by the Park Chung Hee (Pak Chŏng-hŭi) military regime, because the military regime interpreted that the line "Let's go" spoken by the mother means "Let's go to North Korea." See Yi Hyŏn-ch'an, *Han'guk yŏnghwa 100 nyŏn* (*100 Years of Korean Cinema*) (Seoul: Munhak sasangsa, 2000), 124. Director Yu added in the interview performed by me in summer 2002—that the regime also criticized the film's depressing portrayal of society, particularly the representation of the dark side of war veterans. The regime established through a military coup would not allow the negative image of war veterans to be shown.

5. I am using Mulvey's hypothesis on the scopic regime to gauge its theoretical limitations in relation to the historical specificity and cultural difference of postwar South Korea. I am also drawing from the work of subsequent theorists who have critiqued and revised Mulvey's assertion to account for differential constructions of masculinity. Paul Willemen, for instance, in "Voyeurism, the Look and Dwoskin," *Afterimage* 6 (1976): 43, asserts that the scopophilic drive, central to Mulvey's thesis, is autoerotic at the beginning. It does not, therefore, exclude the possibility of taking one's sexual like as an object to be looked at, and therefore includes men and the male body as objects of the gaze. Peter Lehman observes that Mulvey's argument replicates patriarchal ideology by exclusively assigning the position of being looked at to women. He explores the male body as object of the gaze in his *Running Scared: Masculinity and the Representation of the Male Body* (Philadelphia: Temple University Press, 1993). Feminist critic Gaylyn Studlar challenges masculine subjectivity as the powerful active agent of the gaze in her book *In the Realm of Pleasure: Von Sternberg, Dietrich, and the Masochistic Aesthetics* (Urbana: University of Illinois Press, 1988). Linda Williams and Marsha Kinder also assert the presence of the female subject of the gaze, respectively, in *Hard-Core: Power, Pleasure, and the "Frenzy of the Visible"* (Berkeley: University of California Press, 1989) and "Individual Responses," in *Camera Obscura* 20–21 (1989).

6. Laura Mulvey, "Visual Pleasure and Narrative Cinema," *Screen* 16, no. 3 (1975).

7. This film has always been lauded for its realism; critics and historians of Korean cinema have predominantly categorized the film as a central text of realism following the tradition of Na Un-gyu's *Arirang* (1926), Yi Kyu-hwan's *A Ferryboat with No Ferryman* (*Imja ŏmnŭn naruppae*, 1932), and Ch'oe In-gyu's *Victory of Freedom* (*Chayu manse*, 1946), which have been established as the center of the genealogy of Korean film history. See Lee Yŏng-il's *Han'guk yŏnghwa chŏnsa* (*History of Korean Cinema*) (Seoul: Han'guk yŏnghwain hyŏphoe, 1969), 232–33, and Lee Yŏng-il, "Yu Hyŏn-mok: Pan hŏgu yŏngsang ŭi ch'ehŏm" ("Yu Hyŏn-mok: Experience of Anti-Fiction-Image") and Pyŏn In-sik, "Yu Hyŏn-mok yŏnghwa e p'yoch'uldoen sin kwa in'gan ŭi k'ŏmyunik'eisyŏn" ("Communication between God and

Man in Yu Hyŏn-mok Films") in Chŏn Yang-jun and Chang Ki-ch'ŏl, eds., *Tathin hyŏnsil yŏllin yŏnghwa* (*Closed Reality Open Cinema*) (Seoul: Chesam munhaksa, 1992). Another interesting remark on the film as a realist text is found in the director's own comment. In the same interview aforementioned, responding to my explanation that essays on his film, *The Stray Bullet*, will be included in a volume on melodrama of the 1960s and published in the United States, he emphasized that the film is not a melodrama, but a realist one much influenced by Italian Neorealism.

8. See Jinsoo An's discussion of *Until the End of My Life* (chapter 3 this volume) for another treatment of a military prostitute.

9. Benedict Anderson, *Imagined Communities* (London: Verso, 1983), 11–12. Partha Chatterjee has critiqued Anderson's account of colonial and postcolonial nations. See *The Nation and Its Fragments: Colonial and Post-Colonial Histories* (Princeton: Princeton University Press, 1993). See also Julian Stringer's "Sopyonje and National Culture" in *Im Kwon-Taek: The Making of a Korean National Cinema*, ed. David E. James and Kyung Hyun Kim (Detroit: Wayne State University Press, 2002).

10. Chatterjee, *Nation and Its Fragments*, 5–6.

11. When a country undergoes a crisis such as a war or colonization by another country, it inevitably suffers the violation of its women, as in the notorious example of Korean comfort women kidnapped and forced into sexual servitude by the Japanese army during World War II. Such an alignment of the violated country with violated femininity takes place in a symbolic as well as in the corporeal way. When a country is invaded by other countries, for example, it is often said that their "mother land" is taken; their "sisters" are ruined. Woman is mobilized as object to signify lost nationhood. See Youme Park, "Against Metaphor: Gender, Violence, and Decolonization in Korean Nationalist Literature," in *In Pursuit of Contemporary East Asian Culture*, ed. Xiaobing Tang and Stephen Snyder (Boulder, CO: Westview Press, 1996).

12. Anderson, *Imagined Communities*, 7.

13. George L. Mosse, *Nationalism and Sexuality: Middle-Class Morality and Sexual Norms in Modern Europe* (Madison: University of Wisconsin Press, 1985).

14. In a colonized nation this repression involves the censorship of suspect female sexuality; women are suspected of prostituting themselves to the colonizer. They are thus easily charged with collaborating with the colonial power. For a detailed argument along these lines see Chungmoo Choi's "Nationalism and Construction of Gender in Korea," in *Dangerous Women: Gender and Korean Nationalism*, ed. Elaine H. Kim and Chungmoo Choi (New York: Routledge, 1998).

15. Kaja Silverman, *Male Subjectivity at the Margins* (New York: Routledge, 1992), 54.

16. Ibid.

17. In *Until the End of My Life* (*I saengmyŏng tahadorok*, 1960) while the husband is hospitalized, his wife (played by Ch'oe Ŭn-hŭi) experiences strong affection for another man. Although her affair is never consummated and she

114

quickly comes back to the position of a sacrificial wife, it is implied that the handicapped husband has strong anxiety about his married life. To reassure him about his lost masculinity, female sexuality is repressed. In *The Way Back Home* (*Kwiro*, 1967) the wife of the handicapped male protagonist (played by Mun Chŏng-suk) also falls in love with another man. In both films the maimed male body is tied to the lack of masculinity and to the loss of control of female sexuality.

18. Such a representation of war veterans is similar to that of *The Best Years of Our Lives* (William Wyler, 1946), one of the well-known Hollywood war films that was released in Korea in 1958. Silverman deals with the image of war veterans in the film and failed masculinity in the context of postwar America (Silverman, *Male Subjectivity*, 65–90).

19. I would like to thank David James for this idea that the move of Ch'ŏr-ho is directed to block the overall traffic of gazes activated by the scene.

20. Similar instances of such a troubled male gaze are found elsewhere in the film. When Ch'ŏr-ho picks up Myŏng-suk in police detention (she gets caught while flirting with American GIs at night on the street), he never looks at her. Afterward, walking along the street as if they don't know each other, they keep a certain distance between them. By not seeing her he avoids the perception of her "degraded" sexuality and his disempowered position as a male subject.

21. The sequence of Ch'ŏr-ho spotting Myŏng-suk on the bus is noteworthy in terms of its use of sound as well. During the sequence, two sharply contrasting kinds of music collide: American popular song, jazz, and Korean traditional music, *p'ansori*. Chungmoo Choi argues that the music is deployed as "trope of popular resistance." That is, the traditional music is mobilized as cultural resistance to the U.S. domination visualized through the relationship of Myŏng-suk and the American GI (see Choi, "The Magic"). Choi's inspiring argument invites a way of reading the scene as an expression of the split psyche of Ch'ŏr-ho. While disavowing the vision of the female body, his split subjectivity would still desire to resist the colonial power, which is articulated through the music in the scene. His repressed will to resistance in the visual track is thereby rendered via the soundtrack.

22. Lehman also deals with the image of the wounded male body in westerns in light of failed masculinity. See chapter 3 of his book, titled "Men Called Scarface, Scar, and Stumpy." As for the issue of the male body and spectacle in the context of Western film theory, see Steve Neale's "Masculinity as Spectacle," *Screen* 24, no. 6, and Paul Willemen's "Anthony Mann: Looking at the Male," in *Frameworks* 15–17 (Summer).

23. The phrase said by Yŏng-ho sounds like a quote from the title of *The Best Years of Our Lives*. The film was released in Korea in 1958. *The Stray Bullet* shares certain features with the film, for example, the crippled body of war veterans and their masculinity in crisis. Yŏng-ho's phrase and similarities between the two films provide an instance of *The Stray Bullet*'s quoting Hollywood, which I will explore in the rest of the essay.

24. For a detailed explanation of the concept of "cultural hybridity" see Homi K. Bhabha's "The Third Space," in *Identity: Community, Culture, Difference,*

ed. Jonathan Rutherford (London: Lawrence and Wishart, 1990) and also "Dissemination: Time, Narrative, and the Margins of the Modern Nation," in *Nation and Narration,* ed. Homi K. Bhabha (London: Routledge, 1990).

25. Bhabha, "Dissemination," 292–302.

26. Homi K. Bhabha, "Of Mimicry and Man: The Ambivalence of Colonial Discourse," *October* 28, no. 2.2 (Spring 1990): 129.

27. Ibid., 129.

28. About the panoptic gaze of the colonizer see Bhabha, "Of Mimicry."

29. When it was first built in 1907, Tansŏngsa was mainly used for theatrical performances. After it was remodeled into a full-scale film theater in 1918, it became a central place for Korean national cinema. See Lee, *History of Korean Cinema,* 21–22.

30. The fact that the overall plot of Yŏng-ho was created through the process of adaptation from short story version to film version further connotes the self-reflexive dimension of his story. Although Yŏng-ho's robbery is still the main event involving him in the short story, a detailed description of the event is not given. Rather, the short story focuses on Ch'ŏr-ho's response to it, rendering it filtered through his consciousness and narrated by him as in the rest of the short story. Yŏng-ho's episode in the film studio, characters such as Mi-ri and Sŏr-hŭi, and his relationship to them are the pure product of adaptation. The plot and characterization of Yŏng-ho were, therefore, brought forth through what we can call "a cinematic imagination." Using the cinematic imagination, the director incorporates the self-referential perspective into the film.

5

Toward a Strategic Korean Cinephilia:
A Transnational *Détournement* of Hollywood Melodrama

HYE SEUNG CHUNG

A slight yet significant gesture: a man lights a cigarette with the graceful elegance and casual demeanor of someone whose cool exterior belies a passionate, romantic streak. He hands another unlit cigarette to a young woman standing opposite him. She brings it to her lips and leans seductively toward him. Face to face, the couple poses as if on the verge of a kiss. As they slowly draw nearer to each other, the ends of the two cigarettes touch, one lighting the other. By visualizing the convergence of two cultures, one ostensibly bound to tradition, the other representative of modernity, this blissful contact not only seals the pact of their newfound affection but also inscribes, at a deeper level, the complex cultural hybridization bound up in the symbolic image of the romantic couple.

Any American movie fan worth his or her salt will recognize this famous "nicotine kiss" between William Holden and Jennifer Jones as the most memorable scene in Henry King's sweeping East-meets-West melodrama *Love Is a Many-Splendored Thing* (1955), a film that taught would-be-lovers around the world a particularly Hollywood way of igniting both cigarettes and passions.[1] Aficionados of South Korea's cinematic Golden Age, however, may recall a different scene upon hearing the above description. In place of a picturesque Hong Kong beach, dramatically framed in Cinemascope and populated by a swimsuited twosome, a drab black-and-white apartment in poverty-stricken Seoul might flicker in their minds. This is one of the settings of director Yu Hyŏn-mok's critically acclaimed *The Stray Bullet* (*Obalt'an*, 1961), a postwar classic that ingeniously rearticulates and recontextualizes the scene in *Love Is a Many-Splendored Thing* by situating its cigarette-lighting couple within a claustrophobic interior. The male hero is not the American correspondent played by Holden, a personification of the escalating U.S. imperial presence in the British crown colony, but rather an unemployed, battle-

Cross-cultural *détournement:* The "nicotine kiss" from *Love Is a Many-Splen-dored Thing* (above) and *The Stray Bullet* (below)

scarred Korean War vet played by matinee idol Ch'oe Mu-ryong, emasculated by his lack of financial means to court and marry another woman,
his movie star fiancée. His partner in this scene, unlike her Hollywood
counterpart (the financially stable Eurasian medical doctor played by
Jones), is a struggling part-time college student who earns her tuition by
spending four hours a day in a smoky cellar as a factory worker. Coun-
terpoised against Hollywood's star-crossed lovers who whisper sweet-
nothings against a swelling musical score, the Korean couple confesses
familial loss and destitution while mimetically enacting the romantic
Holden-Jones pose accompanied by a soundtrack featuring little more
than caged birds chirping offscreen.

Yu's film subtly critiques Hollywood's Orientalist geopolitical imaginary by decisively refusing its fantasy settings and romantic excess. Like
French Situationist guru Guy Debord,[2] director Yu mobilizes the tech-
nique of *détournement,* whereby the tropes of dominant popular culture
are appropriated, rerouted, and reconfigured so as to provoke a counter-
hegemonic disarticulation of meaning. The Korean *détournement* of the
melodramatic scene cleverly registers the squalor and despair of postwar
Seoul in which a young, handsome couple is literally caged inside slum
walls while their Hollywood counterparts leisurely engage in touristic
consumption in exotic Hong Kong and neighboring Macao. *The Stray
Bullet* is a remarkably modernist text that not only hybridizes Korean and
Euro-American signifiers (costumes, languages, and soundtracks) but
also commingles and intermixes Hollywood melodramatic tropes and
realist South Korean aesthetics. Golden Age South Korean melodrama
diverges from its American equivalent of the Eisenhower era due to the
former's focus on ordinary lower-middle and working-class citizens
(*sosimin*) as opposed to the latter's gravitation toward upper-middle-class
bourgeois housewives and widows.[3] In this respect, one could argue that
South Korean film melodrama offers a more discursive range of spectatorial positions than that engendered by Hollywood's 1950s family melodrama, which, as Christine Gledhill points out, opens up a cross-class fantasy and identification conduit for petite bourgeois or working-class
audiences vis-à-vis screen surrogates basking in "lavish furnishings and
consumer goods"[4] whose fetishistic potency represents America's postwar
prosperity and abundance. In marked contrast, the South Korean society
of the 1950s and the 1960s was torn apart by postwar poverty and chaos.
Melodrama sided with underprivileged masses suffering social and familial alienation in the shadowy margins of modernization and economic
development. Thus, in terms of its aesthetic characteristics and semantic

ingredients, South Korean melodrama was seldom divested of its realistic, socially conscious core.

Although many commentators observe the influence of Italian Neo-realism and German Expressionism in *The Stray Bullet*,[5] few scholars have pointed out the film's intertextual relationship with Hollywood melodrama. By linking South Korean Golden Age cinema and Classical Hollywood melodrama within a comparative paradigm, this essay addresses not only the cross-cultural translation and adaptation of particular scenes and star-images but also Korean audiences' unique cinephilic fixation on often overlooked Hollywood films. Korean audiences' infatuation and identification with Hollywood cinema should be historicized in the postwar cultural context rather than being simply frowned upon as a symptom of U.S. cultural imperialism. The post–Korean War generation's intense nostalgia for sentimental Hollywood melodrama is a significant indicator of the cultural displacement that occurs when spectatorial desire for the "other" operates within a postcolonial setting. Before embarking upon specific comparative case studies, a brief examination of the otherwise discursive cultural forces intermingled within and responsible for the formation of South Korean melodrama will provide a historical backdrop against which to frame intertextual relations.

Origins of South Korean Melodrama: *Sinp'a, Han, and Hollywood*

In her book-length study of Korean melodrama, feminist film scholar Yu Chi-na identifies three origins of the genre that figured decisively in the context of an emergent national cinema.[6] The first source is the Japanese *sinp'a* (new school) drama introduced and localized during the colonial era (1910–45). In the late-nineteenth-century *Meiji* period, the *sinp'a* drama arose in Japan as a popular alternative to the *kup'a* (old school) drama, *kabuki*.[7] Set in a modern milieu, it usually features a sentimental plot revolving around family tragedy and heterosexual romance. After Japan's annexation of Korea in 1910, the *sinp'a* drama strongly influenced Korean theater, film, and literature, injecting Japanese theatrical modes of storytelling into the syntactical core of Korean cultural productions. Famous silent *sinp'a* films include *Twin Jade Pavilion* (*Ssangongnu*, Yi Ku-yŏng, 1925), *Arirang* (*Na Un-gyu*, 1926), *Long Cherished Dream* (*Changhanmong*, Yi Kyŏng-son, 1926), and *Fallen Blossoms on a Stream* (*Nakhwayusu*, Yi Ku-yŏng, 1927). During the Golden Age of South Korean cinema in the 1950s and 1960s, the *sinp'a* drama became associated with female audiences, identified by such derogatory nicknames as "handkerchief army" (*sonsugŏn pudae*), "tear gas" (*ch'oerut'an*), and "rubber shoes" (*komusin*: trademarks of married, middle-aged women who migrated to the metropolis from rural areas).[8] The term *sinp'a* is still used by South Korean critics and audiences to derogatorily designate old-fashioned melodramas filled with unlikely coincidences and fortuitous reversals as well as excessive sentimentality.[9]

In addition, Yu and other scholars[10] claim that Korean melodrama hinges upon the national sentiment of *han*, a slippery and subtle term that, depending on context, denotes everything from "resentment" and "lamentation" to "unfulfilled desire" and "resignation." *Han* can be vaguely defined as the deep-rooted sadness, bitterness, and longing sparked by prolonged injustices and oppression. Various scholars have identified the sociopolitical sources of Korean *han* to include: a long history of foreign invasions by the Chinese, the Japanese, and the West; patriarchal Confucian traditions that have silenced and enslaved women for hundreds of years; the inhumane treatment and exploitation of the subaltern class under the feudal caste system as well as during the full-throttle modernization process; and the gross violations of civil rights by successive authoritarian military regimes in the postcolonial period.[11] Indeed, the recuperation of the abiding sense of *han* in South Korean melodrama seems to facilitate our appreciation of the indigenous and dormant forces behind a genre deeply influenced by colonial cultural import. However, over-dependence on this elusive, psycho-phantasmic concept for the explication of generic categories intrinsic to a particular national cinema risks generating what can be labeled "critical nationalism." By "critical nationalism," I refer to the attitude of filmmakers, critics, and scholars alike who contend that *han* is uniquely Korean, a concept that almost, if not completely, escapes translatability in other cultural lexicons. Im Kwŏn-t'aek (Im Kwon-Taek)—a household name in South Korea and a director whose oeuvre brims with *han*-centric films that aestheticize Korean history, tradition, and culture in melodramatic modes[12]—concisely sums up this position: "*Han* is not a concept that Koreans can agree on. I can't even count the number of books that have been written about *han*. . . . However, *han* is a specific emotion that has profound links to the history of the Korean people, and as such, might be a difficult concept for non-Koreans to grasp fully."[13] The critical over-emphasis on such an ambiguous concept as definite marker of Korean-ness contributes to the erection of "imagined [emotional] communities" of the nation and its culture.

From the point of view of genre studies, *han* can be better understood as a historically and culturally specific mobilization of what Peter Brooks defines as the "melodramatic imagination" or "melodramatic mode."[14] *Han* indeed connotes melodramatic affect and sensibility in the Korean context. However, what is unique about Korean *han* is its *context* rather than *affect* in and of itself. The overlooked transnational valency of the concept becomes salient once we examine the etymological roots of this monosyllabic Sino-Korean character. According to a Chinese-English dictionary, "*han* is *hen* ('hate') in Chinese, *kon* ('to bear a grudge') in Japanese, *horosul* ('sorrowfulness') in Mongolian, *korsocuka* ('hatred,' 'grief') in Manchurian, and *hân* ('frustration') in Vietnamese."[15] Although similar concepts exist throughout East and Southeast Asia, only *han* has emerged as a privileged marker of national culture and identity. Instead of essentializing the uniqueness of Korean melodrama on the grounds of the ontologically uncertain *han,* it is useful to examine how similar concepts function in other national cinemas and how they converge with and diverge from it. For example, in exploring the transnational circulation of filmic *han* as it cross-pollinates into neighboring cultural arenas, attention could be directed to the historical epics and melodramas of Zhang Yimou, Chen Kaige, and other Chinese Fifth Generation filmmakers who anchor their stories in the imagery of suffering female bodies. Is the *han* expressed by the Korean surrogate childbearers in Im Kwŏn-t'aek's *Surrogate Mother* (*Ssibaji,* 1986) fundamentally different from the pain and suffering of the Chinese concubines in Zhang Yimou's equally exoto-ethnographic melodrama *Raise the Red Lantern* (1991)? Or does the difference lie in the cultural and historical crevice separating these two nations?

One can similarly cast doubts on the concept of *mono no aware* as being distinctively Japanese. Defined by Donald Richie as "sympathetic sadness . . . a serene acceptance of a transient world" and by David Bordwell as "the pathos of things,"[16] *mono no aware* is an underlying emotional chord struck in the meditative family melodramas of Yasujiro Ozu and other Japanese auteurs sensitive to quotidian poetics. It is tempting to argue that *mono no aware* is what distinguishes tranquil Japanese melodramas from their more emotionally intense South Korean counterparts. However, many Japanese audiences appear to have experienced *mono no aware* when they saw Hŏ Chin-ho's *Christmas in August* (*P'arwŏl ŭi K'ŭrisŭmasŭ,* 1998), a critically lauded pan-Asian success already canonized as a representative South Korean melodrama. According to film critic Deruoka Sojo, many Japanese who compared this film to Ozu's work were surprised to discover that Korean sentiments were, after all, very similar to their own.[17] This casts in relief prejudiced perceptions about South Korean cinema as alienating and defamiliarizing due to its imagined exoticism and emotive primitivism. As evidenced by the Japanese reception of *Christmas in August, mono no aware* as well as *han* can be unraveled as a discursively radiating transnational experience rather than as a uniquely indigenous manifestation of a given culture's resignation to or transcendence of sorrow. Granting that *han* and *mono no aware* have different origins, histories, and connotations, both concepts have been similarly mobilized by critics as the aesthetic purveyors of national identity. If it is true that South Koreans can sense *han* in Zhang Yimou's melodramas and the Japanese can feel *mono no aware* in *Christmas in August,* both concepts need to be reexamined from a critical perspective more attuned to the cross-cultural implications of not one but many melodramatic imaginations.

While many Korean film scholars have emphasized *sinp'a* and *han* as two foundational determinants of South Korean melodrama,[18] the third influence, Hollywood melodrama, remains notably understudied. The unabated influx of American films since the U.S. military occupation (1945–48) and the Korean War (1950–53) significantly affected the genre formations of the embryonic South Korean industry. Golden Age melodramas of the 1950s and 1960s register palimpsestic traces of Hollywood's tropes and iconography, which undergo a process of cross-cultural translation or, as Stuart Hall defines it, a "continuous process of re-articulation and recontextualization, without any notion of a primary origin."[19] These visual and aural motifs and semantic elements are recycled and recast in specifically South Korean contexts. South Korean melodrama furthermore complicates American melodrama's entrenched country/city binary as well as its nostalgia for a preindustrial past, both of which, as Gledhill asserts, replaced the class oppositions permeating European melodrama and created the myth of American egalitarianism.[20] Rather than vilifying the city like in early American melodramas (especially those directed by D. W. Griffith), South Korean melodramas represent Seoul as bearing the imprint of modernization—as a polyphonic center that mediates confrontations, conflicts, and compromises among rivaling values and camps: European, American, Japanese, and Korean; tradition and modernity; the ruling class and the working class; male and female; the urban and the rural. Perennial favorite *The Stray Bullet,* for example, does more than simply evoke or copy Hollywood melodramas, specifically Mervyn LeRoy's *Waterloo Bridge* (1940) and the aforementioned *Love Is a Many-Splendored Thing.* Its translation and *détournement* of Hollywood melodramatic scenes lay bare the artificial constructs and ideological spuriousness of larger-than-life romantic trappings that often obscure the disparity of power among various nations, races, genders, and classes.

Waterloo Bridge and Postwar Korean Cinephilia

Waterloo Bridge in particular is one of the top ten favorites of South Korean audiences. According to the Korean Broadcasting System (KBS)'s nationwide survey of "100 Films That Audiences Want to See Again" (conducted in 1996), the ten most requested films were, in order of preference: *Roman Holiday* (1952), *Gone With the Wind* (1939), *Romeo and Juliet* (1968), *The Sound of Music* (1965), *Breakfast at Tiffany's* (1961), *Ben-Hur* (1959), *Waterloo Bridge* (1940), *Doctor Zhivago* (1965), *The King and I* (1956), and *Casablanca* (1942).[21] The popularity of these films remained strong across generations, from parents who saw them in theaters during the 1950s and 1960s to their children who encountered them through television reruns dubbed in Korean. Considering that 6,523 out of 11,064 participants responded by means of local computer networks (such as Chollian [*Ch'ŏllian*] and Hitel [*Hait'el*]) rather than conventional postcards, it can be inferred that the voice of the younger generation was considerably amplified in the survey. In fact, among the top fifty were a number of 1980s and 1990s films including *Dead Poets Society* (1989, #14), *The Shawshank Redemption* (1994, #19), *The Mission* (1986, #22), *The Terminator* (1984, #24), *Forrest Gump* (1994, #25), *The Last Emperor* (1987, #26), *Once Upon a Time in America* (1984, #29), *Amadeus* (1984, #31), *Out of Africa* (1985, #32), *A River Runs Through It* (1992, #37), *Ghost* (1990, #38), *Rain Man* (1988, #39), *Schindler's List* (1993, #40), *Top Gun* (1986, #41), *Back to the Future* (1985, #44), *Raiders of the Lost Ark* (1981, #45), *Braveheart* (1995, #47), and *Scent of a Woman* (1992, #48). However, the fact that the top ten list consists primarily of Classical Hollywood films clearly attests to South Korean audiences' general preference of what they call "unforgettable classics" over New Hollywood blockbusters. Although *Love Is a Many-Splendored Thing* ranks relatively low on this list (#84), its status would likely have been much higher if more fans from the older generation had participated in the survey. Regrettably (and tellingly), only one South Korean film, Im Kwŏn-t'aek's *Sŏp'yŏnje* (1993),[22] broke into the list, coming in at #74. Despite the fact that the survey was conducted before the arrival of South Korean cinema's fin-de-siècle renaissance initiated by a series of box-office hits such as *Contact* (*Chŏpsok*, 1997), *A Promise* (*Yaksok*, 1998), *Whispering Corridors* (*Yŏgo koedam*,

124

1998), *Shiri* (*Swiri*, 1999), *Attack the Gas Station* (*Chuyuso sŭpkyŏk sagŏn*, 1999), *Nowhere to Hide* (*Injŏng sajŏng polgŏt ŏpta*, 1999), *Joint Security Area* (*Kongdong gyŏngbi guyŏk*, 2000), and *Friends* (*Ch'in'gu*, 2001), it is both curious and disturbing that not a single Golden Age South Korean film appears on a list dominated by Classical and post-Classical Hollywood cinema.

The distinctive characteristics of South Korean cinephilia should be analyzed and contextualized before such preferences are dismissed as the by-product of U.S. cultural imperialism in general and of Hollywood hegemony in particular. For many post–Korean War theatergoers, whose mania for "Dream Factory" products and whose celebration and recognition of the "genius of the system" rivaled that of contemporaneous *Cahiers du Cinéma* critics in Paris, American films offered much more than an entertaining night out with friends and family. With few exceptions, classic Hollywood films, packed with glossy images and blessed with wholesome, innocent characters and storylines, represented the hopes and dreams of poverty-stricken masses in the underdeveloped country. Like the poor Sicilian child Toto and his undereducated projectionist friend Alfredo in *Cinema Paradiso* (1988) (the highest-ranked Italian film [#11] on the KBS list), cinephilic Koreans managed to endure postwar poverty and hardships in the therapeutic glow of the movie screen. From a political standpoint, it is indeed problematic that audiences were passively sutured into a cross-racial set of identificatory gazes and were often oblivious to the ideological transparency normalizing the implicit white, male-subject position. However, the enormous spectatorial pleasures and comfort provided by classic Hollywood films, as well as the emergence of a cinephilic competency and potential to engage the act of cross-cultural *détournement*, should be recuperated as a critical intervention in the cultural history and memory of the 1950s and 1960s.

In renowned South Korean journalist-writer Ahn Junghyo (An Chŏng-hyo)'s novel, *The Life and Death of the Hollywood Kid* (*Hŏlliudŭ k'idŭ ŭi saengae*, 1992),[23] the narrator dreamily reminisces about the period's obsessive theatergoing:

> We chased dreams and escaped the sorrows of our ugly lives through the films. We sought outlets for our anger and longing for happiness at the cinema. Although we missed the early silent era when such screen legends as Greta Garbo, Rudolph Valentino, and the Barrymores reigned, we still had many names to evoke our fantasies: Rudolph Maté, Henry King, Henry Hath-

away, Cecil B. De Mille, Frank Capra, George Cukor, Michael Curtiz, Delmer Daves, Edward Dmytryk, Fred Zinnemann, Howard Hawks, Fritz Lang, Jean Negulesco, Mervyn LeRoy, Lewis Milestone, Mark Robson, George Seaton, George Stevens, King Vidor, Raoul Walsh, Robert Wise. . . . Upon my first encounter with the world of cinema, I was, like a drug addict, unable to resist the magical power of the screen. . . . Absorbing diverse models of life manufactured in Hollywood . . . we came to believe that the wide plains of the American West were our beautiful, lost home from some previous life. Denying our poverty-stricken home and dirty streets, we came to mistake the screen world as our idealized reality. For us, going to the movies was a religious act, like going to a Mass.[24]

Although the starstruck, auteurist narrator is retrospectively critical of his and his friends' (a group of schoolboys who proudly proclaim themselves the "Magnificent Seven") blind fascination with classic Hollywood films, which caused them to "misrecognize white faces as [their] own faces" and "misconstrue Indians as [their] enemies and genocidal American and English troops as [their] allies,"[25] the novel unmistakably evinces nostalgia for a bygone era—a time when South Korean audiences had access to thousands of North American and European classics, many of them now available only as faded images flitting about in failing memories due to the severely limited South Korean video and DVD markets. Although South Koreans were so engrossed by Occidental cultural productions that they deemed indigenous films were inferior to their Western counterparts, the reception of Hollywood products remained emphatically Korean in terms of canon formation and cross-cultural hermeneutics.

My experience (as both a student of Korean and Hollywood cinema and a fledgling cinephile during my formative years living in Seoul) has shown that Koreans often gravitate toward sad stories centering around star-crossed lovers separated by war, death, or social prejudice—melancholic films, in other words, that demand a certain willingness to withhold ironic judgment in the face of providential coincidences and emotional excess. Except for *The Sound of Music,* all of the films in the aforementioned top ten list depart from Hollywood's conventional happy endings. Tragic romances—unconsummated due to the intervention of social upheaval, familial opposition, or cruel fate—form the narrative trajectory of many of these films. Although Ahn Junghyo's narrator unfurls an impressive list of favorite directors, South Korean audiences generally flock to star vehicles in lieu of auteur films. Remarkably, yet tellingly, not a single Hitchcock, Ford, or Welles film broke into the KBS one hundred list, whereas four romantic comedies starring Audrey Hepburn (*Roman Holiday* [#1], *Breakfast at Tiffany's* [#6], *Sabrina* [#16], and *My Fair Lady* [#33]) were included in the top fifty. It is noteworthy that the quoted passage from *The Life and Death of the Hollywood Kid* lists Henry King and Mervyn LeRoy, who directed *Love Is a Many-Splendored Thing* and *Waterloo Bridge,* respectively, without a trace of such legends as Douglas Sirk and Nicholas Ray, film melodrama's preeminent auteurs whose combined work is crucial to the academic legitimization and canonization of the genre. Mervyn LeRoy's MGM melodramas and literary adaptations—including *Waterloo Bridge, Random Harvest* (1942), *Madame Curie* (1943), *Little Women* (1949), and *Quo Vadis* (1951)—are considered classics by South Korean audiences, while his critically acclaimed Warner Brothers gangster and social problem films such as *Little Caesar* (1930) and *I Am a Fugitive from a Chain Gang* (1932) remain virtually unknown. *Screen* (*Sk'ŭrin*), a leading South Korean movie magazine, described Mervyn LeRoy as "The Father of Melodrama Who Made *Waterloo Bridge*" and referred to the film as one of the five best melodramas ever made,[26] an audacious statement in light of the Western canon's preference for such films as *Stella Dallas* (1937), *Casablanca* (1942), *Letter from an Unknown Woman* (1948), *Rebel Without a Cause* (1955), and *Imitation of Life* (1959).

Indeed, *Waterloo Bridge* and *Love Is a Many-Splendored Thing* are the archetypal sentimental melodramas popular among South Korean audiences. The older generation of theatergoers who saw these films upon their original release during or not long after the Korean War could easily identify with the tragic stories of two lovers who suffer the separation and loss caused or exacerbated by wars.[27] During the three-year civil conflict, 3 million Koreans were killed, wounded, or missing. Another 10 million people endured familial breakups.[28] This transpired only a decade after the Japanese colonial government mobilized millions of Koreans for labor, military service, and sexual slavery to expedite their war efforts across Asia and the Pacific Islands, dividing countless families and lovers.[29] South Korean audiences wept for Vivien Leigh's Myra, a ballet dancer-turned-streetwalker in *Waterloo Bridge,* just as they shed tears for Jennifer Jones's Han Suyin, a Hong Kong Eurasian doctor who loses her American lover during the Korean War in *Love Is a Many-Splendored Thing.* These unfortunate female characters whose ill-fated lives were ravaged by war, functioned—in the collective spectatorial consciousness—as surrogates for millions of Korean daughters, mothers, and sisters who either lost their fathers, husbands, and sons during World War II and the Korean War or became sex slaves ("comfort women") for the Japanese Imperial Army and prostitutes for American GIs.

The theme of military prostitution, a shadow looming over Korean femininity, plays a pivotal role in *Waterloo Bridge*. Robert E. Sherwood's eponymous play was adapted into three very different studio films over a twenty-five-year period. Director James Whale's Universal Studio version (1931) is most faithful to the original story and stars Mae Clark as the heroine. Two MGM remakes followed: Mervyn LeRoy's 1940 film, held dear by South Koreans, and director Curtis Bernhardt's *Gaby* (1956), unanimously panned as the worst of the three despite the endearing, pixielike presence of Leslie Caron and a revised happy ending. Sherwood's original play is regarded by literary critics as "melodramatic, and . . . as sentimental as the author warns in his preface it is going to be . . . the sophomore's story of the Fallen Woman and the Nice Young Man . . . [which] can in no sense establish a claim to literary distinction."[30] The play's setting is World War I. Myra is an expatriate American chorus girl who is stranded in London and enduring German air raids. After befriending Kitty, a cockney British prostitute, Myra—penniless and desperate—descends into a life of soliciting sexual bargains from GIs on furlough. The chorine-turned-prostitute soon falls in love with an innocent compatriot soldier enlisted in a Canadian regiment, Roy Cronin, who offers tender affection to Myra, mistaking her as a decent girl. Roy is even willing to desert the military to stay with his loved one. Myra persuades him to return to his duties as a soldier, assuring him that she will wait steadfastly for him. After parting with her lover on Waterloo Bridge, where the two first met, Myra, unable to escape her shameful past, invites death by making herself a visible target for German bombers.

Whale's and LeRoy's cinematic adaptations of Sherwood's antiwar play fit conventionally into the category of what Lea Jacobs calls the "fallen woman film . . . the genre [that] is not popular with present-day audiences . . . [but] was a staple of Hollywood melodrama"[31] from the 1920s to the 1940s. Due to its focus on illicit sexuality, the fallen woman genre was subjected to careful scrutiny by the industry and was prone to censorship, which became more systematic after the 1934 installation of the Production Code Administration (PCA) headed by Joseph Breen to enforce the Motion Picture Production Code of 1930. Warner Brothers, a socially conscious studio known for its founders' pro-Roosevelt political affiliation and sensitivity to working-class interests, first attempted to remake Whale's *Waterloo Bridge*. The PCA discouraged the studio by stating, "We regret to inform you that it is our opinion that this story, as treated in the play, is definitely objectionable from the point of view of the Production Code. . . . The story is objectionable on the ground that it glorifies a prostitute, shows details of prostitution, sympathy is created for acts of prostitution, and the sin itself is not shown to be wrong."[32] When David O. Selznick knocked on the door of the PCA again with the same material in tow, Breen this time forwarded the producer a cable from the British Board of Censors that expressed their disapproval of the earlier version: "Film *Waterloo Bridge* submitted for censorship September 1931 considered prohibitive heroine being a prostitute. Film drastically amended to eliminate this characteristic and was passed. Board considers reissue most undesirable."[33]

Once MGM began toying with the project and finally submitted their early draft to Breen's office, the PCA still found the script objectionable on three counts: the details of prostitution; the condoning of prostitution by Roy's mother; and the inclusion of air raids over London, a taboo topic for the British censors. LeRoy and his screenwriters gave the original material a thorough "cleansing" to conform to the PCA's standards and regulations. The details of Myra's descent into prostitution were curtailed and no direct mention of her occupation was made; the dialogue in which Roy's mother condones Myra's past was eliminated; and Myra's death scene was rewritten so that the heroine commits suicide by throwing herself in the path of speeding army trucks rather than being bombed. One of the notable differences between Whale's and LeRoy's versions is the pre-fall status of Myra. As Cam Tolton comments: "Mae Clark's Myra [in the 1931 version] was a cheap chorine packaged much as she was in *Public Enemy* with James Cagney in the same year. A far cry from the exquisite ballet-hopeful that Myra would become when played by Vivien Leigh. When LeRoy upgraded Myra's cultural status, he upgraded the whole production with her."[34] Just as Vivien Leigh's Myra is a much more polished, respectable variation of Mae Clark's, Robert Taylor's Roy likewise rose from a humble Canadian soldier to a Scottish aristocrat officer. Leigh's character changed from an American-born chorus girl to an English schoolmaster's daughter who works as a ballet dancer under the stern disciplinary watch of Madame Kirowa. Vivien Leigh's Myra turns to prostitution only after she is unjustly fired, is mistakenly informed of her fiancé Roy's death, and learns that, after months of sickness, her best friend Kitty (Virginia Field) has been supporting her with money earned from streetwalking. As Mary Ann Doane points out, the "situation is an impossible one"[35] because prostitution is unspeakable and unrepresentable in Classical Hollywood cinema. For example, Myra manages to make Roy's mother understand her past by answering "You are naive" to the future mother-in-law's question, "Has there been someone else?" Belatedly discovering Myra's secret after her disappearance and suicide, Roy relieves Kitty of the burden of speaking the unutterable word by saying, "I understand—you don't have to say it."

The American censorship of *Waterloo Bridge* contrasts sharply with South Korean censorship of *The Stray Bullet*. While American motion picture censorship, with its principal of self-regulation that precluded the need for federal restrictions, focused on issues of sexual and religious morality so as to prevent local censorship and church boycotts, Korean films have constantly been subjected to stringent state regulations, whether the colonial government's suppression of anticolonial, nationalistic films or South Korea's authoritarian, military regimes' (1961–92) severe censoring of politically subversive subjects. In *The Stray Bullet*, prostitution is unambiguously foregrounded in the narrative and is explicitly named by characters. For the Park Chung Hee (Pak Chŏng-hŭi) regime, which came into power through the May 16, 1961 coup d'état during the original release of *The Stray Bullet*, the threat posed by the film stemmed not from its representation of military prostitution but from its realist critique of social illness and corruption. The anticommunist government banned the film, suspecting a pro-North subtext couched in recurring scenes where the North Korean refugee family's demented matriarch yells, "Let's get out of here!"[36] The ban was not lifted until 1963, when the film was re-released. Unlike in Classical Hollywood film, prostitution and adultery emerged as normative subject matter in South Korean cinema, culminating in the "hostess genre" cycle of the 1970s,[37] under the acquiescence of dictatorial regimes encouraging sexual subjects to divert the public's attention from political oppression. If the story of *Waterloo Bridge* seems deviant by Hollywood's sometimes-puritanical standards, it is completely normal and familiar to South Koreans accustomed to realistic portrayals of illegitimate sexual relations.

Interestingly, at the time of its original release, *Waterloo Bridge* was not deemed an "impossible text," as contemporary cine-feminists may be predisposed to label it. The film was instead promoted and reviewed as a typical Hollywood romance with top stars. Much publicity has been generated from the fact that this was Vivien Leigh's first starring role after her Academy Award–winning portrayal of Scarlett O'Hara, a compelling performance in *Gone With the Wind* (1939) that turned a little-known

British actress into a big-name marquee attraction. The studio also milked what was being touted as the "happiest reunion in Hollywood"— that between Leigh and Taylor, who first co-starred in MGM's *A Yank at Oxford* (1938), one of the studio's many productions shot in England. The film additionally marked LeRoy's anticipated return to the director's chair after overseeing the production of *The Wizard of Oz* (1939) and other big-budget MGM projects of the late 1930s.

Although *Waterloo Bridge* is now nearly forgotten or ignored by critics and the public alike in the United States, the film received glowing reviews upon its release. Commentators, for the most part, described the film as a fine love story or a woman's picture, calling it "a persuasive and compelling romantic tragedy that will sweep through for smash grosses . . . adult entertainment, particularly aimed at femme customers" (*Weekly Variety,* May 11, 1940), "a sure fire woman's picture headed for important coin" (*Daily Variety,* May 11, 1940), "a beautiful, tender love story that should have special appeal for femme fans" (*Film Daily,* May 16, 1940), and a picture with "deep appeal for women patrons, as evidenced by the extensive use of handkerchiefs at the preview" (*The Hollywood Reporter,* May 11, 1940). Considering this observation of the film's universal appeal to female audiences, it is peculiar that *Waterloo Bridge* continues to fall by the wayside whenever the feminist film canon is revamped or reformulated.[38] One interesting aspect of the film's American reception is that it did much better at the box office when re-released in 1944 than it did on its original release in 1940. On October 4 of that year, the *New York Times* reported "astonishment over at MGM these days [concerning] the success being enjoyed by the current reissue of the 4-year-old *Waterloo Bridge.*" As the newspaper elaborates, "In thirteen out of the fourteen cities it has played so far, managers of Loew's Theaters have reported grosses ranging from 24 percent to 179 percent above business done by the film when it was brand new."[39]

Even though many reviewers commented on the film's "timeliness" upon its original release in the wake of Great Britain's entrance into World War II (the historical frame of the film encapsulating Roy Cronin's flashback), the United States of 1940 was only a precariously situated yet distant observer of conflicts brewing in the European political arena. By the time the picture was re-released four years later, its story was no longer foreign or abstract. No doubt, after the Japanese attack on Pearl Harbor in 1941, American audiences could better appreciate the immediacy of a narrative depicting the tragic effects of the war on the lives of sympathetic young men and women. The same was true for South

Korean audiences who encountered the film for the first time during the Korean War. Myra—a respectable ballerina who sinks into prostitution for GIs when her fiancé is mistakenly reported dead—is an all-too-familiar figure in the minds of South Koreans: she is the image of the *yanggongju*. As Hyun Sook Kim succinctly defines her: "Historically, the term 'Yang-gongju' has referred to Korean women who engage in sexual labor for foreign soldiers. . . . Used derogatorily, it means, 'Yankee whore,' 'Yankee wife,' 'UN lady,' and/or 'Western princess.' This epithet, 'Yang-gongju,' relegates Korean women working in militarized prostitution with foreign men to the lowest status within the hierarchy of prostitution."[40]

Following the Korean War, U.S. troops became permanently installed in South Korea so as to protect the host country from the communist threat from the North. Accordingly, over 1 million Korean women have served as "entertainment hostesses" to accommodate the sexual needs of American military officers and soldiers—VIPs of the South Korean government.[41] Although Vivien Leigh's Myra is not a prostitute for foreign soldiers of different racial backgrounds, her suggestive smile at uniformed GIs carries an unsettling resemblance to that of South Korea's cinematic *yanggongju*s, from the evening gown-clad seductress Sonya in *Hell Flower* (*Chiokhwa*, 1958) to the peasant widow-turned-"UN Lady" Ŏl-lye in *Silver Stallion* (*Ŭnma nŭn oji annŭnda*, 1991). Raven-haired, brown-eyed Myra even physically approximates the ubiquitously inscribed filmic *yanggongju* image.

Throughout the cinematic Golden Age, *yanggongju*s were portrayed either as temptresses equivalent to the dangerous, powerful, and sexually promiscuous *femmes fatales* of American film noir or as tragic fallen women forced to sell their bodies due to postwar poverty and familial duties. For *Hell Flower*, director Sin Sang-ok cast his wife, Ch'oe Ŭn-hŭi (a Golden Age actress who is best remembered as the chaste widow in *The Houseguest and My Mother* [*Sarangbang sonnim kwa ŏmŏni*, 1961]), against type. In the film, Ch'oe plays an egoistic, decadent *yanggongju*—a bad "spider woman" who lures male characters into her web of deceit and is ultimately punished for her transgression by an avenging husband who kills her. In *The Stray Bullet*, Myŏng-suk (Sŏ Ae-ja), the decent-minded daughter of an impoverished North Korean refugee family, slides into the life of a *yanggongju* when rejected by her disabled Korean War vet fiancé for whom a marriage is too heavy a burden. When her brother Ch'ŏr-ho's wife (Mun Chŏng-suk) gives birth, it is Myŏng-suk's savings earned from military prostitution that pay for the hospital fee, despite the fact that Ch'ŏr-ho, in an earlier scene, turned his face in shame when he spotted his sister with an American GI. Myŏng-suk is emblematic of the tens of thousands of postwar Korean women who were forced into military prostitution out of economic urgency.

The pro-democratic, antiauthoritarian, anti-American labor union and student demonstrations that comprised the *minjung* movement of the 1980s and early 1990s instigated a new perception of and interest in *yanggongju*s. Having been long neglected and despised as the lowest of the low, these women emerged as the victimized "sisters and daughters" of the nation enslaved by American imperialists, so long as their legacy was couched within the rhetoric of nationalist activism and political dissidence urging the withdrawal of the U.S. military and the reunification of the Korean peninsula. One case in particular—the brutal rape and murder of a bar woman, Yun Kŭm-i, by Private Kenneth Markle (who stuffed a cola bottle into Yun's vagina and an umbrella into her anus after killing her) in 1992—sparked nationwide rage and stoked protests against the U.S. military. As a convenient corporeal metaphor for the oppressed nation and the disenfranchised classes, the *yanggongju* conspicuously haunted the margins of the New Korean cinema throughout the 1980s and 1990s (from *In the Heat of the Night* [*Pam ŭi yŏlgi sok ŭro*, 1985] to *Spring in My Hometown* [*Arŭmdaun sijŏl*, 1998])—a period dominated by intellectual New Wave male directors emerging from the leftist student movement, such as Chang Sŏn-u (Jang Sun-woo), Pak Kwang-su, and Chŏng Chi-yŏng.

The Hollywood "Scene of Misrecognition" vs. the Korean "Scene of Recognition"

Returning once again to the question of intertextuality linking *The Stray Bullet* and *Waterloo Bridge*, I would like to draw attention to two contrasting yet parallel scenes—one from each film—in which the same event of the fallen woman's accidental encounter with her lover at a place of prostitution is repeated in radically different configurations. Built upon dissimilar gaze structures and moving toward different narrative outcomes, these scenes provide a mutually enriching case study through which to unmask the ideological mechanisms undergirding the construction of a transnational imaginary. In the former, Myra makes her usual trip to Waterloo Station to solicit a customer. She enters the station, sending inviting glances and smiles toward a crowd of arriving soldiers. When she greets one, saying, "Welcome home," the soldier condescendingly responds "Thanks, ducky," and exits. The camera dollies in to a close-up of Myra's face overwhelmed by shame and pathos. Looking blankly into the camera, her sad, trancelike visage suddenly beams with a combination of shock and joy. The following shot cuts to several soldiers walking toward the camera along the platform, a milling crowd from which Roy emerges. The point of view immediately shifts to Roy, who spots Myra and rushes toward her, frantically calling her name. With climactic orchestral accompaniment, the lovers reunite in each other's arms, gazing at each other adoringly in tightly framed shot-reverse-shots. The officer's excitement and euphoria overflows into a torrent of words in contrast to a speechless Myra who can barely utter, "Roy, you're alive." The miraculously returned fiancé seems unaware of any change in Myra's appearance and status despite her tawdry dress and tell-tale makeup as well as her feeble excuse that she has come to the station to meet "no one in particular."

There are two moments when Roy makes a deliberate effort to *look* at Myra, to subtly fix his gaze on a woman who no longer conforms to the ideal image of virginal heroine. The first moment occurs when he tells her that he cannot believe what has happened: "Darling, let me look at you. I'm not dreaming, am I?" The second instance takes place in the following scene set in a teashop, where they sit and talk. "Let me have a squint at you," Roy says, as he inspects Myra up and down after she improvises the meager excuse that she cannot accompany him to his family mansion in Scotland because she looks unfit and has no decent wardrobe. Although Roy reluctantly agrees with her, stating, "Now I look at you, there is something in what you say," he misreads her dress code as a sign of destitution rather than prostitution. In both cases, Roy's scrutinizing gaze fails, for he does not see what the spectator sees. Oblivious to Myra's dilemma and internalized agony, Roy takes charge and dominates the scene, pouring tea for the sobbing woman, telling her that she will quit her job and marry him, calling his mother to inform her of their impending arrival, and suggesting a trip to the clothing store. Once again, Roy misunderstands when Myra musters courage to say that she cannot go with him. He asks if she has someone else, a suspicion Myra adamantly denies, assuring him, "I loved you. I never loved anyone else. I never shall"—a statement which will resurface during middle-aged Roy's oral flashback in the film's last scene. Roy's momentary doubt evaporates and his ego remains intact due to Myra's oath of platonic devotion, which the unknowing fiancé self-servingly misrecognizes as sexual fidelity.

In the corresponding scene of *The Stray Bullet*, Myŏng-suk—dressed in Western attire—is shown in a deep-focus shot standing alone with her head hung low as she sets up "shop" on a street corner where nightly transactions between Korean women and American GIs take place. The background shows the traditionally coded gate of the Chosŏn Hotel, which displays a bilingual sign. Into the middle distance streams a group of men and women. The "new face" is noticed by a GI who addresses Myŏng-suk in English, fishing for her name. The flirtation between the two is juxtaposed with a long shot of Myŏng-suk's disabled ex-fiancé, Kyŏng-sik, limping toward the scene from afar. Laughing mischievously, Myŏng-suk runs away from the GI who claims her for the evening. The scurrying woman and her Korean lover with crutches bump into each other and fall to the ground. Recognizing Myŏng-suk, Kyŏng-sik flashes a smile, in a rare close-up shot, which quickly turns south into a frown against a grim musical cue. Myŏng-suk's reaction shot is suppressed. The camera stays with Kyŏng-sik's point of view as he watches her flee the scene with the American GI chasing after her. The wounded veteran immediately comprehends the gravity of his lover's situation as he stands alone, looking in the direction where Myŏng-suk has disappeared. His horrific recognition is visually accentuated as a *yanggongju*-GI couple emerges from the left side of the frame and crosses the foreground. Picking up his crutches, Kyŏng-sik despondently starts limping away. A bilingual traffic sign is clearly visible in the background, indicating the Korean man's displacement in a space reserved for American masculinity. Kyŏng-sik eventually sinks into a nearby bench, sobbing uncontrollably. The scene of his breakdown is intercut with a shot of an escaped Myŏng-suk, guilty but relieved, leaning against a tree.

These two scenes are symptomatic of the aesthetic and ideological ruptures separating a classical Hollywood text and a Golden Age South Korean text. In *Waterloo Bridge*, the use of close-ups and shot-reverse-shots are pronounced. As the station scene progresses, shots get tighter and tighter until Myra and Roy look into each other's eyes in a self-contained and flattened romantic space winnowed from its external setting. Background passers-by, though occasionally visible in frame, are conveniently out of focus so that the spectator's attention stays fixed on the main couple. The scene in *The Stray Bullet*, by contrast, extends and maximizes focal depth and suppresses close-ups in favor of long shots so as to accentuate the surroundings in which the characters are situated. As André Bazin argues, the use of deep-focus cinematography "brings the spectator into a relation with the image closer to that which he enjoys with reality" and invites a "more active mental attitude on the part of the spectator."[42] The Korean scene not only reworks a transnational melodra-

Roy misrecognizes Myra in a close-up from *Waterloo Bridge*

Kyŏng-sik recognizes Myŏng-suk as *yanggongju* in a deep-focus shot from *The Stray Bullet* (Courtesy of the Korean Film Archive)

matic trope across more realistic deep-focus shots, which effectively stage simultaneous actions from foreground to background, but also complicates the Hollywood gaze structure. Yet more than reflecting the realist style of the South Korean film, this contrast suggests a greater emphasis on the larger social context of the latter film. *Waterloo Bridge*'s close-ups emphasize the personal psychological crisis of its female character, whereas *The Stray Bullet*'s long shots suggest that the lovers' problem is societal, not merely individual.

The "scene of misrecognition" in *Waterloo Bridge* involves three looking positions: Myra, Roy, and the spectator. Myra initially functions as the subject of the gaze when she accidentally spots Roy after being rejected by a potential customer. Her eyes look vacant in a way that recalls an earlier scene when she peered through a misty and steam-covered window to see Roy who was supposed to have left for the front. Because her vision is fuzzy, unstable, and shaky, it reveals the underlying anxiety of looking. This anxiety grows from a psychological split, the gap that emerges when the female subject usurps the privileged position of the "bearer of the look," which—according to feminist film critic Laura Mulvey—belongs to the active male protagonist in mainstream narrative cinema.[43] When the camera cuts to what she sees, Roy enters the frame and takes control of the gaze. Roy, however, misrecognizes Myra. He sees her as the same innocent girl that he had left years ago. Unlike the soldier who correctly ascertained her role as prostitute and labeled her a "ducky," Roy is incapable of imagining her as erotic spectacle despite her "slutty" make-up and dress. His misrecognition is a form of disavowal. In the narrative logic of classical Hollywood cinema, it is not possible for Roy to *see* Myra's scene of prostitution, which fortunately transpires prior to his disembarkation. Roy's knowledge must remain inferior to that of the knowing spectator if his own sense of phallic power is to be kept intact. For Roy, the recognition of Myra's prostitution stands for the acknowledgment of his own figurative castration or emasculation. Hence, he disavows her excessively coded sexuality as a prostitute and de-specularizes her (as proven by her erasure of lipstick upon his temporary absence) with his nonsexual, paternal gaze and infantilizing attitude. Actual recognition comes much later in the film only after the threat of marrying an ex-prostitute is eliminated, as Myra disappears and is about to commit suicide. Roy maintains his and his family's aristocratic status through her sacrificial act. Myra's death is inevitable because, according to Doane, "the woman associated with excessive sexuality resides outside the boundaries of language; she is unrepresentable and must die."[44]

The man's immediate recognition of his ex-fiancée's status conspicuously distinguishes the parallel scene in *The Stray Bullet* from its Hollywood counterpart. In the Korean "scene of recognition," the gaze structure is much more complicated due to the introduction of a third embedded look commanded by the American GI. Whereas the soldier whom Myra approaches ignores her and passes by, the GI in *The Stray Bullet* aggressively pursues Myŏng-suk, declaring "You are mine for tonight, baby." In actuality, it is the American GI who misrecognizes. He sees Myŏng-suk only as a "new face," another streetwalker, not as someone's daughter, sister, and lover, as the spectator sees her. The ignorant GI aggravates the situation by chasing the woman who has run into her lover at the scene of prostitution. One notable difference from *Waterloo Bridge* is the excision of the female perspective (except for an insert shot of Myŏng-suk after she flees the scene). Myŏng-suk is literally caught in-between two male gazes—that of the GI on the left side of the frame and that of Kyŏng-sik on the right side. After the GI codifies her as a *yanggongju* (whore), the point of view promptly swivels to Kyŏng-sik's position as he collides with Myŏng-suk, whom he first identifies as his lover and then as a fallen woman. Quite opposite to *Waterloo Bridge,* it is the disabled Korean fiancé who literally vanishes from the screen after painfully witnessing the white male's appropriation of "his" woman. In *The Stray Bullet* and other South Korean films, the spectral nonappearance of the powerful patriarch and the emphatic focus on the *yanggongju* as a signifier of modernity function not only as an allegory of the (neo)colonized nation but also as a symptom of Korean male trauma precisely because she bears the traces and thus is a reminder of the infiltration and domination of American masculinity in South Korea.

What Kyŏng-sik—already emasculated by his crippled leg—recognizes in the scene is his symbolic castration, the annihilation of his masculinity in a postcolonial space packed with *yanggongjus* and U.S. soldiers. Like Myra in *Waterloo Bridge,* he is an unrepresentable sign that must be eradicated from the narrative at all costs. Myŏng-suk stays on, but she must redeem herself in the end. The only way "guilty" cinematic women (running the gamut from an unfaithful professor's wife, Sŏn-yŏng in *Madame Freedom* [*Chayu puin,* 1956], to the *yanggongju* mother Ŏl-lye in *Silver Stallion*) can redeem themselves is to return to their maternal role, the most honored female function in neo-Confucian society. It is Myŏng-suk who stands by her baby nephew, acting as a surrogate mother, in the penultimate scene after her sister-in-law dies immediately following childbirth. Her eldest brother, the head of the family, is reduced to a "stray bullet" (as a taxi driver describes him), roaming the city aimlessly without knowing which obligation he should attend to first: the crazed mother and his young daughter at home, the younger brother in prison, or the baby son in the hospital. Affectionately gazing at the newborn nephew, Myŏng-suk soliloquizes, "Brother, come back. . . . We can help the baby smile, can't we?" Her hopeful wish for the baby's future implies that she will quit sex work and devote herself to raising her motherless nephew, her surrogate maternalism thus canceling the earlier *yanggongju* image. While in classic Hollywood narratives conflicts usually develop and are resolved in the tightly circumscribed world of the romantic couple, Golden Age South Korean cinema, for the most part, situates young couples in the thickly woven web of familial obligations. Clashes arise because traditional Confucian values often prioritize the family over heterosexual love. Whereas Myra's unwitting infidelity to Roy is unpardonable from the viewpoint of the sexual mores and Christian doctrines governing individual, man-to-woman relationships, Myŏng-suk's prostitution is forgiven by the family-centric society in light of her willingness to assume maternal duties for the newborn heir and to provide unpaid domestic labor.

From *Aesu* to *Obalt'an:* Transnational Reception and Canon Formation

Many South Korean audiences might not immediately recognize the English-language titles of *Waterloo Bridge* and *Love Is a Many-Splendored Thing*. For them, these films are respectively known as *Aesu* (translated as "Sorrow" or "Grief") and *Mojŏng* ("Affectionate Love"). The Sino-character-based titles were originally created in Japan and imported to South Korea along with the film prints. Ahn Junghyo's novel, *The Life and Death of the Hollywood Kid*, elaborates the Sino-Japanization of Hollywood film titles:

> Back then, when a foreign film was imported to South Korea, it came with a title made in Japan. . . . We had a hard time distinguishing one Sino-Korean title from the other because many of them sounded alike and their meanings were ambiguous. . . . We confused *Aesu ŭi yŏro* ("Sad Journey Road": *Separate Tables*) with *Yŏjŏng* ("Journey Love": *Summer Time*), *Aesim* ("Sad Heart": *The Eddy Duchin Story*) with *Aejŏng* ("Sad Love": *Wuthering Heights*), and *Param kwa hamkke sarajida* (*Gone With the Wind*) with *Param kwa hamkke chida* ("Fallen with the Wind": *Written on the Wind*).[45]

139

As Ahn's novel suggests, many postwar cinephiles were also keen on collecting Japanese film magazines such as *Aeigano Domo* ("Cinema Friend") or *Screen,* which likely affected the South Korean canonization of foreign films and stars. My own adolescent experience of collecting Japanese film books and magazines has demonstrated that the Japanese-constructed pantheon of classic Hollywood texts has much in common with its South Korean counterpart as shown in the KBS list. In fact, the enormous popularity of *Waterloo Bridge* seems to be a pan-Asian, rather than exclusively South Korean or Japanese, phenomenon. When former Beijing Film Academy professor Chuanji Zhou visited UCLA to teach a post-1949 Chinese film course in the spring of 2001, he screened *Waterloo Bridge* for curious graduate students, arguing that one can only make sense of emotionally excessive Chinese melodramas after comprehending the affective appeal of this film to Chinese audiences.[46] It would not be an exaggeration or conjectural leap to argue the same for South Korean cinema.

What is unique about the South Korean reception of *Waterloo Bridge* is its centrality to the cultivation of the *Aesu* cycle. The Korean Film Archive's website[47] lists nine films that use the word "aesu" in their titles: *Yujŏn ŭi aesu* (*Hereditary Grief,* 1956), *Aesu* (1959), *Aesu e chŏjŭn t'oyoil* (*Sad Saturday,* 1960), *Aesu ŭi namhaeng yŏlch'a* (*South-Bound Train of Sorrow,* 1963), *Aesu ŭi pam* (*A Sorrowful Night,* 1965), *Aesu* (1967), *Aesu ŭi ŏndŏk* (*Hill of Sadness,* 1969), *Aesu ŭi Saenp'ŭransisŭk'o* (*Sad San Francisco,* 1975), and *Aesu ŭi hamonik'a* (*The Harmonica of Grief,* 1996). Inheriting the narrative tradition of *Waterloo Bridge,* *Hereditary Grief*—directed by none other than the director of *The Stray Bullet,* Yu Hyŏn-mok—recounts a love story between a prostitute and a man from a wealthy family, an amorous affair that tragically yet inevitably culminates with female suicide. *Sad Saturday* likewise features a female protagonist who slides into prostitution after being separated from her lover during the Korean War. She reunites with the soldier, but eventually commits suicide to set him free. The other *Aesu* films are melodramas thematizing tragic love affairs, the exigencies of prostitution, illegitimate motherhood, and so on. Besides these films, which either cross-culturally adapt *Waterloo Bridge*'s paradigmatic plot or simply borrow its famed title and melodramatic spirit, a number of foreign titles were deemed *Aesu* offspring upon their South Korean release. Two Hollywood tearjerkers, *Daisy Kenyon* (1947) and *Never Say Goodbye* (1956), were re-titled as *Aesu ŭi sarang* ("Sorrowful Love") and *Aesu ŭi ibyŏl* ("Sad Goodbye") in an attempt to recapitulate *Waterloo Bridge*'s legendary success. Vivien

Leigh's *The Roman Spring of Mrs. Stone* (1961) transformed into *Roma ŭi aesu* ("Sad Rome") in oblique homage to *Aesu*'s leading actress. The German biopic of Clara and Robert Schumann, *Fruhlingssinfonie* (*Spring Symphony*, 1983), was renamed as *Aesu ŭi T'ŭroimerai* ("Sorrowful Traumerei [Dreaming]"). More recently the Graham Greene adaptation, *The End of the Affair* (1999) was released as *Aesu*, probably because the film is set in a wartime London and focuses on a fated romance that must end sadly. Most South Korean reviewers of the film did not forget to mention the original *Aesu*.

Indeed, the celebration and recirculation of the same narrative and/or title during the past five decades attests to the fact that *Aesu* (*Waterloo Bridge*) is not simply a single film but a discursive and mobile ur-text melodrama favored as an emotional outlet for South Korean audiences whose tears were shed in the wake of national division, the Korean War, familial separation, political tyrannies, economic crises, and gender and class oppression. The connection between *Waterloo Bridge* and Korean national discourse is further solidified by the film's foregrounding of the Scottish folk song "Auld Lang Syne"—theme music supplying the quixotic yet doleful sonic backdrop against which Roy and Myra dance their last waltz in the Candlelight Club on the eve of Roy's departure for the front. Before the 1948 inauguration of the ROK government, "Auld Lang Syne" provided the melodic foundation for the Korean national anthem, "Aegukka" ("Patriot Song").[48] Although An Ik-t'ae's newly composed anthem had already been officialized by the time *Waterloo Bridge* was first released in South Korea in the early 1950s, "Auld Lang Syne" must have still carried special meaning and emotional resonance for South Korean audiences who had weathered the colonial years singing "Aegukka."

Now I would like to shift focus back to *The Stray Bullet* and its transnational reception. Although audiences did not vote it as one of their one hundred choices in the KBS list, the film is widely considered as an indisputable masterpiece of realist cinema by critics, scholars, and journalists. The Motion Picture Promotion Corporation's 1995 list of the "10 Best Korean Films" consists of (in order): *The Stray Bullet*, *P'iagol* (1955), *Late Autumn* (*Manch'u*, 1966), *Mandara* (1981), *Viva Freedom* (*Chayu manse*, 1946), *A Sea Village* (*Kaet maŭl*, 1965), *The Marines Who Never Return* (*Toraoji annŭn haebyŏng*, 1963), *March of Fools* (*Pabodŭl ŭi haengjin*, 1975), *The Coachman* (*Mabu*, 1961), and *Declaration of Fools* (*Pabo sŏnŏn*, 1982).[49] The 1998 *Chosun Daily* poll of the "50 Best Korean Films" confirms the number one status of *The Stray Bullet*, which is followed by *Mandara*, *The Housemaid* (*Hanyŏ*, 1960), *Late Autumn, Sŏp'yŏnje, Why Has Bodhi-Dharma Left for the East?* (*Talma ka tongtchok ŭro kan kkadak ŭn*, 1989), *The Houseguest and My Mother*, *P'iagol*, *The Coachman*, and *Kilsottŭm* (1985).[50] The film was presented at the 7th San Francisco International Film Festival, an entry that contributed to its domestic re-release in 1963 after the two-year ban mentioned earlier. According to one-time producer and film historian Ho Hyŏn-ch'an, *The Stray Bullet* did not enjoy an enthusiastic reception in San Francisco. Ho quotes Yu having said that the Korean situation depicted in his film was difficult for Western audiences to fully understand.[51] Although the film was not commercially successful in South Korea, it appealed to intellectuals in the audience and cinephiles who appreciated its artistic values and political messages. Sadly, the original print was lost and the film was unavailable for theatrical screenings for many years. Although in the mid-1970s the Motion Picture Promotion Corporation (now the Korean Film Archive) had struck a restored print from an existing copy submitted to the San Francisco Film Festival, this English-subtitled version was not publicly accessible. Instead, director Yu's personal copy of *The Stray Bullet* was circulated in underground campus screenings organized by activist students during the *minjung* period.[52] When the Korean Educational Broadcasting System, a public broadcaster, aired the film on April 7, 2002, it had to resort to the Korean Film Archive's subtitled print due to the lack of any alternative version. The same copy (with its unremovable English subtitles) was recently transferred to DVD and became available in South Korea, ending the film's long absence in the commercial market.

Although the film remained virtually inaccessible to the general public in South Korea until very recently, *The Stray Bullet* began to creep into the Western art-house canon of East Asian cinema in the mid-1990s. Thanks to the recognition of New Wave Korean cinema in the international festival circuit beginning the late 1980s and early 1990s (especially the works of Pae Yong-gyun, Pak Kwang-su, and Chang Sŏn-u), *The Stray Bullet* was given a second chance to travel to North America after its less-than-stellar San Francisco debut in 1963. Packaged as a part of "Three Korean Master Filmmakers: Sin Sang-ok, Yu Hyŏn-mok, and Im Kwŏn-t'aek"[53] (the first major film series in the United States devoted to South Korean cinema), the film was shown in New York's Museum of Modern Art in late 1996. Since then, *The Stray Bullet* has been added to the MoMA Collection and re-exhibited several times. The "Three Korean Master Filmmakers" program was also sent on a cross-country tour through Canada (Montreal, Toronto, Ottawa, and Vancouver) in 1997. *The Stray Bullet* continued to appear in major Korean film events in North America, including the 1998 "Post-Colonial Classics of Korean Cinema" festival at UC–Irvine; the 2000 "Korean War: The Last 50 Years" series at UCLA; and the 2002 Korean Film Festival at the University of Wisconsin–Milwaukee. In each of these festivals, the film's English title changed from *An/The Aimless Bullet* to *The Stray Bullet*. The closest translation of its Korean title (*Obalt'an*) would be *A/The Misfired Bullet*.[54] Ironically, the West has finally come to "recognize" *The Stray Bullet*—a text bearing the permanent inscription of transnationalism in its indelible English subtitles—as a masterful work of international cinema over three decades after its initial "misrecognition" in the 1963 San Francisco Film Festival. This belated fixing of the epistemological and cinephilic gaze contrasts drastically with South Korean audiences' immediate canonization of *Waterloo Bridge* as an archetypal melodrama, a recognition that still slips through the consciousness of North American and European critics.

Postscript: Vivien Leigh as Cross-Cultural Screen Surrogate for Ch'oe Sŭng-hŭi

In hopes of opening the rhetorical floodgates of this essay even wider, I would like to close with an anecdote that will perhaps allay any doubts or suspicions the reader might have about my earlier attempts to pose Vivien Leigh's Myra as the spectral, cross-cultural image of Korean femininity. The anecdote, which came to me late in the writing of this essay, involves the coincidental connection between Leigh's character and a real-life Korean dancer.

The person in question is Ch'oe Sŭng-hŭi (Choi Seung-hee), a legendary dancer who reportedly received a flirtatious fan letter from Robert Taylor at the height of her international success. Born in Seoul in 1911 and trained in modern ballet in Japan, Ch'oe (who adopted the Japanese name, Sai Shoki) became the first Korean artist to debut internationally in the late 1930s. Between 1937 and 1940, she gave five hundred performances throughout the United States, Europe, and Latin America. She became acquainted with Hollywood stars such as Charlie Chaplin, Gary Cooper, and Robert Taylor as well as novelist John Steinbeck during her West Coast tours. Her 1939 co-performance with American dance legend Martha Graham received enthusiastic reviews in New York. Her Paris performances of the same year were attended by famous artists including Henri Matisse and Pablo Picasso, who drew a sketch of Ch'oe in pencil.

Despite her worldwide fame, Ch'oe was criticized after the Liberation for her alleged collaboration with Japanese officials, for whom she performed. In 1946, she defected to North Korea (with her writer-husband An Mak) and continued to dance, choreograph, and teach until she was' purged by the Communist Party and mysteriously disappeared in the mid-1960s. Ch'oe's life and career, having been long ignored due to political censorship against defecting artists, was eventually re-evaluated in South Korea thanks partly to the recent release of the Japanese documentary *Legendary Dancer Ch'oe Sŭng-hŭi: Kim Mae-ja's Search for the Nation's Spirit* (*Densetsu no maihime Ch'oe Sŭng-hŭi*, 2000), produced by female director Fujiwara Tomoko.

According to an article in the *Kukmin Daily*, dated January 21, 2002, Robert Taylor's fan letter to Ch'oe had been acquired by documentarist Chŏng Su-ung, who recently finished his eight-year project on the dancer.[55] The newspaper quotes Chŏng: "The letter expresses Taylor's admiration and praise for Ch'oe and conveys his wish to make a film with her." Although the report does not specify the date of the letter, it can be inferred to have been written sometime in the late 1930s when Ch'oe performed in Los Angeles and was being introduced to Hollywood royalty. Not long thereafter, Robert Taylor became involved in a film project in which he plays a character falling head-over-heels for a dancer: *Waterloo Bridge*. During the film's production, Vivien Leigh sent a letter to her barrister husband, complaining about the ballet lessons she was forced to undertake (during which, to borrow the actress's own ironic wording, she was placed "between two strong girls" who could "prop [her] up")[56] for the one brief scene in which she performs in Tchaikovsky's *Swan Lake*.

One wonders if Taylor, perhaps still infatuated with the extraordinarily gifted Korean dancer, envisioned Ch'oe in place of Leigh, whose ballet performance comes across as awkward and amateurish. Maybe this hypothetical scenario is a mere reflection of my own romantic inclinations—my own "melodramatic imagination" intensified by years of viewing Hollywood tearjerkers and woman's films. Regardless, after stumbling upon this footnote to history, I now find myself lamenting the unrealized cinematic union between Robert Taylor and Ch'oe Sŭng-hŭi. Although it could not have been possible in light of the antimiscegenation politics dominating studio-era filmmaking, such a coupling would have been infinitely more persuasive as a manifestation of cross-cultural hybridity and exchange than all of the "many-splendored" cigarettes brought together by the William Holdens and Jennifer Joneses of the world.

Legendary Korean dancer Ch'oe Sŭng-hŭi (Courtesy of Susan Ahn and the Ahn Family Collection)

Notes

The author is especially grateful to Kathleen McHugh, whose warm and intelligent mentorship greatly influenced the writing of this essay. Thanks also to David Scott Diffrient for proofreading early manuscripts and improving them immensely with his advice and affection.

1. Another famous Hollywood scene of stylized smoking takes place in *Now, Voyager* (1942), when Paul Henreid lights two cigarettes in his mouth and hands one to a teary-eyed Bette Davis. Canonized as one of the representative woman's films in the United States, *Now, Voyager* is not nearly as ingrained in South Korean audiences' spectatorial consciousness as *Love Is a Many-Splendored Thing*.

2. In his documentary video version of *The Society of Spectacle*, Guy Debord mobilizes clips from classic Hollywood films such as *The Shanghai Gesture* (1941) and *Johnny Guitar* (1954) to articulate a Neo-Marxist critique of mass-produced popular culture. The Situationist International's method of *détournement* was subsequently inherited by American filmmakers and video artists such as Marlon Riggs, Valerie Soe, and Rea Tajiri, who hijack and recontextualize Hollywood images to challenge their stereotypical representations of ethnic minorities.

3. Although some Golden Age melodramas such as *Madame Freedom* (*Chayu puin*, 1956) and *Free Marriage* (*Chayu kyŏrhon*, 1958) center on bourgeois female protagonists, a far greater number of films thematize the sorrows and conflicts of underclass families, as in *Mr. Pak* (*Pak sŏbang*, 1960), *The Stray Bullet* (1961), and *The Coachman* (*Mabu*, 1961).

4. Christine Gledhill, ed., *Home Is Where the Heart Is: Studies in Melodrama and the Woman's Film* (London: BFI, 1987), 11.

5. Korean film scholar Kyung Hyun Kim, for instance, notes that the "visual presentation and the thematic concerns of the film recall both the styles of German Expressionism and Italian Neo-Realism." See *Post-Colonial Classics of Korean Cinema*, ed. Chungmoo Choi (Irvine, CA: Korean Film Festival Committee, UCI, 1998), 17.

6. Yu Chi-na, ed., *What Is Melodrama* (*Mellodŭrama ran muŏt in'ga*) (Seoul: Minŭmsa, 1999), 16–17.

7. Since 1897, the *sinp'a* drama developed in Japan, reaching its heyday between 1904 and 1910. The Japanese *sinp'a* drama was influenced by European literary and stage melodrama.

8. See Soyoung Kim, chapter 7 in this volume.

9. In the past few years, South Korean cinema has given rise to new *sinp'a*-style melodrama; exemplary films include *The Letter* (*P'yŏnji*, 1997), *My Heart* (*Chŏng*, 2000), *Kiss Me Much* (*Pesamemuch'yo*, 2001), and *Bitter but Once Again* (*Miwŏdo tasi hanbŏn:* a remake, 2002). Among recent American films, *Sweet November* (2001) was cross-culturally labeled as a *sinp'a* melodrama by South Korean critics.

10. See, for instance, Ahn Byung-Sup's "Humor in Korean Cinema," *East-West Film Journal* 2 (1987) and Rob Wilson's "Melodramas of Korean National Identity," in *Colonialism and Nationalism in Asian Cinema*, ed. Wimal Dis-

sanayake (Bloomington: Indiana University Press, 1994).

11. For a more thorough English-language elucidation of *han,* see M. Sapiro, *The Shadow in the Sun: A Korean Yea of Love and Sorrow* (New York: Atlantic Monthly, 1990); Andrew Sung Park, *The Wounded Heart of God: The Asian Concept of Han and the Christine Doctrine of Sin* (Nashville: Abingdon, 1993); Jae Hoon Lee, *The Exploration of the Inner Wounds-Han* (Atlanta: Scholars, 1994); Uichol Kim and Sang-Chin Choi, "Indigenous Form of Lamentation (Han): Conceptual and Philosophical Analyses," in *Korean Cultural Roots: Religion and Social Thoughts,* ed. Ho-Youn Kwon (Chicago: North Park College and Theological Seminary, 1995), 245–66; and Chang-Hee Son, *Haan of Minjung Theology and Han of Han Philosophy* (Lanham, MD: University Press of America, 2000).

12. Im's filmography is inundated with historical melodramas centering on beautiful yet suffering female bodies, such as *Surrogate Mother* (*Ssibaji,* 1986), *Adada* (1988), *Sŏp'yŏnje* (1993), and *Chunhyang* (*Ch'unhyangjŏn,* 2000).

13. Quoted in Julian Stringer's "*Sopyonje* and the Inner Domain of National Culture," in *Im Kwon-Taek: The Making of a Korean National Cinema,* ed. David E. James and Kyung Hyun Kim (Detroit: Wayne State University Press, 2002), 171–72.

14. I am indebted to Kathleen McHugh for her generosity in sharing this and many other insights with me in personal correspondences. For an elaboration of the term "melodramatic imagination," see Peter Brooks, *The Melodramatic Imagination: Balzac, Henry James, Melodrama, and the Mode of Excess* (New York: Columbia University Press, 1985).

15. *Matthew's Chinese-English Dictionary* (Cambridge: Harvard University Press, 1963), 310, quoted in Andrew Sung Park (1993), 180.

16. See Donald Richie, *Ozu* (Berkeley: University of California Press, 1974), 52; and David Bordwell, *Ozu and the Poetics of Cinema* (Princeton: Princeton University Press, 1988), 28.

17. "Neighboring Land, Unknown Sentiment (*Kakkaun nara, miji ŭi kamsŏng*)," *Cine 21,* 244 (March 28, 2000): 68.

18. See Yu Hyo-in's "About Modernity in *Sinp'a*-Style Melodrama (Sinp'ajŏk mellodŭrama ŭi kŭndaesŏng e taehae)," *Korean Film Critiques* (*Yŏnghwa p'yŏngnon*) 7 (1995); Ahn Byung-Sup, "Humor in Korean Cinema"; and Isolde Standish, "Korean Cinema and the New Realism: Text and Context," as well as Rob Wilson's "Melodramas of Korean National Identity," in Dissanayake, ed., *Colonialism and Nationalism.*

19. "Cultural Studies and the Politics of Internalization," an interview with Stuart Hall by Kuan-Hsing Chen, in David Morley and Kuan-Hsing Chen, eds., *Stuart Hall: Critical Dialogues in Cultural Studies* (London: Routledge, 1996), 393.

20. Gledhill, *Home Is Where the Heart Is,* 24.

21. KBS press kit, dated February 25, 1996.

22. Attracting record-breaking audiences (the top-grossing South Korean film before *Swiri*) and enormous media attention upon its release, *Sŏp'yŏnje* became a cultural phenomenon in South Korea, reviving the popularity of the waning indigenous operatic storytelling art form, *p'ansori.*

23. Ahn himself translated two of his novels into English, both of which were published in the United States: *White Badge* (New York: Soho, 1989) and *Silver Stallion* (New York: Soho, 1990). *The Life and Death of the Hollywood Kid* was adapted into the same title film in 1994 by Korean New Wave director Chŏng Chi-yŏng.

24. Ahn Junghyo, *The Life and Death of the Hollywood Kid* (*Hŏlliudŭ k'idŭ ŭi saengae*) (Seoul: Minjok kwa munhwasa, 1992), 88–91.

25. Ibid., 24, 80.

26. *Screen* 45 (November 1987).

27. *Waterloo Bridge* was first released in the provisional capital Pusan during the Korean War, and *Love Is a Many-Splendored Thing* was released in 1956, three years after the end of the war.

28. William Steuck, *The Korean War: An International History* (Princeton: Princeton University Press, 1995), 361.

29. During the Asia-Pacific War, over 360,000 Koreans were mobilized as soldiers, 240,000 as military personnel, and 2 million more as laborers. Between 100,000 and 200,000 women were also forcefully drafted as sex slaves (so-called comfort women) for the Japanese military and sent to comfort stations (military brothels) across Asia. For more information, see Chin Sung Chung's "The Origin and Development of the Military Sexual Slavery Problem in Imperial Japan," in *Positions* 5, no. 1 (Spring 1997): 219–53.

30. R. Baird Shuman, *Robert E. Sherwood* (New York: Twayne, 1964), 77.

31. Lea Jacobs, *The Wages of Sin: Censorship and the Fallen Woman Film, 1928–1942* (Madison: University of Wisconsin Press, 1991), 5.

32. Joseph Breen's letter to Jack Warner, dated February 14, 1936, *Waterloo Bridge* PCA file, the Margaret Herrick Library, Academy of Motion Picture Arts and Sciences (AMPAS).

33. Joseph I. Breen's letter to David O. Selznick, dated October 5, 1939, ibid.

34. Toronto Film Society's Film Buff Program 5, Sunday, December 6, 1981, *Waterloo Bridge* clippings file, the Margaret Herrick Library, AMPAS.

35. Mary Ann Doane, *The Desire to Desire: The Woman's Film of the 1940s* (Bloomington: Indiana University Press, 1987), 119.

36. A direct translation for the Korean mantra "Kaja!" is "Let's go!" The authoritarian government suspected that it meant "Let's go to North Korea!" Director Yu defended his film against the charge, arguing that the line expressed a desire for a utopian society. See Ho Hyŏn-ch'an, *Korean Film 100 Years* (*Han'guk yŏnghwa 100–nyŏn*) (Seoul: Munhaksasangsa, 2000), 124.

37. Exemplary works include *Hometown of Stars* (*Pyŏldŭl ŭi kohyang*, 1974), *Yŏng-ja's Heyday* (*Yŏng-ja ŭi chŏnsŏng sidae*, 1975), and *Miss O's Apartment* (*O-yang ŭi ap'at'ŭ*, 1978), each focusing on the exploits of heart-of-gold concubines, "hostesses," or prostitutes.

38. To my knowledge, Mary Ann Doane is the only feminist film critic to analyze, albeit briefly, scenes from *Waterloo Bridge* (*Desire to Desire*, 119, 122).

39. *Waterloo Bridge* clippings file, the Margaret Herrick Library, AMPAS.

40. Hyun Sook Kim, "Yanggongju as an Allegory of the Nation: The Representation of Working-Class Women in Popular and Radical Texts," in *Danger-*

ous Women: Gender and Korean Nationalism, ed. Elaine H. Kim and Chung-moo Choi (New York: Routledge, 1998), 178.

41. There are several English-language sources on U.S. military prostitution in South Korea. Kim and Choi, eds., *Dangerous Women,* contains two essays on these women: Katharine H. S. Moon's "Prostitute Bodies and Gendered States in U.S.-Korean Relations" and Hyun Sook Kim, "Yanggongju as an Allegory of the Nation." Katherine H. S. Moon also published a book, *Sex among Allies: Military Prostitution in U.S.-Korea Relations* (New York: Columbia University Press, 1997). In addition, two documentaries on the subject, Diana Lee and Grace Lee's *Camp Arirang* (28 min. video, 1995, Third World Newsreel) and J. T. Takagi and Hye-jung Park's *The Woman Outside* (58 min. documentary film, 1996, Third World Newsreel) provide illuminating testimonies of sex workers themselves as well as feminist activists.

42. André Bazin, *What Is Cinema?* vol. 1, trans. Hugh Gray (Berkeley: University of California Press, 1967), 35–36.

43. Laura Mulvey, "Visual Pleasure and Narrative Cinema" (1975), reprinted in Constance Penley, ed., *Feminist and Film Theory* (New York: Routledge, 1988), 57–68.

44. Doane, *Desire to Desire,* 119.

45. Ahn, *Life and Death of the Hollywood Kid,* 40.

46. Chuanji Zhou also told me that when he criticized the film on television, many Chinese female audiences cried or became upset because *Waterloo Bridge* was their favorite film.

47. See http://www.koreafilm.or.kr (accessed August 2004). The Web site has both Korean and English versions.

48. Samuel Fuller's Korean War film *The Steel Helmet* (1951) incorporates this fact as a narrative component in a scene featuring a South Korean orphan nicknamed "Short Round," who baffles American soldiers when he sings "Aegukka" to the melody of "Auld Lang Syne."

49. Chŏng Chong-hwa, *Korean Film History through Primary Materials, 1955–1997 (Charyŏ ro pon han'guk yŏnghwasa)* (Seoul: Yŏrhwadang, 1997).

50. *Chosŏn Ilbo,* July 16, 1998.

51. Ho, *Korean Film 100 Years,* 124.

52. I thank Korean film scholar Jinsoo An for providing this information through personal correspondence.

53. Other films in the series included Yu Hyŏn-mok's *Daughters of the Pharmacist Kim (Kim yakkuk ŭi ttaldŭl,* 1964), *Martyr (Sun'gyoja,* 1965), *Rainy Days (Changma,* 1979), and *Son of Man (Saram ŭi adŭl,* 1980); Sin Sang-ok's *The Houseguest and My Mother* (1961), *Sam Ryong, the Deaf-Mute (Pŏngŏri Sam-ryong-i,* 1964), *Dream (Kkum,* 1965), *Eunuch (Naesi,* 1968), and *Women of the Yi Dynasty (Ijo yŏin chanhoksa,* 1969); and Im Kwŏn-t'aek's *Daughter of the Flames (Pul ŭi ttal,* 1983), *Kilsottŭm* (1985), *Adada* (1987), *Ticket (T'ik'et,* 1986), and *Sŏp'yŏnje* (1993).

54. In fact, the "Three Korean Master Filmmakers" series introduced the film in its original title with the translation "Aimless Bullet" in parentheses. Throughout Asia, *The Stray Bullet* has been showcased in several festivals,

such as the "Rediscovered Korean Classics" program at the 20th Hong Kong International Film Festival (1996) as well as in the Yu Hyŏn-mok retrospective held at the 5th International Film Festival of Kerala, India (2000), where Yu's films were featured alongside the works of such world-renowned auteurs as Pier Paolo Pasolini and Nagisa Oshima. Domestic festivals quickly responded to the rise of the film's international fame by spotlighting it in the 4th Puch'ŏn International Fantastic Film Festival (2000), the 6th Pusan International Film Festival (2001), and the 3rd Chŏnju International Film Festival (2002).

55. Chŏng's documentary on Ch'oe Sŭng-hŭi was broadcast on both Asahi Television (Japan) and KBS (South Korea) in 2002. The Japanese documentary by Fujiwara Tomoko was introduced to South Korean audiences a year earlier.

56. Hugo Vickers, *Vivien Leigh* (Boston: Little, Brown, 1988), 120–21.

6

Han'guk Heroism: Cinematic Spectacle and the Postwar Cultural Politics of *Red Muffler*

DAVID SCOTT DIFFRIENT

Owing to its historical links to anticommunist propaganda, the war film continues to be one of the most critically neglected genres of South Korea's cinematic Golden Age. While many scholars and critics have largely focused attention on the realist dramas and family melodramas growing from the democratic spirit of the April 19 Revolution (1960), state-supported films dealing explicitly with the Korean War have by and large been deemed ideologically suspect, inferior to their socially progressive brethren. However, the Golden Age war film exhibits greater flexibility and fluidity than its Hollywood counterpart and, though coded as a masculine genre (one which ostensibly relegates female characters to the margins), frequently adopts the exaggerated postures and emotional excess typically associated with melodrama and the woman's film. Indeed, the radical intermixing of generic tropes undermines critical preconceptions usually brought to this most "conservative" of genres. Moreover, the Golden Age war film's generic multivalency is conducive to the disentangling of various social and historical issues, such as class and gender; tradition and modernity; and the influence of foreign (particularly American) cultures on South Korea's full-throttle drive toward industrialization. In this essay, I seek to expand preexisting critical paradigms subtending the study of South Korean cinema by recuperating the ideological complexities lurking behind narratives of heroic soldiers and patriotic pilots.

Although critical interest in U.S.-produced Korean War films has grown since the 1997 publication of Paul M. Edwards's groundbreaking *Guide to Films on the Korean War,* very little is known by Western scholars about cinematic representations of the war produced within South Korea.[1] Beginning with Son Chŏn's 1951 drama about a landowner forced to take sides, *The 38th Parallel* (*Nae ka nŏmŭn samp'alsŏn*), the Korean War as literal or allegorical plot element held considerable sway over South Korea's booming film industry of the 1950s and 1960s—a Golden Age unrivaled even by today's vibrant batch of internationally distributed blockbusters. The decade and a half stretching from 1955 (the year Yi Kang-ch'ŏn's path-clearing *P'iagol* was released) to the early 1970s witnessed a spate of notable motion pictures from the likes of Sin Sang-ok, Yi Man-hŭi, Kim Ki-yŏng, Yu Hyŏn-mok, Kim Su-yong, and Cho Kŭng-ha. These auteurs cut their teeth on fictionalized retellings of important Korean War battles while injecting melodramatic pathos, comedic levity, and jaunty if anachronistic musical numbers into the proceedings. Indeed, the so-called military enlightenment films produced by these and other directors, though sometimes freighted with jingoistic or anticommunist sentiments and sprinkled with historical anachronisms, treat the subject of the Korean War with sensitivity to the kind of genre-mixing, textual interplay, and self-reflexivity rarely witnessed in Hollywood war films. By bringing South Korean films into a generic fold thought to be the exclusive province of North American and European filmmakers, this essay seeks to remedy a critical oversight.

Despite their value as snapshots of the McCarthy-era cultural landscape, the ninety-odd American films taking the Korean War as their narrative focus do little more than sketch the geopolitical coordinates upon which Korea could be imagined by the Western spectator. In place of historical insight into the events leading up to the war, audiences are given dollops of screen action set against "Oriental" backdrops with a smidgen of sex and romance to attract moviegoers. War films produced in South Korea not only add nuance, detail, and emotional shading to these sketches, but they also proffer images heretofore unseen by Western spectators. In lieu of filming in the American Southwest, works such as *The Hill of the Phoenix* (*Pulsajo ŭi ŏndŏk*, Chŏn Chang-gŭn, 1955), *Five Marines* (*Oin ŭi haebyŏng*, Kim Ki-dŏk, 1961), *The Men of YMS 504* (*YMS 504 ŭi subyŏng*, Yi Man-hŭi, 1963), and *Red Muffler* (*Ppalgan mahura,* Sin Sang-ok, 1964) offer the kind of authenticity of setting and cultural verisimilitude that could only otherwise be achieved through documentary reportage.[2] While the glaciated landscapes of northwest Montana and the barren deserts of Arizona function as geographical stand-ins for the frozen corn stubble and rice paddies of Korea, local films capture the actual sites where many of the war's most famous operations were staged—from the coastal city of Chinhae (base of operations for the

ROK Navy) to Kimp'o Airfield (northwest of Seoul) to Mount Chiri (in the southwestern part of the peninsula).[3]

With few exceptions, when Korea's indigenous populace appears in Hollywood films, they are monolithically stereotyped as either faceless hordes from the North, war orphans in need of Western paternalism and charity, or hunchbacked geezers whose frailty casts in relief the physical prowess of their American saviors. South Korean films paint a more diverse cross-section of social life, and focus on doomed heroes whose masculinity, though troubled, is the screen upon which the nation's virtues and tribulations can be projected. In *Red Muffler*, for example, a decorated pilot successfully destroys a military target after thirty-six failed attempts (!) by American pilots. Whatever this episode lacks in historical accuracy or documentation is made up for by the sheer ambition and political moxie needed to step outside the long shadow of the U.S. military occupation. Political theorists may be led to reject such displays of "*Han'guk* heroism" as a kind of psychological defense mechanism on a national scale—a way of projecting and perpetuating flag-waving fantasies at the behest of a military government. But when these films are understood as excessive cinematic moments propelled by the twin engines of genre—uniting the war film and the woman's melodrama—a more judicious assessment of South Korean cinema's connection to both the political status quo and postcolonial forces might come into focus.

Besides aggressively mixing genre elements, Golden Age war sagas collapse the typology outlined by Edwards. This typology consists of four major camps: the combat action film; the psychological trauma film; the brainwashing film; and the home front movie.[4] All four categories are connected to separate spaces (combat zone, POW camp, domestic arena, and so forth) and different periods (before, during, and after the fighting) that are collapsed in South Korean films—their intermixing indicative of the spatio-temporal slippage unique to a country where battlefield, training ground, and home front are all only a grenade's throw away from one another and where the prewar domination of the Japanese and the trauma of national division finds its counterpart in the American occupation after the war. South Korean war films exploit this fearful proximity and historical continuity, and turn what might appear to be a hopeless situation—the *hopelessly situated nation*—into an occasion for addressing the country's political and cultural adjacency to foreign superpowers.

By the time the armistice was signed at P'anmunjŏm on July 27, 1953 (bringing the "police action" to an unceremonious halt), some

34,000 American troops had died. The war cost the lives of over 1 million Chinese and North Koreans. Approximately 224,000 South Korean civilians had been massacred (only half of that number fell at the hands of the North Korean People's Army [KPA]). If one takes into consideration such factors as starvation and disease, South Korea's total losses number around 900,000. While the Korean War remains a repressed or "forgotten" conflict in American popular discourse (one characterized by an army private in the film *War Hunt* [Denis Sanders, 1962] as "a funny kind of war"), for the men and women living on the peninsula it was and continues to be a traumatic touchstone to which they are eternally bound. Lacking closure, this contentious historical narrative is permanently ingrained in the Korean national psyche and, consequently, has been a constant source of frustration and inspiration for artists working in print and visual media. Given its ideological complexities, the war film genre—so often disparaged as a tainted throwback to a politically repressive era—should not be dismissed as mere propaganda. Rather, these films constitute a mode of *imperfect assimilation* that can be interpreted as a form of cultural resistance.

Borrowing the concept of "double consciousness" elaborated by W. E. B. Du Bois in *The Souls of Black Folk,* this essay argues that, in the wake of the war, South Koreans were impelled to look at themselves, to represent themselves through the eyes and generic conventions of others. This double consciousness was often expressed as "impertinent associations," malapropisms, and uniquely Koreanized Americanisms (pidgin English, for the politically incorrect). In the blending of the woman's film and the war film, of Euro-American and Korean signifiers, the resulting excess and compression can be seen both as a melodramatic maneuver appropriate to the historical reality of the Korean War (wherein there was little distinction between battlefront and home front) as well as a strategic mode of (mis)appropriation in which gaffes, glitches, and gaps figured as an imaginary foil against the United States' military occupation and cinematic-cultural hegemony. In the remainder of this essay, I will take Sin Sang-ok's Air Force love story *Red Muffler* as a case study, focusing on the film, the director, and the film's female star (Ch'oe Ŭn-hŭi) in hopes of elucidating the inner workings of war films in general. Like the film itself, both Sin Sang-ok (who worked in multiple genres) and Ch'oe Ŭn-hŭi (whose career encompassed diverse female roles) assimilated various strands of excess that point toward a uniquely Korean form of cinematic spectacle.

Three Cinematic Sensations: *Red Muffler,* Sin Sang-ok, and Ch'oe Ǔn-hǔi

First screened in Seoul on April 5, 1964, *Red Muffler* drew record crowds to Myŏngbo Theater (where it debuted). Of the roughly 2.5 million people living in the capital, approximately 250,000 saw the film upon its original release—a large number given the fact that, for many people, socioeconomic constraints precluded frequent trips to the movie theater and other such luxuries.[5] In addition to the film's well-publicized inclusion of realistically staged aerial combat footage, an all-star cast (including Sin Yŏng-gyun, Ch'oe Ǔn-hǔi, and Ch'oe Mu-ryong) captured the public's imagination and contributed to *Red Muffler*'s box-office success. Although *Red Muffler* stands out among the ranks of contemporaneous hits such as *The War and the Old Man* (*Chŏnjaeng kwa noin,* Im Kwŏn-t'aek, 1962), *The Fighting Lions* (*Ssaunǔn sajadǔl,* Kim Muk, 1962), *DeMilitarized Zone* (*Pimujang chidae,* Pak Sang-ho, 1965), and *Martyr* (*Sun'gyoja,* Yu Hyŏn-mok, 1965), due to its breathtaking color cinematography and high production values, the film nevertheless exemplifies the thematic preoccupations of more modestly budgeted Korean War epics. Valor, solidarity, and heroic self-sacrifice *pro patria* are saliently figured in the guise of Air Force pilots for whom each new day may be the last.

That this most popular war film of the 1960s—proclaimed in advertisements as "The Greatest Achievement of the ROK Air Force"—kicked off a spate of subsequent flyboy dramas such as Kim Ki's *Angry Eagle* (*Sŏngnan toksuri,* 1965) and Yi Man-hǔi's *We Live in the Sky* (*Ch'anggong e sanda,* 1968) should come as no surprise. What is surprising, however, is that thirty-five years before the blockbuster hit *Shiri* (*Swiri,* 1999) stormed into Asian theaters and sparked comparisons to Hollywood action films based on its technical polish, the internationally distributed *Red Muffler* gave Korean, Japanese, Hong Kong, and Taiwanese audiences of the 1960s an equally kinesthetic thrill—one that did not forego psychological or historical insight in the name of cinematic spectacle. What distinguishes the pan-Asian "*Red Muffler* phenomenon" of the 1960s from the "*Shiri* phenomenon" of the 1990s are the political and economic circumstances of the respective eras, as well as the fact that the former emerged during the most prolific decade of the South Korean motion picture industry—a ten-year span that gave birth to 1,506 films (double the 742 films produced throughout the entirety of the 1990s).

Any film that rises to the top of such a competitive heap must be special both as an aesthetic object and as an object lesson on the driving forces behind cultural consumption during the 1960s.

If *Red Muffler* set a cinematic benchmark of the 1960s, then its maker, Sin Sang-ok, lays equal claim to that decade's directorial throne. After studying at the Tokyo Art School and then apprenticing under legendary filmmaker Ch'oe In-gyu (of *Viva Freedom* [*Chayu manse*, 1946] fame), Sin put his experience and training in fine arts toward a short career in production design, eventually making his directorial debut on *The Evil Night* (*Agya*, 1952), a bleak social drama detailing the lives of a drunken writer and a *yanggongju* prostitute in the war-shattered city of Taegu. Following the release of this 16 mm film, he created his own production company, Shin Sang Ok (Sin Sang-ok) Productions, followed by the 1955 launch of his production and distribution house Seoul Films. His vision of a Hollywood-style studio system came to fruition in 1960 with the creation of Shin Films (Sin Films), the largest production company at that time. The director's most famous films, *Romance Papa* (1960), *The Houseguest and My Mother* (*Sarangbang sonnim kwa ŏmŏni*, 1961), and *Red Muffler* were shepherded to box-office success under the Shin Films banner. A master of Silla and Chosŏn-era historical epics, Sin was equally adept at surreal Buddhist fables (*Dream* [*Kkum*, 1955]), contemporary family melodramas (*Ch'un-hŭi* [1959]), literary adaptations of Japanese stories (*Traces* [*Ijo chanyŏng*, 1967]), travelogue documentaries about his homeland (*Korea* [1954]), omnibus films (*Yi Dynasty Women* [*Ijo yŏin chanhoksa*, 1969]), biopics (*Young Syngman Rhee* [*Tongnip hyŏphoe wa ch'ŏngnyŏn Yi Sŭng-man*, 1959]), ghost and horror films (*Snake Lady* [*Sanyŏ*, 1969]), murder mysteries (*It's Not Her Sin* [*Kŭ yŏja ŭi choe ka anida*, 1959]), combat and military pictures (*War and Man* [*Chŏnjaeng kwa in'gan*, 1971]), and even musicals (*I Love Mama* [*Ai lŏbŭ mama*, 1975]) and Manchurian "westerns" (*Homeless* [*Musukcha*, 1968]).[6]

His 1961 *Chun-hyang* (*Sŏng Ch'unhyang*), the first Korean film exported to Japan as well as the first color film to be shot in Cinemascope, was an "event" movie, an adaptation of a popular Confucian tale that set a spectacular precedent for the box-office success of *Red Muffler* three years later. *Chun-hyang*, like practically all of his films during this era, starred his wife Ch'oe Ŭn-hŭi, perhaps the most photographed face in South Korean film history. Not unlike MGM's "First Lady of the Screen" Norma Shearer, who throughout the 1930s exuded an intelligent and sophisticated aura under the guidance of husband-producer Irving

Thalberg, "Madame Ch'oe" (as she was affectionately dubbed by Sin) parlayed her screen iconicity as both "new woman" and traditional wife into a complex evocation of Korean femininity during a postwar era characterized by competing cultures and values. Interestingly, her character in *Red Muffler*, Chi-sŏn, is a combination of these stereotypic polarities, which are subtly evoked in a passage of dialogue from the film. Questioned about her obstinacy by her new lover, Chi-sŏn responds, "I'm complicated. My personality is sometimes very bright, sometimes depressing. Sometimes I talk like a lark, sometimes I don't feel like talking at all the whole day." These lines reflect Ch'oe Ŭn-hŭi's own complexity throughout a career in which the actress switched back and forth between cinematic images of promiscuous barmaids and sacrificial mothers, flirtatious prostitutes and chaste widows. Her own offscreen life, including her divorce from Kim Hak-sŏng (based partly on postwar financial difficulties and jealousy) and remarriage to Sin Sang-ok, as well as her ability to endure all manner of gender oppression (from the threat of the colonial-era comfort woman draft to her forced conscription as "entertainment" for North Korean officials during the war) while supporting her philandering husband, seems to conform to her dual image.[7] Yet her star persona would not have come into being without the tenacity needed to ascend the scales of the industry as a *modern, professional woman*—an image that culminated with her pioneering stints as film director during the mid-1960s.[8]

Sin Sang-ok's status as the preeminent auteur of his generation is similarly contingent upon artistic as well as his ideological inconsistencies. An entrepreneurial populist who proves to be politically slippery, Sin (who counts among his cross-cultural influences Jean Renoir, Julian Duvivier, Charlie Chaplin, George Stevens, and author Guy de Maupassant) is both a wholly original talent and a filmmaker adept at assimilating and synthesizing the influences of others. A man of apparent contradictions, he remains a vocal advocate of Confucian ideology yet has exposed its virulent oppression of women in historical epics and melodramas that are lauded by conservatives and feminists alike. Sin disliked pretentious claims to Art and—like the sometimes-irascible John Ford—often shot down the critical hyperbole brought to his work. Yet over the years he has become increasingly self-promotional in his appearances at international film festivals. His career benefited from his close ties with the Park administration. During the 1960s, Sin was a frequent guest at the presidential mansion, playing cards with Park Chung Hee (Pak

Chŏng-hŭi), who professed that he wept when he saw the director's *Evergreen Tree* (*Sangnoksu*, 1961), while less sycophantic filmmakers were denied work and left feeling like outsiders.[9] Predictably, his affiliation with the Park regime—at least prior to their falling-out in 1975 (when his Producer's Permit was canceled)—led to a backlash, though his dynastic reign over the film industry was never jeopardized in the least.

The filmmaker's fame only increased after his alleged abduction in 1978 by North Korean officials. Although details about this notorious episode remain sketchy, Sin claims that, after flying to Hong Kong in search of his missing wife in January of that year, the couple was kidnapped six months later by the North Korean government. They eventually escaped to Austria in 1986 and took up temporary residence in the United States, but not before Sin had appeased the famously cinephilic Kim Jung-il (Kim Chŏng-il) by making and/or supervising eleven films for the "Great Leader." His life-altering trip to Hong Kong was based partly on the quixotic idea of rekindling a rocky romance, but his underlying motivation was the possibility of jump-starting a flagging career in a city that had imported many of the director's films with open arms.

One of the unfortunate consequences of his abduction is that half of the original 35 mm negative of *Red Muffler* was in his possession at the time, and was subsequently confiscated by North Korea, where it remains today.[10] Luckily, Sin had the foresight to smuggle a videotape version upon his escape, and eventually linked the bits back together again, but not without a considerable reduction in picture and sound quality. Today, watching the film is like peering through a fine wire mesh that occasionally breaks up the image. Although the film's fate is lamentable, media scholars should celebrate the fact that any version exists at all.[11] The opening title crawl of *Red Muffler* informs the audience of its tortured history, stating "the complete film is not able to be seen in South Korea, but this version was made possible by transferring videotape into film. For that reason, the quality of the film is sometimes not clear." Indeed, watching the reconstructed, film-video hybrid—aired by the Korea Educational Broadcasting System on January 5, 2003—necessitates a certain resignation to the fact that *Red Muffler* is "not all there," that its radiant colors and mise-en-scènic precision have been defiled through intermedia transfer. Sin was not referring to the film's storyline or characters when, during a recent interview, he called *Red Muffler* a "tragic film"— a work whose material separation echoes the tragic history of Korea, which likewise suffered a partition that today casts doubts on hopes of reunification. In this sense, the very surface of the movie provides an enticing theoretical entryway into the devastated nation's heart. The almost palpable grain, the celluloid rips and electronic noise that might otherwise detract from the enjoyment and appreciation of a film, in this case add to our understanding of the psychic and emotional ruptures exacted in national division.

Neither Here nor There, Neither Today nor Tomorrow: Spatial and Temporal Tropes

Red Muffler's story revolves around the training and military exploits of a group of rookie pilots in the ROK Air Force, whose bomber planes are periodically deployed from their Kangnŭng base in Kangwŏn Province to P'yŏngyang, capital of the North. Led by Major Na Kwan-jung, a brave flier who has risen from working-class origins to become a man of honor (having broken the record for the number of successful combat missions), the nine ragtag yet disciplined men eventually cast off their fresh-faced demeanor to reveal a battle-weary understanding of the physical and spiritual toll of war. Rounding out the cast of characters are three women: Chi-sŏn, the widow of a fallen pilot who now works as a prostitute; Madam Yu, a permanent fixture on Na's arm whenever he and his men descend upon the local bar (a kind of poor man's cocktail lounge catering to Koreans only); and finally Na's ashen-faced mother who appears at the end of the film, bearing a basket full of rice cakes for the squadron only to discover that her son has died in a suicide mission. To this tightly knit network of fraternal, sexual, and familial relations, one additional person might be added: Na's best friend No, an ROK pilot who—we learn via flashback—met a tragic end only days after marrying Chi-sŏn. Much of the emotional poignancy of the film comes not from the stratospheric pressure of combat, but from the many encounters between Na and Chi-sŏn—scenes in which the irate pilot reprimands his colleague's widow for her licentious, less-than-ladylike behavior at the bar. Tensions are finally resolved when Pae Tae-dong, a strait-laced pilot nicknamed "Prude," chivalrously steps in to console and eventually marry the woman. Ironically, though Major Na eagerly sponsors their marriage, it exacerbates his feelings of inadequacy and self-deprecating class-consciousness. Harboring romantic feelings for Chi-sŏn, Na can only admire her from afar due to his lower-class status.

While this abbreviated summary evokes the melancholic and melodramatic undertow of the narrative, *Red Muffler* is far from being just a morose or tearfully sentimental piece of propaganda. Although sobering in terms of its depiction of the psychological fallout of war, this veritable feast for the senses is celebratory in tone and (despite its video-to-film degradation) resplendent in image. Unlike the monochrome minimalism of the title cards prefacing *The Marines Who Never Return* (*Toraoji annŭn haebyŏng*, Yi Man-hŭi), big, bright red letters leap onto the screen during *Red Muffler*'s credit sequence, which shows F-86 Sabre jet airplanes in formation streaking through billowing clouds. Set to the jubilant title tune, "Red Muffler,"[12] whose lyrics ironically warn women not to cling to the heart of a pilot (whose "youth can be snuffed out like lightning"), the introductory credits give way to a booming voiceover informing the audience that the story takes place sometime during the "last stages of the Korean War." Lacking specificity of time if not milieu, this commentary might seem to correspond with the willfully oblivious approach to setting typical of Hollywood's Korean War films. Even *Men in War* (Anthony Mann, 1957), a film in which Koreans are all but invisible, at least begins with the expository caption "Korea, September 6, 1950."[13]

Indeed, few people besides military experts can be expected to identify the allusions embedded in *Red Muffler*, which takes dramatic license in depicting one of the greatest accomplishments of the ROK Air Force—the destruction of the Sŭngho-ri Railroad Bridge near P'yŏngyang on January 15, 1951. But in opting not to pin its story of sacrifice and mourning to any one temporal marker, the film diffuses history into, paradoxically, a more concentrated evocation of the pain wrought by the Korean War, whose legacy has been felt by millions. As the omniscient narrator concludes, "These pilots have neither today nor tomorrow," one is momentarily struck by the appropriateness of the sentiment, which finds its visual equivalent in the nebulous patches of clouds and vapor trails speckling the expansive sky. This temporal diffusion, this intentional vagueness, at least within a Korean context, has something curiously specific about it, and opens the historical frame of reference to encompass more than fifty years of preempted tomorrows.

Moreover, the rhetorically rich yet ambiguous voiceover—a trademark of Golden Age cinema observable in everything from *Wŏr-ha's Public Cemetery* (*Wŏr-ha ŭi kongdong myoji*, Kwŏn Ch'ŏl-hwi, 1967) to *Yi Dynasty Women*—is rooted in the performative tradition of *pyŏnsa*, Korea's equivalent to the *benshi* commentaries in Japanese *sinp'a* dramas of the Meiji era. As a transmuted version of *pyŏnsa*, *Red Muffler*'s narration points toward the nation's indeterminate future while gesturing back to the troubled colonial past, the period from 1910 to 1945 when the *sinp'a* form was introduced into Korean society by the Japanese.

After the breathtaking title sequence concludes, the pilots receive the requisite pep speech and are each handed, in ceremonious fashion, a red muffler—the emblem of the ROK Air Force. At this point, there is much talk of the apparel's symbolic connection to blood, to fiery patriotism and consciousness.[14] The mufflers are to remind them to become ferocious when confronted with injustice, but to act restrained ("as benevolent as a mother") when faced with something sad or pitiful. However, not until their three-day advanced training is complete will the men have earned the honor of wearing the red mufflers.[15] Thankfully, the days go by in a flash, as if any narrative time devoted to scrutinizing maps and the geographic coordinates of future bombing sites could be (and indeed is) better spent cinematically rendering the actual terrain of Korea, which appears in abundance throughout the film. Maps of the country are indispensable to Hollywood's Korean War films, but this kind of authenticating device is unnecessary in South Korean cinema, whose validity rests on its situational and emotional proximity to the war itself. The topography of tears traced by this and other Korean War films can be effectively "mapped" once sky and earth are brought into alignment, something that the pilots' commander (who has an idiosyncratic habit of speaking in metaphors) does in his opening lecture: "We live in the sky, but we eat on the earth," he says, adding, "That's why when you are upright on earth you can be courageous in the sky."[16] Although few among us would dare sort out the logic of these statements, the humorously tautological wordplay seems to convey the slipperiness and seriousness of the men's mobile yet unstable position in the text—their vacillation between earth (its plebeian desires of the flesh) and the heavens (nobly associated with loftier ideals, the transcendence of personal vice for spiritual virtue). The film analogously parcels out a version of this dichotomy to its female characters as well, the symbolic import of earth and sky transformed into the more mundane seesaw movement between the domestic sphere (home to chaste housewives) and the public space of bars and brothels (where promiscuous prostitutes service men). The alignment and confusion of gender-coded genre elements attached to the war film and the woman's film opens a provocative if problematic window onto the sexual politics of the 1960s, when the aforementioned stereotypes predominated among the limited variety of cinematic femininities available to women.

For all of its thorniness, the sense of topographical or spatial slippage issuing from the commander's speech effectively structures the entire narrative, wherein categorical differences between men and women are asserted only to blend, to become unstable, or to collapse. This process is evident in the film's focus on the act of naming, which is itself redolent of genre diversification. In an early scene, Major Na inspects the men's barracks and introduces himself as "Santwaeji," or "Mountain Pig"—a rather base description that divulges his earthy sense of humor as well as his inferiority complex. When he fishes for his men's nicknames, one by one the pilots present themselves as "Yamjŏni" ("Prude"), "Ch'adori" ("Sturdy"), "Saennim" ("Sissy"), "Nogada" ("Construction Worker"), and so on.[17] The members of the squadron will eventually be assigned numbers once they take to the skies, but this unusual roll call of character types and occupations mimics the kind of military lingo and nomenclature that, during the Korean War, provided the names for such battles as Operation COURAGEOUS (March 22–31, 1951), Operation DAUNTLESS (April 11–22, 1951), and Operation RUGGED (April 3–6, 1951). More importantly, their patent attempts to differentiate themselves from one another places ironic quotation marks around the very process of naming, and suggests that, for all its racial homogeneity, Korean society—particularly within the microcosmic lens of the military—is built upon clearly delineated, top-to-bottom lines of class and rank. However, in continuously shuttling between the "sturdy" iconography of the war film and the "prudish" or "sissy" elements of melodrama, *Red Muffler* both asserts and eventually flattens the vertical stratification implicit in militaristic or hierarchical chains of command.

Un-Gendering Genre

Against the advice of his superior, Na takes his men to a smoky nightclub to celebrate their successful completion of training. There, he sees Chi-sŏn prostituting herself and becomes furious. Through a point-of-view zoom-shot, the camera captures the sudden appearance of the fallen woman in the arms of a lecherous drunkard. Although this image underscores the male's status as subject of the film and the female's function as spectacle and object of the male gaze, conventional gender dichotomies are problematized throughout *Red Muffler* in its occasional foregrounding of female gaze structures. Exerting his (patriarchal) authority over the woman, Na censures her, demanding that she no longer come to this place of ill repute. In a passage of dialogue that recalls *The World of Suzie Wong* (Richard Quine, 1960), when William Holden's American architect scorns Nancy Kwan's prostitute after he spots her wearing a revealing dress (bought for her by a businessman-client),[18] the major urges Chi-sŏn to replace her trashy Western clothing with a traditional *hanbok*. He

Hand-in-hand: The men of the ROK Air Force, from *Red Muffler* (Courtesy of the Korean Film Archive)

is momentarily pacified by the Madam of the bar, who acts as a voice of reason throughout the film and informs him that "this is a vocation too . . . there is no high or low in vocation," yet he continues to bristle at the sight of Chi-sŏn behaving so indecently. Na harbors romantic as well as fatherly feelings toward his best friend's widow. He wants to protect Chi-sŏn, yet—as a subsequent scene indicates—he adopts a caustic, even destructive attitude toward her. Spotting Chi-sŏn once again being hit on by patrons of the bar, Na cannot hold back his emotions and slaps her.

As the diegetic representatives of two seemingly irreconcilable genres—the combat war film and the woman's melodrama—Na and Chi-sŏn forge a tantalizingly complex relationship built on respect and aggression. Their forced reconciliation, though qualified by Chi-sŏn's compliant attitude toward remarriage, registers the Korean film industry's push toward a form of genre hybridity that promoted, rather than curtailed, dialogue between the sexes. Woman's melodrama and combat action are the main ingredients in most South Korean war films. Although there are fleeting glimpses of other genres, such as the musical, the gangster film, and even slapstick comedy, it is principally the tension between the war film and the woman's film that gives such works as *Red Muffler, Inchon Landing Operation* (*Inch'ŏn sangnyuk chakchŏn,* Cho Kŭng-ha, 1965), and *The Mythical Marine Corps* (*Sinhwa rŭl namgin haebyŏng,* Sŏl T'ae-ho, 1965) their emotional charge. Stylistically, visual excess and spatial claustrophobia characterize the woman's melodrama. A premium is placed on extravagant lighting, color schemes, and camera movements, on lush décor and costumes. Sin Sang-ok's decorative signature is indelibly inscribed in *Red Muffler,* a film whose flamboyant mise-en-scène externalizes the characters' moral and emotional dilemmas.

This bifurcating paradigm is complicated by the fact that Na is as much a part of the woman's melodrama syntax as Chi-sŏn is central to the war film's formula. As mentioned earlier, Chi-sŏn is both demure and flirtatious. Similarly, Na is a swaggering leader given to braggadocio, yet he is sensitive to the needs of his men (who, significantly, are to act heroically and be as "benevolent as a mother"). To see them only as figures of their respective genres is to fall back on prescribed and tautological notions concerning the genrification of masculinity and femininity and the gendering of genre. This approach misses other substantive criteria that might account for a more symbiotic or interactive relationship that, in the words of Rick Worland (in his exploration of *The Bridges at Tokori* [Mark Robson, 1954]), "creates an off-balance combination of resolve and regret that complicates readings of these films as jingoistic reinforcements of official policy."[19] While it is true that Hollywood's Korean combat films "are about American families back home, American families waiting in Japan, and about love and romance in both places,"[20] war films made in South Korea collapse male-female conflicts through spatial integration—bringing the heterosexual union into the direct path of bullets and bombings. Even those Hollywood films that are most attuned to the peaceful coexistence of melodrama and war (such as *Bombers B-52* [Gordon Douglas, 1957], a "combat-romance" starring Natalie Wood as the daughter of an Air Force sergeant and the lover of a young colonel) lack the immediate proximity between battlefield and home front found in the chronotopically claustrophobic South Korean films.

The combat action film has been historically coded as a masculine text whose explosive poetics and rigidly defined codes of both group and individual behavior align it with other ostensibly "male" genres such as the western and the action-adventure film. In the war film, one is likely to find showy displays of technological hardware and firepower, the kind of testosterone-fueled iconography (guns, ships, tanks, airplanes) that appeals to the boy in every man. Paul Edwards has suggested that part of the war film's attraction lies in the child's fascination with toys, an engagement with the tactility or "thing-ness" of playthings. This subject is broached in many of the Korean War films produced in Hollywood. Lacking personal incentive, many of the grunts on the ground are motivated by acquisition, the promise of a consumable object as payment for services rendered, whether a bottle of scotch in *Hold Back the Night* (Allan Dwan, 1956) or a box of cigars in *The Steel Helmet* (Samuel Fuller, 1951).[21] Interestingly, the title of Fuller's film, which draws attention to Sgt. Zack's life-saving headgear, is rare insofar as it foregrounds not a person but a *thing*, a piece of protective apparel. Similarly, *Red Muffler*'s title refers to a piece of clothing worn by enlisted men, albeit one that lacks the functional "manliness" associated with ground combat.

The red muffler functions, then, as an objective correlative, one that erodes distinctions between the war film and the woman's film by suggestively bringing femininity into the fold. Film and stage melodramas spill over with similarly cathected objects. Not unlike the Wedgwood teapot in Douglas Sirk's *All That Heaven Allows* (1955) or the fragile unicorn in Tennessee Williams's "The Glass Menagerie" (1945), the flashy red muffler is an everyday object imbued with metaphoric meanings and emotional residue, registering in material form the film's simultaneous appeal to the mind and the eye. Like the blood-red scarves draped around the necks of the pilots, the film *Red Muffler* is an aesthetically attractive object, a spectacular achievement in the history of Korean cinema when production values kept pace with the Herculean ambitions of the artists behind the lens. Although there are other Korean films whose titles call attention to metonymic objects rather than people—whether things such as *Money* (*Ton*, Kim So-dong, 1958) and *Rice* (*Ssal*, Sin Sang-ok, 1963) that are essential to sustenance; or practical if supplementary items such as *Swivel Chair* (*Hoejŏn ŭija*, Yi Hyŏng-p'yo, 1966) and *Apron* (*Haengjuch'ima*, Yi Pong-nae, 1964), which signify office work and housework, respectively—few mine the ideological complexities of nationhood so dramatically as does *Red Muffler*, a film whose titular insignia is both a symbolic flourish and a moralistic mandate. As the commander says, "Just because this is wartime, don't mistreat someone else's daughter. Make sure that the red muffler doesn't cry"—a statement that brings together in one material metaphor the responsibilities of men, the historical subjugation of women, and national pride.

The object itself conjures a host of literary, cinematic, and cultural associations outside the textual horizons of this particular film. Red mufflers have graced the throats and shoulders of everyone from Horne, one of the militant anarchists in Joseph Conrad's "The Informer" (who gave the narrator "the impression of being strung up to the verge of insanity"), to the lovelorn peasant girl played by Zhang Zi-Yi in *The Road Home* (*Wode fuqin muqin,* 2000). This proletariat fable by Fifth Generation filmmaker Zhang Yimou foregrounds the clothing's connection to provinciality, the lower-class milieu of a girl whose trademark attire—red padded jacket and red muffler (accentuated by red barrette)—parodies the iconography and revolutionary fervor of China's Cultural Revolution (also referenced in Ji-Li Jiang's 1997 memoir, *Red Scarf Girl*). The color alone is densely packed with political suggestiveness, connoting everything from Mao-era communism to Coca-Cola capitalism. As a cold war catchword linked to danger and aggression, "red" has functioned as a symbol of socialism dating back to the 1917 Russian Revolution. For most South Koreans, the red muffler is as much the regalia of North Korean schoolchildren as it is of the ROK Air Force—a connection that casts in relief the familial or blood ties linking the two Koreas. This last link—referenced in films such as *Shiri* and *Joint Security Area* (*Kongdong kyŏngbi kuyŏk,* Pak Ch'an-uk, 2000)—is tweaked in Chang Chin's black comedy *The Spy* (*Kanch'op Yi Ch'ŏl-chin,* 1999) when the main character strolls drunkenly through an entertainment district in Seoul only to hallucinate seeing North Korean children distinguished by their red mufflers. In light of the post–2002 World Cup frenzy that saw a sea of "Red Devils" cheering the South Korean soccer team to Cinderella-style victory, this most political of colors appears to have been recuperated as a national symbol, an expression of solidarity apparently stripped of its negative denotations.

To anyone familiar with the work of Oscar Wilde, a red muffler might evoke the three-hundred-year-old chain-rattler in "The Canterville Ghost," a disconsolate blue blood who—unable to spook the new American occupants of Canterville Chase—creeps about the corridors "with a thick red muffler round his throat for fear of draughts."[22] What this reference to Wilde underlines is the red muffler's fanciful connection to dilettantism and "male femininity"—one that expands the hermeneutic horizons of the film to encompass both queer and politically transgressive forms of visual pleasure. It is a flourish, a decorative gesture on the wearer's part to visibly signify his individuality, which, in this case, is recouped by the collective élan of the pilots (who are less emotionally inhibited in their relationships with other men than their American counterparts). Decorating the fighting men of the ROK Air Force, the red

Major Na (left) looks on as newlyweds No (center) and Chi-sŏn (right) begin their connubial life together, from *Red Muffler*

mufflers announce in exuberant hue the indomitable spirit of the nation. Apart from its aesthetic properties and ideological connotations, the red muffler serves practical purposes as well. A shield against the cold, the red muffler protects each pilot from sub-zero temperatures. It can even save lives, as when Prude wraps a red muffler given to him by Chi-sŏn—one originally made for her first husband—around the bullet wounds in his leg to stop the bleeding. It is this coexistence of the poetic and the pragmatic, passion and reason, that makes the red muffler especially applicable to the exploration of a collective Korean psyche or national character.

Because it passes from one person to another in a hand-me-down fashion, the borrowing and shifting ownership of the red muffler resonates with the thematic predilection in Korean War films for women as *possessions*—women who, like the hand-me-down muffler, are objects of exchange, passed from one person to the next. After being "discovered" traipsing alone through the snow, Chi-sŏn is given a lift by the men to Madam Yu's bar, where—following the death of her husband No—she ingratiates herself into the lives of its patrons as a prostitute. Once she remarries, Chi-sŏn is able to put her past behind her, thereby re-assuming the persona of a steadfast wife. Securing his status as protector of the woman, Major Na acts as mediator, overseeing her passage from one pilot

167

to the next. Yet in addition to her diegetic transformation from wife to prostitute to wife again, this shifting "ownership" can be read as a movement from one genre to the next.

The two men/one woman configuration in *Red Muffler* is a plot device that dates back to director Hong Sŏng-gi's *The Attack Order* (*Ch'ulgyŏk myŏngnyŏng*, 1954), the first ROK Air Force drama. Another Korean War film, *South and North* (*Nam kwa Puk*, 1984), brings this configuration as well as the themes of appropriation and possession front and center. *South and North*—director Kim Ki's same-title remake of Kim Ki-dŏk's 1965 classic—depicts the pain of familial separation and, like the original, imbues its story of two men in love with the same woman with humanism. Having defected to the South in search of his wife, Chang Il-gu, a major from the North, is captured by an ROK Army unit and grilled for information. Chang will not comply until his one conditional request is granted: to be reunited with Ŭn-a, a woman he married seven years earlier. Only at the end of the film does Chang learn that, during that period of absence, Ŭn-a had married another man, indeed the very person who captured and interrogated him: Army Captain Yi. This unlikely situation is the stuff of melodrama, an association reinforced by the film's maudlin string music as well as the emphatic burst of piano chords accompanying Yi's earlier shock upon seeing Chang's photo of his/their wife. Although Chang protests when his photo of Ŭn-a is circulated among the soldiers, he ultimately consents to his wife living with her second husband, Captain Yi, thereby giving up his "custody" if not memory of the woman. Leading up to this dénouement is an unintentionally comical scene that likewise registers an act of appropriation, albeit one that reflects the film industry's "hijacking" of historical imagery: a blast of trumpets announces the sudden appearance of a Douglas MacArthur look-alike—an ROK division commander who has come to assess the situation. Wearing trademark pipe and sunglasses, this Korean version of the supreme commander of U.N. forces would seem out of place were it not for an earlier reference, made in passing, to (the real) MacArthur's desire to bomb Manchuria.

In both *South and North* and *Red Muffler,* women not only shuttle from one man to another, but in their situational indeterminacy are also exposed to the physical and psychological repercussions of the war. In the former film, Captain Yi hesitatingly fetches his wife under the ruse that he will be awarded a medal at a ceremony so that she will return with him to headquarters where, unbeknownst to Ŭn-a, her first husband is de-

Romance in the ruins: Tae-dong comforts an ailing Chi-sŏn, from *Red Muffler* (Courtesy of the Korean Film Archive)

tained. Significantly, he is forced to drive by jeep because the transport plane is not working—a point that reflects both the lack of dependable equipment in Korea during the war as well as the budget limitations of this and other films grappling with large-scale combat. After Yi picks up Ŭn-a and his seven-year-old stepson in the city of Chŏnju (where she has been washing the U.S. Army's laundry), the family drives through a rain-soaked obstacle course of bombs and fallen bridges. The image of the wife and child in the midst of the action corroborates Lynne Hanley's claim that modern warfare "vaporizes the myth of a protected zone, of woman's exclusion from war."[23] In her study of the "breathtaking male-ness of the terrains of both the military and its symbiotic sciences and technologies," Hanley argues that "war and its kindred sciences divide the sexes in Western culture more radically than any other human activi-ties with the exception of childbearing and, possibly, sports." However, unlike the Southern fiancée in *Sayonara* (1957) or the pregnant wife in *Battle Hymn,* safely removed from the war yet confined to their domestic ghettos, Korean women like Ŭn-a and Chi-sŏn (refugees from the North) walk an ontological tightrope. They are exposed to disease, hypothermia, and other residual effects (not to mention the nocturnal reality of the war: sexual violence) that disprove what Hanley calls a "radical separation of men from women and children." In *Red Muffler*, Chi-sŏn's exposure to the war is connoted by her cramped living quarters and her weakened health. Her ramshackle hovel, wallpapered in newspaper and furnished with little more than a bed on which to lie, offers scant sanctuary from the shelling outside.[24] Interestingly, *Red Muffler*'s most moving transaction takes place not between two men, but between two women—an old mother and a young prostitute. In the penultimate scene, Madam Yu receives a handmade muffler intended for Na. Leading up to this visual fulfillment of the film's melodramatic pact is a climactic air battle that culminates with Na's kamikaze collision into a bridge at Maengjung-ri. Having earlier scoffed at the American pilots' feckless attempts to destroy the bridge, the gung-ho pilot soon finds himself hit by a North Korean Yak fighter and, rather than bail out, crashes his flaming jet into the intended target.[25] The tragic death of Na brings *Red Muffler*'s generic affiliation to the combat picture to an explosive end, and makes way for the unexpected entrance of his mother in the next scene. Her appearance at the barracks, coinciding with the reading of Na's last will and testament to the weeping men, overwrites the previous scene's combat footage with the ameliorative imprint of maternal melodrama. Emphasizing once again the lowly status of this self-proclaimed "Mountain Pig," Na's words from beyond the grave are humble, stating that his remains should be sprinkled in the fields like fertilizer so that "you smart and educated guys might grow out of my ashes."

Dressed in tatters and on the brink of death herself, Na's physically weak mother exerts a commanding aura, a spiritual strength that suggests that her providential arrival in the text is an act of almost supernatural proportions (in fact, there is something shamanistic about the mother's ghostly complexion). Holding court over the lugubrious men, whom she takes to the bar to toast her late son, the maternal figure physically manifests the words spoken at the beginning of the film, when the red muffler was connected to the benevolence of all mothers. This benevolence is passed along to Madam Yu, who receives a red muffler made by Na's mother and then dissolves into tears. Na is not dead, the commander reassures the grieving women, but lives on in the hearts of these and future pilots.

And indeed, the film follows through on that promise, offering in epilogue form a spectacularly choreographed air show put on for an appreciative crowd of onlookers. This last-minute resurgence of war film iconography in *Red Muffler,* this image of demonstrable firepower and fanfare, has no narrative function. Yet there is great national significance attached to the act of wasting ammunition and glorifying technology. Although he is not shown, President Park Chung Hee is a palpable off-screen presence in this epilogue, the proverbial wizard behind the curtain insuring that military pomp and pageantry contribute to a feeling of national euphoria. It would therefore seem to be ideologically consistent with the political imperatives of the post–May 16 era,[26] when development, speed, and economic prosperity masked the more unsavory aspects of this repressive period, which depended on propagandistic narratives to legitimize Park's authoritarian rule. Sin Sang-ok's collaborationist connection to South Korea's charismatic yet tyrannical leader recalls the critical rhetoric surrounding Sergei Eisenstein's state-sanctioned *Alexander Nevsky* (1937), a morale-boosting epic that sparked patriotic fervor among a Soviet populace who were, at the time of the film's release, concerned about German invaders. Just as Eisenstein's portrait of a thirteenth-century prince has been branded propaganda for enhaloing the Stalinist regime, so too has *Red Muffler* been positioned as a fantasy of military autonomy, a film that presents a sovereign ROK Air Force operating outside the umbrella of the United Nations.[27] But read in a recuperative light, the thrill of pyrotechnic display elicits an ironic gaze that disturbs the hegemonic disposition of the text. It is possible, then, to acknowledge this superfluous burst of flag-waving spectacle as the film's last-ditch attempt to accommodate the earlier, melodramatic moments of visual excess—one that liberates both male and female subjectivities dominated by American military presence and provides a means of recouping cinematic pleasure.

Impertinent Associations: (Mis)Appropriations, Malapropisms, and the English Language

As contemporary theorists have argued, film genres are never stable. They continuously mate and mutate, discovering an unexpected affinity for one another in shared textual, epistemological, and historical preoccupations. This is especially true of works produced during the Golden Age of South Korean cinema—generically promiscuous films like *Red Muffler* that seized upon and devoured the themes, iconography, and technical sheen of other national cinemas until, from that intimate union, a stronger, more circumspect sense of self and sovereignty crystallized. Because *Red*

From left to right: Major Na, Madam Yu, Chi-sŏn, and Tae-dong are caught in the headlights of the commander's jeep outside a bar during New Year's Eve festivities, from *Red Muffler*

Muffler's generic multivalency is conducive to the disentangling of various social and historical issues, a further extrapolation of the film's impertinent associations, or anachronistic affinities, is in order.

The notion of impertinent associations—here related to the (mis)appropriation of material, stylistic, generic, and linguistic conventions—is a particularly apt way of describing the complex array of multicultural allusions embedded in this and other Golden Age texts. *Red Muffler*, like many films of the 1950s and 1960s, rewards the remarkable visual literacy of cinephilic South Koreans by mobilizing transnational signs, re-articulating images and icons associated with the West so as to cast in relief the economic disparity between two nations bound by paternalistic contract even as it renders "old" and "new" simultaneous and interchangeable. Just as the red muffler—an object of fetishistic allure and material comfort—allegorizes a proudly nationalistic ethos through, ironically, its integration of cultural anomalies and historical anachronisms, so too do the film's other visual and aural signifiers reinforce the ongoing generic slippage between war film and woman's melodrama.

172

A brief moment of joy: Line dancing to an American tune on New Year's Eve, from *Red Muffler* (Courtesy of the Korean Film Archive)

Truth be told, the bold associations in *Red Muffler* are at once inappropriate, insofar as they exceed the perceived limits of metaphoric propriety (that is, they are aggressive and intrusive), and appropriate, insofar as they are intrinsic to the matter at hand (that is, they pertain). This inappropriate yet oddly appropriate form of cultural appropriation is exemplified midway through the film: Prude and Chi-sŏn go to a Catholic Church where, kneeling, she prays that "her precious one will be protected from danger" to the tune of *Ave Maria*. Meanwhile, Christmas and New Year's Eve festivities are sweeping through the region. Na and his men sing "White Christmas" at the bar and, at the stroke of midnight, embrace just as the commander (nicknamed "Hong Kil-tong," Korea's version of the omnipresent Robin Hood) suddenly appears and instructs them to return to the base. Earlier in the scene, Madam Yu—whose spangled, feathery dress and diamond tiara evoke Marilyn Monroe with a hint of 1920s flapper-girl[28]—responds to Na's question if she will be his protector. As if to recall the United States' sentinel-like relation to its protectorate South Korea, she answers in English: "Yes."

173

Many Golden Age films incorporate bits of English into the dialogue, a sonic phenomenon that parallels the onscreen intermixing of visual icons (architecture, sports cars, costumes, coiffures) and cultural milieus (boutiques, dance halls, cafés, jazz clubs) in postwar Seoul. At a deeper, systemic level, these appropriations reflect a more troubling manifestation of a collective identity crisis spawned by rampant modernization and Americanization.[29] This unwarranted intrusion of English reflects the era's fractured, mangled Korean subjectivity dominated by Western influences. The jarring contrast of English and Korean languages is not only a reminder of the first full-scale intercultural encounter between the United States and South Korea during the war; it also lays bare the postwar promise of economic development and cultural assimilation that—powered by American capital—sometimes alienated the lower-class majority of the populace.[30]

English phrases likewise sprout up in the naval comedy-cum-musical melodrama *The Men of YMS 504*. In one scene, Lieutenant Han—piloting an American-made ship—orders "All engines stop" in English and yells "Man overboard" when a sailor leaps to his presumable death. An earlier irruption of English occurs in a bar for enlisted men—a sequence boldly announced by a burst of American jazz (with a rock-and-roll backbeat). Among the obviously fake cherry blossoms festooning the barroom is a sign on the wall that reads "Well Come Navy." The misspelling of "welcome" can be read any number of ways (being divided in half, the word could conceivably connote the nation torn asunder, split in two), but it unwittingly reflects a general unease about newly introduced cultural and linguistic elements from abroad.

If less jaundiced than other Golden Age films in its vision of a postwar melting pot, if governed by the political machinations of the Park Chung Hee regime, *Red Muffler* nevertheless proves to be equally significant as a barometer of public opinion during a decade when cultural imperialism and interest in the West were at an all-time high. That the "mahura" in the film's Korean title originates from the English word "muffler" by way of Japanese phonetic transformation is symptomatic of the multilayered colonial and postcolonial legacies inscribed in the national language. Moreover, as one of the many migratory references lending *Red Muffler* a transnational sweep, it allegorizes the dual influence of Japanese and American disciplinary and material resources in the formation of South Korea's military branches and film industry.[31]

Because it is passed from one person to another in a hand-me-down fashion, the red muffler flutters outside the narrative to represent the miraculous recovery of the South Korean film industry during the Golden Age, when Arriflex cameras and other equipment donated by American companies were utilized to aesthetically pleasing affect.[32] The recycling of U.S.-originating film supplies further relates to the ways in which the ROK's meagerly equipped military branches came into possession of used artillery, aircraft, and tanks during the early months of the war. World War II weaponry and technical know-how, after a five-year hiatus, were put to use again during the Korean War, much as the visual tropes and stylistic patterns of 1950s Hollywood war films, musicals, and melodramas would resurface in dramatically reconfigured form during the 1960s, when directors such as Sin Sang-ok appropriated the "second-hand goods" of Douglas Sirk and Vincente Minnelli.

Indeed, *Red Muffler* finds its director in Douglas Sirk mode—Sin's dynamic manipulation of the film image accentuating the emotional cadences of each scene as few contemporaneous works did. In fact, Sin frequently out-Sirks Sirk, showing the disparity between national goals and personal incentives through a seemingly arbitrary use of candy-colored gels, filters, and unmotivated red and blue lighting schemes. The red and blue halves constituting the South Korean flag—a Pepsi-like yin-yang symbol in which two parts create a whole—provide not only a metonymic insignia of the divided nation emblazoned on aircraft, but also a structuring element underscoring the film's visual and thematic interest in fire and ice. The many reconciliations throughout the narrative (between red-suited Na and devil-in-a-blue-scarf Chi-sŏn, between the melodrama and the war film, between past and present, between communist and capitalist iconography) are made visible at moments when fire and ice literally collide. For instance, Prude at one point risks his life to save his plane without landing gear. Upon touchdown, the underbelly of the aircraft catches fire, and can only be salvaged by the collective efforts of the rescue team, who send a spray of ice and water onto the burning plane.

Prude's decision not to bail out foreshadows Na's death at the end, and also recalls his earlier, daredevil heroics against enemy planes during his first outing—an individual as opposed to collective stab at glory that almost got him killed. Back on the ground, Prude is berated by one of the commanders. Slapping him in the face for his insolence, the commander barks, "We have fewer than one hundred planes. . . . Do you know how much money was spent on your training? Do you know how much time and manpower was spent on your training?" Although the ROK Air Force actually had fewer than half that number of aircraft and fighters at its disposal during the war, the commander's erroneous remark casts light

Pae Tae-dong and an expensive "gift" from the United States—an F-86 Sabre jet, from *Red Muffler*

on the scarcity of supplies and the relative value of these men, who are responsible for keeping their expensive "gifts" from the United States intact. Prude's apologetic response to his commander thus parallels South Korea's obsequious relation to U.S. command. Interestingly, the F-86 Sabre jets shown in *Red Muffler* were not flown by South Koreans until three years after the war, when a total of eighty-two such aircraft were received from the United States—aircraft that had contributed to America's air superiority during the war.[33] If the appearance of the jets is anachronistic, it nevertheless reflects the South Korean film industry's appropriation and creative re-deployment of even the most hackneyed Hollywood images.

Reflecting Back, Looking Ahead

Like Na, *Red Muffler* lives on in the hearts and minds of many South Koreans. In fact, just as the dead major's spirit is evoked in the air-show epilogue, the film has made similar returns: first as the germinal seed for Im Wŏn-jik's *The Man in the Red Muffler* (*Ppalgan mahura ŭi sanai*, 1971), starring Sin Yŏng-gyun (the actor who had played Na in the original); then as the titular inspiration for celebrated Japanese Gen-X filmmaker Shinji Aoyama's 8 mm student film *Red Muffler* (*Akai mafuraa*). Ask any South Korean under the age of thirty about *Red Muffler*, and the likely response will have something to do with South Korea's most notorious bootleg sex video of the 1990s (a scandal due to the commercial exploitation of its underage participants): "Red Muffler." Whether explicitly referenced (in the case of the latter's inadvertent, porno-parody of a "sacred" text), or visually alluded to in such recent melodramas as *Failan* (*P'airan*, Song Hae-sŏng, 2001) and *Untold Scandal* (*Sŭk'aendŭl*, Yi Chae-yong, 2003), *Red Muffler* continues to circulate in the spectatorial consciousness as an appropriative property or impertinent association in its own right—as a marker of a past forever consigned to the present. This paradox has not been lost on South Koreans who are hesitant to invoke or return to the past—to the political climate of the Korean War—yet compelled to shuck anticommunist rhetoric and bring closure to this most protracted of national traumas.

The theme of reflecting back to the past while looking ahead is negatively conjured at several junctures in the narrative. After bombing his old hometown of Yŏnbyŏn, a place of childhood memories to which he can never return, Pae Tae-dong (a.k.a. Prude) tells his lover Chi-sŏn, "Forget the past . . . there is no time to look back." This echoes a thought voiced by No, Chi-sŏn's first husband, prior to their marriage: making an impromptu proposal, No manages to convince her by saying, "Our pasts don't matter." After No's death, Prude has misgivings about pursuing his senior's widow, but these are quickly assuaged by Major Na, who advises, "If you are going to give, give it all, so there will be no time to look back and think about the past." Although spoken forty years ago in the context of personal, as opposed to national or collective, compulsions, these nihilistic yet strangely comforting replies are like echoes of echoes, "cryptic common senses" reverberating through the decades while providing much-needed solace for Korea's unduly strained souls.

Notes

I would like to thank Dr. Paul Edwards and his staff at the Center for the Study for the Korean War (Independence, Missouri) for their kindness in providing resources and documents related to this topic. Thanks also to Hye Seung Chung for her research assistance and for translating films and Korean-language articles.

1. Paul M. Edwards, *A Guide to Films on the Korean War* (Westport, CT: Greenwood Press, 1997). There has since been one additional English-language guidebook to Korean War films published in the United States, Robert J. Lentz's comprehensive survey *Korean War Filmography: 91 English Language Features through 2000* (Jefferson, NC: McFarland, 2003). This text fills many gaps in historical research, and even includes, in its appendix, synopses of forty South Korean films (compiled by Darcy Paquet and available online at www.koreanfilm.org [accessed August 2004]).

2. Whenever actual combat footage was inserted into U.S.-produced Korean War films, it often derived from World War II archives.

3. During the Korean War, Mount Chiri was the site of numerous anti-guerrilla campaigns spearheaded by General Paek Sŏn-yŏp. One in particular, the infamous Operation RATKILLER (December 2, 1951–March 14, 1952), resulted in the death or capture of thousands of resistance forces—a campaign that forms the backstory of such Korean War films as Im Kwŏn-t'aek's *The Taebaek Mountains* (*T'aebaek sanmaek*, 1994).

4. To these four categories, Edwards appends five equally salient characteristics of the Korean War film: (1) the biographical focus on the exploits of a famous individual, (2) the emphasis on men who have fought in two wars (the Korean War often serving as a redemptive or curative experience to wipe away any pain or guilt associated with World War II), (3) the relative lack of location shooting, (4) the near absence of superheroes (men whose unparalleled battle skills and acumen raise them above the average soldier), and (5) a rather equivocal picturing of the returning war veteran assimilating into American daily life. See Edwards, *Guide to Films on the Korean War,* 31–36.

5. See Kim Hak-su, *Off-Screen: Korean Film History,* vol. 1 (*Sk'ŭrin pak ŭi yŏnghwasa 1*) (Seoul: Inmul kwa sasangsa, 2002), 206. Professor Kim Hong-jun puts the figure at 220,000, and claims that roughly one out of ten people saw the film upon its original release. Kim Hong-jun is the host of South Korea's weekly Educational Broadcasting System program "Han'guk

yŏnghwa t'ŭksŏn" (Korean Film Special), which has aired many Korean War films such as *The Men of YMS 504* (July 14, 2002), *Red Muffler* (January 5, 2003), and *South and North* (January 26, 2003).

6. Besides his work as director, Sin produced several noteworthy films, among them Kim Muk's prize-winning documentary *All Quiet on the Vietnamese Front* (*Wŏllam chŏnsŏn isang ŏpta*, 1966), which acknowledges the role of South Korean soldiers in the Vietnam War.

7. For more information on Ch'oe Ŭn-hŭi's life and screen persona(s), see Kwak Hyŏn-ja, "Widow and *Yanggongju*: Korean Modern Woman's Dream and Burden Seen through Ch'oe Ŭn-hŭi," in *Korean Cinema and Modernity* (*Han'gukyŏnghwa wa kŭndaesŏng*), ed. Chu Yu-sin (Seoul: Yŏrhwadang, 1996).

8. This notion of Ch'oe Ŭn-hŭi as a modern, professional woman willing to make certain concessions to the industry is perhaps best articulated through her early starring role in Sin Sang-ok's *A Certain College Woman's Confession* (*Ŏnŭ yŏdaesaeng ŭi kobaek*, 1958), a social drama for which she won Best Actress at the First Annual National Film Awards. This compelling film—a mixture of Mizoguchi mise-en-scène and Puccini operatics that is thematically reminiscent of the Hollywood classics *Stage Door* (1937) and *Adam's Rib* (1949)—finds Ch'oe's virtuous yet alienated and unemployed law student scaling the heights of her profession by means of a ruse. Like Chi-sŏn in *Red Muffler*, the morally upstanding yet downhearted So-yŏng (who, when not job hunting, spends her time despondently drifting past storefront windows of shops named "Paris" and "Seoul New York") is contradictory in action and thought. Unlike Chi-sŏn, however, this twentysomething friend of the dispossessed refuses to be used as a sexual pawn by her potential employers, and pushes away the lecherous men who mistake her for a prostitute. Yet she is not above resorting to a form of extortion to further her fledgling career. Pretending to be the long-lost daughter of a congressman, So-yŏng deceitfully insinuates herself into a life of wealth and luxury, though not without a nagging sense of guilt that eventually compels her to come clean. Her ultimate redemption lies in her desire to right the many wrongs thrust on subjugated women and defenseless children at home and in court. Indeed, after passing her bar exam with honors, she acts as the defense lawyer for a young woman on trial for murdering her ex-lover—ultimately appealing to the emotions of the jury and audience by way of an eerily autobiographical account of the accused woman's numerous hardships.

9. Kim So-hŭi and An Chŏng-suk, "Interview with Director Sin Sang-ok," *Cine 21*, 327 (November 13–November 20, 2001): 46.

10. Besides *Red Muffler*, two other films were in Sin's possession and subsequently snatched away by North Korean officials: *Red Gate* (*Yŏllyŏmun*, 1962) and *Pyongyang Bombing Squad* (*P'yŏngyang p'okkyŏktae*, 1971), the latter another Air Force love story.

11. The prints for many of Sin's early works (such as *The Evil Night* and *Dream*) have been lost or destroyed—acetate casualties of an apathetic industry that, prior to the creation of the Korea Film Storage (a centralized archiving infrastructure created in 1975 by the Motion Picture Promotion Corpora-

tion), thought little of film as a cultural document worth preserving.

12. Composer Hwang Mun-py'ŏng's and lyricist Han Un-sa's "Red Muffler" was the first in a series of theme songs to achieve widespread popularity during the 1960s, followed by "Miss Camellia" (*Tongbaek kkot agassi*) and "Barefoot Youth" (*Maenbal ŭi ch'ŏngch'un*). Only the lachrymose single "Does Anybody Know This Person?" from Kim Ki-dŏk's *South and North* (*Nam kwa Puk,* 1965), was more popular—a tune that was revived eighteen years later when the Korean Broadcasting System televised "The Search for Divided Family Members of North and South" (beginning in June 1983). Korean cultural memory is indelibly tied to these theme songs, which often linger in the mind well after thoughts of the films have evaporated. Part of the lasting appeal of the song "Red Muffler" (a snippet of which is whistled by a flight instructor in the recent melodrama *A Smile* [*Miso,* 2003]) is its delicate equilibrium of celebratory and fatalistic inflections. Envisaging the death of the pilots, the lyrics betray a sentiment that runs counter to the fist-pumping performances in other Korean War films such as *The Men of YMS 504* (which concludes with the lyrics, "Let's go back to our maidens who wait for us").

13. At their best, Hollywood films such as *Men in War, Pork Chop Hill* (Lewis Milestone, 1959), and *Retreat, Hell!* (Joseph H. Lewis, 1952) deal with specific areas, events, or periods of the Korean War, treating it not as an ideological showdown between the United States and the USSR but rather as one fought by shell-shocked soldiers unsure about the motives of nation-states. At their worst, they regurgitate stale formulas while making casual, derogatory references to "gooks," as in the 1958 AIP production *Jet Attack,* a seat-numbing exercise in brainless ballistics that begins with the telltale intertitle "Somewhere in Korea."

14. Compare the fiery patriotism of the red muffler to the bleak connotations of color in Kim Ki-dŏk's *Black Muffler* (*Kŏmŭn munŭi ŭi mahura,* 1966), the story of a woman who seeks revenge for the death of her only son.

15. There are several other South Korean films that depict the rigors of military training. One, Sin Sang-ok's *Private First Class Kim* (*Yukgun Kim ilbyŏng,* 1969), is partially set at the Nonsan Training Center, where men from all walks of life converge. Correspondingly, a handful of Hollywood Korean War films are geared toward the training of the ROK Air Force; two of which— *Battle Hymn* and the 3-D *Dragonfly Squadron* (Lesley Selander, 1954)— benefited from having real-life USAF pilot Colonel Dean Hess on hand as technical advisor.

16. This topographical slippage also emanates from *The Men of YMS 504,* when Lieutenant Chang asks Myŏng-hŭi (a woman he has been searching for), "Did you sink into the sea or did you fly up into the heavens?" Likewise, in *The Marines Who Never Return,* one of the ten men waiting for impending Chinese attack asks, "Where is the enemy?" His buddy responds by silently pointing up to the heavens—a gesture that might remind the audience of the film's first image of shadowy ROK Marines scaling down rope lattices from some unspecified height.

17. There are similar nicknames bestowed upon the main characters in *The*

Marines Who Never Return, this time by Yŏng-hŭi, an orphaned girl adopted by the unit. Pointing at the men one by one, she assigns the names "Skinny," "Toad," "Big Nose," "Hairy," "Sister," and "Tiger." As in *Red Muffler,* this emphasis on descriptive sobriquets resonates with the process of genrification. Moreover, as the marines' individual identities are submerged under nicknames or familial appellations (such as "brother" or "sister"), the group's unity is conversely solidified.

18. Holden took a gentler approach to the racialized female subject's attire in the Korean War romance *Love Is a Many-Splendored Thing* (Henry King, 1955): He tells Jennifer Jones's Eurasian doctor that he prefers her in cheong-sam (traditional Chinese gown) rather than in Western garb. For an elaboration of the "brutality over clothes and correct behavior" in *The World of Suzie Wong,* see Gary W. McDonogh and Cindy Hing-Yuk Wong's fascinating ethno-anthropological study, "Orientalism Abroad: Hong Kong Readings of *The World of Suzie Wong,*" in *Classic Hollywood, Classic Whiteness,* ed. Daniel Bernardi (Minneapolis: University of Minnesota Press, 2001).

19. Rick Worland, "The Korean War Film as Family Melodrama: *The Bridges at Toko-ri,*" *Historical Journal of Film, Radio, and Television* 19, no. 3 (August 1999): 363.

20. Jeanine Basinger, *The World War II Combat Film: Anatomy of a Genre* (New York: Columbia University Press, 1986), 178.

21. Edwards, *Guide to Films on the Korean War,* 12.

22. Oscar Wilde, "The Canterville Ghost," in *Lord Arthur Saville's Crime, The Portrait of Mr. W. H., and Other Stories* (London: Methuen, 1912), 91.

23. Lynne Hanley, *Writing War: Fiction, Gender, and Memory* (Amherst: University of Massachusetts Press, 1991), 136.

24. Besides being exposed to the war as mothers, wives, sisters, and daughters on the homefront, nearly five hundred Korean women were very much in the thick of things as noncombatant *soldiers*—a fact that often goes unnoticed in historical accounts of the Korean War. Produced by the Bureau of Public Information, Cho Chŏng-ho's *A Woman Soldier* (*Yŏgun,* 1954) is a documentary about the Republic of Korea Women's Army Corps (ROKWAC), which was established in 1948 and modeled after the American WAC, giving servicewomen the opportunity to lend their administrative, stenographic, and telecommunication skills as well as weapons-training to the war effort. According to Seungsook Moon, despite their importance to the war, women soldiers—even today (after the 1990 initiation of Women's Military Academy)—have been "systematically denied . . . access to and control over the direct use of organized force." See "The Production and Subversion of Hegemonic Masculinity: Reconfiguring Gender Hierarchy in Contemporary South Korea," in *Under Construction: The Gendering of Modernity, Class, and Consumption in the Republic of Korea,* ed. Laurel Kendall (Honolulu: University of Hawai'i Press, 2002), 90.

25. Although bridge-bombing is a plot component of a several Korean War films produced in Hollywood, from *Hell's Horizon* (Tom Gries, 1955) to *The Bridges at Toko-Ri,* few of these manage to evoke either the combined terror and thrill of jet-to-jet combat or the explosive impact of collision as effec-

tively as *Red Muffler*. Incidentally, while the Korean War marked the first time in history that jet-versus-jet air battles took place, it hardly gave Korean pilots (many of whom were trained by the Japanese during World War II to kamikaze U.S. ships and bridges) a chance to enact a romanticized notion of death in battle by smashing their expensive planes into targets.

26. Major General Park Chung Hee seized executive power in a May 16, 1961 coup d'état, beginning a long military dictatorship that came to an end with his 1979 assassination. The coup is obliquely alluded to in a number of morality tales, social dramas, and even period pieces, including *Koryŏ Funeral* (*Koryŏjang*), *My Dear Lover, Come Back!* (*Appa dora wayo*, Im Won-jik, 1965), and *44 Myŏngdong* (*Myŏngdong 44bŏnji*, Ko Yŏng-nam, 1965).

27. Even though the Allied effort throughout the Korean War fell under United Nations Command, this multinational force was led by the United States. It is not surprising, then, that so few Hollywood and independent American films treat the war as a U.N., as opposed to U.S., concern (*The Glory Brigade* [Robert Webb, 1953], concerning Greek guerrilla fighters, and *Target Zero* [Harmon Jones, 1955] being the notable exceptions). Moreover, there was very little integration of international troops, discounting that of American and South Korean units. Known as the Korean Augmentation to United States Army (KATUSA), this plan forced soldiers from opposite sides of the world to surmount language barriers and cultural differences so as to combine strategic theory with homegrown expertise—a kind of "buddy-system" that, though unsuccessful at first, continues to this day.

28. Koreans were well aware of Marilyn Monroe's star persona even as early as 1952, when the up-and-coming actress toured Korea as part of a four-day USO tour, bringing a tantalizing taste of the home country to some 65,000 troops.

29. Besides incorporating bits of English into dialogue, there are several Golden Age films whose phonetic English titles attest to the influence of American culture. Consider, for instance, two 1963 films: Sin Sang-ok's *Romaensŭ kŭrei* ("Romance Gray") and Pak Sŏng-ho's *K'isŭmi* ("Kiss Me"). *Kutpai Chyon*, Song Kuk's 1964 war film, takes its title from the words cried by a Korean woman who sits beside the hospital bed of her dead lover (a U.S. Air Force pilot), "Goodbye John."

30. Another film, Yi Pong-nae's *Third Rate Manager* (*Samdŭng kwajang*, 1961), takes a more lighthearted approach, going so far as to include a smattering of German and French vocabulary—"new and modern words," as one character says, that are useful to know. A wall-to-wall talkfest about the sometimes demoralizing demands of white-collar employment, *Third Rate Manager* examines the generational schisms of the Ko family, who nevertheless share a fascination with foreign doggerel and double entendres (only the grandfather, who finds such talk confusing, remains out of the loop). This fascination extends to daughter Yŏng-hŭi (who, while performing calisthenics in bed, chants "one, two, three" in English); slacker son Yŏng-gu (who, tired of his lackluster life of leisure, tries his hand at "arbeit"—a German word meaning "part-time work"); and their mother (who, when referring to her bribe of a tax collector, repeats the Gallic phrase "ça va, ça va"). Their

father, the manager of the film's title, at one point dons a beret and—mimicking his philandering employer—muses, "Que será será." Other words popular in South Korea during the 1960s such as "smart," "sabotage," and the French-English hybrid "après girl" (a term that, linked to "d'après guerre," or the postwar generation, denotes sexual liberation) are referenced in the film, allegorizing one character's facetious desire "to tear [Yŏng-hŭi's] tongue out" into a defensive yet defensible critical position against cultural hegemony.

31. This is attested by Colonel Dean Hess of the U.S. Air Force, who arrived in South Korea in the first months of the war to train cadets of the newly inaugurated ROKAF. In his autobiography, Hess states, "Some of these Koreans were veteran flyers who, ironically, had flown for Japan in World War II—an indication of how during their [thirty-five-year] occupation of Korea the Japanese had attempted to absorb these people." Dean E. Hess, *Battle Hymn* (Reynoldsburg, OH: Buckeye Aviation, 1987), 76.

32. In addition to U.S.-originating cameras, many lenses were of German origin and most film development during the 1960s was done in Japan.

33. See both volumes of the *Encyclopedia of the Korean War: A Political, Social, and Military History,* ed. Spencer C. Tucker (Santa Barbara, CA: ABC-Clio, 2000), 29, 353–54.

7

Questions of Woman's Film:
The Maid, Madame Freedom, and Women

SOYOUNG KIM

The development of the postcolonial South Korean film industry has been closely intertwined with the emergence of the "woman's film" and the modernities associated with multiple layers of colonialism. Films featuring female protagonists made for and consumed by women have been an important revenue source for the South Korean film industry since 1955. Examining these films, which explore feminine sexuality and gendered modernity, provides a way of examining the nation's postcolonial period in which technologies of gender, sexuality, and cinema are inscribed by modernity.

The history of the colonization of South Korea—Japanese, American, and European—has created a hyphenated national identity that structures the nation's cinema. The hybrid formation of modernity(ies) associated with the multiple layers of colonization over a short period of time contributed to a re-structuring of gender roles. It intensified the surveillance of gender roles and feminine sexuality that have been regulated under the aegis of nationalism and modernization during the postcolonial period. The inauguration of a military government in 1961 launched the project of state-initiated modernization, which involved exploiting cheap female labor by controlling female workers' sexuality.[2] In response to this social phenomenon, the South Korean film industry produced a series of films about Western Princesses (*yanggongju*: military prostitutes), bar girls, and hostesses that narrativize the rural migrant female workers' failed incorporation into the labor-intensive industry.

Postcolonial South Korean cinema came into full existence with the box-office success of *Ch'unhyangjŏn* (*The Story of Ch'un-hyang*, Yi Kyu-hwan, 1955) and *Madame Freedom* (*Chayu puin*, Han Hyŏng-mo, 1956). The success of these two films, which center on female sexuality, helped build a cottage-style film industry in South Korea. *Ch'unhyangjŏn*

185

was adapted from the well-known medieval fiction that praises the virtue of feminine chastity, and *Madame Freedom* deals with a female identity constructed through American modernity and consumerism. These films played a crucial role in the early formation of South Korean cinema by reflecting the shifting identities of women during this period through the depictions of the feudal woman, Ch'un-hyang, and the modern woman, Madame Freedom. At the same time, moviegoing allowed women to extend their sphere of mobility outside the privates space of the home into the public space of the movie theater.

The new field of interest both in the representation and spectatorship of women after the war also anticipated the emergence of South Korea's first woman filmmaker, Pak Nam-ok. Her film, *The Widow* (*Mimangin,* 1955) was shown at the opening night of the First Women's Film Festival held in Seoul in 1997. The screening of *The Widow* was accompanied by landmark European and American feminist films such as Claudia Von Aleman's[3] *The Trip to Lyon* (*Die Reise Nach Lyon,* 1980) and Lizzie Borden's *Born in Flames* (1983). In such a viewing situation, where feminist readings were highly encouraged, the largely female audience not only responded enthusiastically to *The Widow* but also attempted to re-articulate its meanings in relation to current feminist concerns in South Korea such as sexuality and identity politics. South Korean social critics have argued that these feminist issues as well as (post)modernity have drawn attention away from other issues including class and nationalism in the 1980s. The First Women's Film Festival emerged as a forum to address these concerns. In addition the Festival served as a vehicle for placing the first woman filmmaker's work in South Korean film history and for relating *The Widow* to urgent questions within 1990s South Korean feminist film theory.

The most pressing issues included the critical appropriation of the woman director's text, the practice of "reading against the grain" textual analysis, the (dis)articulation of feminism with Marxism, and the construction of the festival site as an alternative public sphere. To Western readers who are interested in the development of Asian feminist film movements over the last two decades, this scene must look rather familiar. Indeed, Debbie Zimmerman, executive director of Women Make Movies, excitedly commented upon the heated ambience of the event as she listened to the ongoing debates: "It's just like our 70s."[4] The analogy sounds both incisive and puzzling if one considers the list of films screened at the festival, which ranged from the re-visioned South Korean films from the 1950s to Mary Harron's *I Shot Andy Warhol* from the 1990s. This encounter has stayed with me for a while and alerted me to the complex meanings generated in the screening and reception of women's and feminist films in a film festival influenced by decades of Western cine-feminism. Without a doubt, the legacy of cine-feminism has enabled South Korean film critics to view South Korean films from a feminist perspective. At the same time, the cultural specificity inscribed in South Korean cinema practices tends to be overlooked in the circulation of cine-feminism. For instance, the women's film as an object of study in Anglophone feminist criticism would never find its equivalent in the South Korean context in spite of the fact there is a genre and a set of films that anticipate and solicit a female audience. On the one hand, it is a truism to say that the South Korean women's cinema is different from the Hollywood women's cinema in the 1940s. The development of feminist film criticism in South Korea, on the other hand, doesn't seem particularly conscious of this difference.

In retrospect, the image of "woman" in the "woman's film" in South Korea did not reference women in as generalized a sense as is common in Western industry cinema. Rather, this general category came into common cultural parlance when feminist film critics subsequently framed these films, targeted for a female audience, as such. In the Golden Age "woman's film," female characters were categorized first as wife, widow, maid, and mother—that is, delimited by kinship and class positions that nuanced their signification of "woman" in an overall sense. The visual and narrative conventions South Korea absorbed from Western industry cinema that purveyed iconic representations of a generalized woman therefore existed in some tension with local linguistic and cultural significations of gender embedded in Golden Age film texts. In this context, it is necessary to point out the difficulty attached to the translation of "she" into Korean although "he" is easily translatable. Furthermore, there is no commensurate term for the plural of "she" (*kŭnyŏdŭl*) while a plural form of "he" (*kŭdŭl*) is available.[5]

"Yŏsŏng" Film

The term *yŏsŏng yŏnghwa* or "woman's film" is a recently invented category, which only dates back to the early 1990s. *Yŏsŏng* in *yŏsŏng yŏnghwa* refers to "woman." In fact, the generic "women" in English can be translated both as *yŏja* and *yŏsŏng* in Korean. Often *yŏja* has derogatory connotations.[6] In the Korean dictionary *yŏja* designates a person who is born

as, who in turn is defined as a woman with an emphasis on sexual difference, as distinct from *yŏsŏng* which suggests a social gender distinction.
The re-appropriation of *yŏsŏng* in 1990s feminist discourse among the
many female-related identities—*yŏja, yŏryu,* feminist and *yŏsŏng undongga*
(feminist activist), for instance—might be related to the growing interests
in the politics of sexual difference derived from the feminist and gay
movements in South Korea.

Before the *yŏsŏng yŏnghwa,* of the 1990s, films for female audiences
were simply labeled weepies (*ch'oerumul*) or other similarly derogatory
terms. Following the example of Anglophone cine-feminists' pioneering
work, in the 1990s South Korean critics re-read the *ch'oerumul* through a
feminist lens and recuperated them as examples of the *yŏsŏng yŏnghwa.*
Well-known weepies such as *Bitter but Once Again* (*Miwŏdo tasi hanbŏn,*
Chŏng So-yŏng, 1968) were brought under feminist scrutiny. The discussion ensued with contemporary films that featured *yŏja* explicitly in their
titles, films that typically focused on women characters caught between
their families and their careers. Thus films from both periods were viewed
as examples of the "woman's film." At the time, the lack of a developed
South Korean feminist cinema encouraged feminist film theorists to critique films intended for female audiences, in a mode similar to that of
Mary Ann Doane's reading of 1940s Classical Hollywood women's cinema. She writes: "Because female identity in the cinema is constructed in
relation to object-hood rather than subject-hood, an investigation of the
contradictions resulting from an attempt to engage female subjectivity in a
textual process such as the 'woman's film' can be particularly productive."[7]

In 1993 South Korean feminist cultural workers made an attempt to
introduce Euro-American feminist film practices to South Korean audiences. Information and reviews of films by feminist filmmakers Chantal
Akerman, Helke Sander, Michelle Citron, and Sally Potter were dissemi-
nated in film magazines, public lectures, and books. In addition, the
women's video festival Riddles of the Sphinx screened Euro-American feminist avant-garde works. Within this context, *yŏsŏng* designated both films
that targeted a female audience, whatever their politics, and explicitly feminist films. Feminist film theory encouraged an active reading of the former
type of films as feminist. Thus, the linguistic use of *yŏsŏng* designates sexual difference but also oscillates between *yŏja* and feminist (no equivalent
term in Korean exists), indicating the negotiated space and moment onto
which the emerging feminism in the cultural arena was grafted.

The choice of *yŏsŏng* among many female-related identities appeared
less threatening not only to women of diverse positions but also to the

mainstream media. For instance, women's magazines and the newly installed culture and women sections in popular newspapers attempted to appeal to women readers, who emerged as powerful consumers, with a new identity such as *Missy.*[8] The outcome of the acceptance of the *yŏsŏng* identity was that contemporary locally produced films by Kim Yu-jin, Pak Ch'ŏl-su, and Yi Hyŏn-sŭng that focused on women were categorized as *yŏsŏng* films. In other words, critics were re-categorizing the *yŏja* film as the *yŏsŏng* film. Kim Yu-jin's *Only Because You Are a Woman* (*yŏja*) (*Tanji kŭdae ka yŏja ranŭn iyu manŭro,* 1990), which was praised as a break-through *yŏsŏng* film, is an example of this tendency. Similarly, Pak's films that explicitly employ *yŏja* in titles such as *Today's Yŏja* (*Onŭl yŏja,* 1989) and *Yŏja Who Walks on the Water* (*Murwi rŭl kŏnnŭn yŏja,* 1990) are particularly notable in terms of how they were re-categorized as *yŏsŏng* films.

During the historical moment in which feminist critics re-categorized the *yŏja* film as the *yŏsŏng* film a number of issue-oriented films and videos produced by the newly formed independent media scene surfaced. *Our Children* (*Urine aidŭl,* Paritŏ: Women Filmmakers Collective, 1990) took up the problem of daycare; *Even Little Grass Has Its Name* (*Chagŭn p'ul edo irŭm issŭni,* Paritŏ, 1990) focused on the labor union movement of women workers in late 1980s; and *Living in Asia as Women* (*Asia esŏ yŏsŏng ŭro sandanŭn kŏt,* P'urŭn Yŏngsang Collective, 1991) explored sex tourism. Even a brief look at the trajectory of the emergence of the *yŏsŏng* film in both the critical and filmmaking contexts of the early 1990s reveals the intersection of the legacy of Anglophone cine-feminism with the "woman's film" produced in both commercial and alternative contexts of the South Korean cinema. In light of the reservations about applying the term "feminist film" to describe South Korean films, I use the term "woman's film" to refer to films produced in both commercial and alternative production contexts. In the *Ch'ungmuro* or the commercial context, the "woman's film" refers to films marketed to and consumed by female audiences.[9] The "woman's film" in the alternative cinema refers to documentary and noncommercial films that are consciously oriented toward women's issues. As a consequence, the commercial film and the alternative film inhabit the same ground known as the "woman's film."

All the Women *Ch'ungmuro* Allows and Disallows: *Madame Freedom, The Widow,* and *The Maid*

As demonstrated by two films that take up the comfort women issue— *The Murmuring* (*Najŭn moksori,* 1993) and *Habitual Sadness* (*Najŭn moksori 2,* Pyŏn Yŏng-ju, 1997)—the *yŏsŏng* film in postcolonial South

Korea inevitably deals with the colonial past, which provides a matrix of unresolved anxiety that spills over into the present. However, between the commercially produced feature *The Widow* (1955) and the independently produced documentary *Habitual Sadness* (1997) lies a wide spectrum of films designed to draw a female audience that does not exactly overlap with the ideal audience constructed by feminist film critics in the 1990s.

"Tearjerkers" (*ch'oerusŏng*), or South Korean films produced between the mid-1950s and late 1960s that targeted female audiences, derisively termed "rubber shoes"[10] and "handkerchief army," can be considered the equivalent of what Anglo cine-feminism has called "the women's film."[11] Instead of the generic term "women," the terms noted above used metonymies to indicate the desired but simultaneously degraded female audiences. The group of female spectators that the film industry favored was *ajumma*,[12] wearing rubber shoes and armed with handkerchiefs. The melodramatic genre was considered an outlet for women to release their *han* (pent-up grief) over their experiences relating to repressive neo-Confucian patriarchy.

Bitter but Once Again provides a good example of this genre. It is not surprising that this maternal melodrama was subjected to heavy criticism in the mainstream press when it was released. It is unlikely that a film with an excessively sentimental tone and a narrative rife with coincidences that pivots on the fall of an innocent girl would qualify as an art or literary (*munye*) film. However, it is the film's emotional excess that attracts the attention of feminist film critics. *Bitter but Once Again* deals with an illicit love relationship between a girl and a married man. As a result of the relationship, the girl ends up as a single parent to a boy who she sends to his father when he reaches schooling age. Her suffering increases as she watches her son being ill treated by his father. Unlike the Hollywood feminist favorite, *Stella Dallas,* however, the female protagonist in *Bitter but Once Again* takes her child back. Although the film's sequel presented a *Stella Dallas* type of ending, the inflated valorization of the maternal in South Korean culture appears, at least in the first film, to dictate a different ending. Along with a detailed depiction of the female protagonist's suffering, the film succeeds in capturing the pain of her lover's wife who not only endures her husband's affair but also faces having to raise his illegitimate child. The film's pathos derives from inarticulate grievances and emotional blockages. As a maternal melodrama, it touches upon the social and emotional constitution of motherhood. One of the contradictions that haunts the female audience lies in the film-

190

maker's ambivalent treatment of the maternal. While the film severely condemns motherhood outside the family, it highly valorizes the emotional and ethical element of the maternal, in particular, the virtue of maternal sacrifice. The film demands female spectators (*ajumma*) to over-identify with the element of the maternal that is inscribed in both women characters. Simultaneously it elevates the spectators to a position where they can cast a condescending gaze on the leading woman characters.

Between the oscillation of these two spectatorial modes lies a gray area that aims to provoke tears, frustration, and anger from female spectators who are asked to derive meanings from the film according to their own experiences as women. This kind of film fully mobilizes the structure of female emotion to allow women viewers to recognize their own sense of entrapment. Unfortunately, however, the recognition does not always lead them to recognize and diagnose the underlying system of patriarchy. Instead, the film provides only a temporary release of "bitterness" and a momentary glimpse of the repressive system.

During the modernization of the 1960s, unmarried migrant female workers like the heroine of *Bitter but Once Again* moved from rural areas to Seoul—a social phenomenon that influenced the depictions of women in films of this period. As South Korea went through a rapid social transformation during the nascent industrialization in the 1960s, young rural girls became the most vulnerable and exploited group in the new urban society. Once they arrived in the city, they provided cheap labor in light industry as factory workers (*yŏgong*) or in upper-class homes as domestic helpers (*singmo*).[13] Two films that dealt with the *singmo* social type were *Singmo* (*The Housemaid*, Pak Ku, 1964) and *Three Singmo Sisters* (*Singmo samhyŏngje*, Kim Hwa-rang, 1969). In these films, unmarried female workers who are suspected of being working-class femme fatales pose dangerous threats to urban middle-class families. Their feminine sexuality combined with their working-class status place them in an abject position. This abjection allows the film to draw maximum emotional affect from the *ajumma* viewers. The success of the film *The Housemaid* (*Hanyŏ*, Kim Ki-yŏng, 1960) can be contextualized in this vein. The reception of the film by female audiences at the time was registered in their reactions to the scene in which the maid seduces her married male employer. It has been reported that female audiences responded to this scene by yelling, "Kill the bitch!"[14] The antagonism among women according to their class differences and marital status is quite strongly marked in this kind of spectatorship. *The Housemaid* (based on a real incident) displaces and disguises class conflicts within threatening feminine sexuality and discloses the anxiety of the newly formed urban middle class toward an emerging lower-class other.

The Housemaid opens with the leading male character (Kim Chin-gyu) reading a newspaper, and it closes with him directly addressing the viewer. In the middle, the film contains a disturbing story seemingly triggered and constructed by his imagination in response to a report he read in the newspaper. The housemaid, who dreams of being upwardly mobile, is presented as a monster within the middle-class family. She is a hybrid monster born out of the repression of feminine sexuality and the lack of opportunities for class mobility. Her uncontainable and dispersed identity is designed to disturb her employer's family and the audience as well. The incoherent development of the character in *The Housemaid*, an often-noted negative attribute of South Korean film, is productively mobilized to a greater extent in order to create a sense of fear and unpredictability.

Sin Sang-ok's *The Houseguest and My Mother (Sarangbang sonnim kwa ŏmŏni,* 1961) is another clear predecessor to *ajumma* films like *Bitter but Once Again.* The director, Sin Sang-ok, is known for his versatility in various kinds of genre films including action, horror, costume drama, and the musical, but he is best known for his melodramas. The overdose of sentiment that often related to *sinp'a* melodrama produced during the Japanese colonial period becomes less pronounced in Sin's melodramas. His subdued and sophisticated approach to melodramatic materials is well manifested in his 1958 film, *Hell Flower (Chiokhwa),* which stars Ch'oe Ŭn-hŭi (legendary actress and wife of Sin Sang-ok) as a "Western Princess" or military prostitute for the U.S. soldiers.[15] The female protagonist becomes involved in a love triangle with her smuggler lover and his brother. Elements of the action genre—a car chase scene, for example—are incorporated in this highly melodramatic narrative. The film reaches a climax when the smuggler kills his lover and himself when he discovers her betrayal, a recognizable element from the *sinp'a* mode. *Hell Flower* resonates with his *Evil Night (Agya,* 1952), which treats a similar subject set in the midst of the Korean War.

Sin Sang-ok's breakthrough film, *The Houseguest and My Mother* set in the 1920s, touches upon the delicate subject matter of widows in Korean society. In this film, a family of three generations of women—the widow (Ch'oe Ŭn-hŭi), her young daughter, and her mother-in-law, together with their maid (To Kŭm-bong) host the deceased husband's friend in their guestroom (*sarangbang*). A mutual attraction develops between the widow and her houseguest, who is a painter. The daughter's point of view is privileged through the use of the devices of the daughter's voice-over narration and shots of her drawings. The narrative takes place in a small city that although provincial is not totally untouched by the constituents of modernity. The church, the widow's piano, and the Western style of painting favored by the houseguest are all signs of modernity. The possibility of the young widow's remarriage also presents a sign of modernity. The final decision made by the widow, however, indicates the immobility imposed on her by the residual Confucian order that still holds influence over the former *yangban* (aristocratic) class. The congenial mode of a collective spirit depicted in the beginning of the film signified by the familiar sight of the neighbors clustered around the alleys quickly becomes claustrophobic when they gather by the riverside and gossip about the widow. The gossip and gazes of the neighbors are presented as a mode of surveillance that functions to safeguard Confucian norms. Although the film concludes with the widow withdrawing from the relationship, it remains critical of the constraints Confucianism places on women.

While *The Houseguest and My Mother* employs a subdued approach to the issue of a widow's remarriage, *The Widow* connects remarriage to other factors including economic independence, motherhood, and the sexuality of middle-aged women. In *The Houseguest and My Mother,* the relationship between the mother and the guest is presented only to be disrupted by the Confucian ideology. *The Widow,* however, reveals the ways in which the leading character seeks the possibility of a second marriage explicitly out of economic, sexual, and maternal necessities. Three male characters who each meet one of the widow's requirements are presented in a schematic way: one offers money, the other offers romance, and another offers paternal care for her daughter. When the widow realizes that her relationships with all three men have problems, she begins to see the obstacles imposed upon a middle-aged widow, a *mimangin* (literally, a person who could not follow her husband to death). Her new self-awareness persuades her to find a more independent way of living without depending on male support. The ending, although missing from the currently available print, is said to capture her determination to start a new life with her daughter. Despite its realistic representation of the status of a war widow, this low-budget independent film did not reach a large audience.

Madame Freedom, a huge box-office hit in 1956, was based on a serial novel in a major newspaper and caused a controversy with its scandalous representation of a professor's wife. From the perspective of the

South Korean film industry, it also played a crucial role in constructing a platform for South Korean cinema. In this respect, we could say that the postcolonial and postwar cinema declared its birth with the discursive construction of a dangerous woman in the form of *Madame Freedom*. Since then films with the same title have been re-made—in 1969, 1981, and 1990—although none of the re-makes broke the box-office records of the original film. In the film, the leading female character, the wife of a well-respected professor, works downtown as the manager of a boutique called Paris. Exposed to the smuggled commodities on display, she gradually transforms into a consumer of Western goods and engages in an affair with her employer.

Madame Freedom's focus on the female character's promiscuity articulates the notion of freedom implicit in Americanization as sexual liberation. When the film was first shown, the kiss scene between the female protagonist and her illicit partner caused a great deal of controversy, which led to the censorship of the film. This expression of feminine sexuality, that of a married, middle-class woman in particular, was severely condemned at the time. In striking contrast with the widow character in *The Houseguest and My Mother*, the wife and mother character in *Madame Freedom* momentarily enjoys freedom outside the home. American modernity under the signifiers of consumerism and sexual freedom slips into the film to converge on the Madame Freedom figure. As discussed before, postcolonial South Korean cinema, in its attempt to confront modernity, has heavily focused on the representation of modern women. In this representation, the elaboration of feminine sexuality is figured as simultaneously dangerous and desirable. Madame Freedom becomes an object of desire, and subsequently of punishment, only when she masquerades in a Western-style costume.

Unlike contemporaneous films such as *The Stray Bullet* (*Obalt'an*, Yu Hyŏn-mok, 1961), *Barefoot Youth* (*Maenbal ŭi ŏch'ŏngch'un*, Kim Ki-dŏk, 1964) and *The Coachman* (*Mabu*, Kang Tae-jin) that investigate the anxiety of the marginalized urban male, *Madame Freedom* focuses on a middle-class female character. Once she obtains a disposable income, Madame Freedom adopts a sexual and consumerist identity. The narrative marks her as both a salesperson and a consumer who is well versed in the names of Western goods. Her changed perspective regarding her husband and her home reveals the shift brought by American modernization in both private and public spheres. Her presence in the public sphere is left ambiguous. On the one hand, her new identity is related to the notion of illegality (a salesperson dealing with smuggled goods) and sexual promiscuity. On the other hand, the display of her tailored suit and free-floating lifestyle also provokes a longing for a consumerist lifestyle on the part of female spectators. The protagonist pays dearly for her "freedom" at the film's conclusion. Her business partner catches Madame Freedom in an erotic embrace with her husband and slaps her. Deeply shamed, Madame Freedom runs home, only to find herself rejected at the threshold of her home by her husband. Despite the imploring cries of her son on her behalf, her husband abandons her at the threshold. The mise-en-scène of the ending indicates the precarious position of women during the period. In comparison with her husband's conventional clothes that suit the traditional-style house, her Western dress clearly signifies her nonbelonging. After tasting a bit of consumer culture, the protagonist faces her final condemnation and punishment. In a society where consumer culture is pervasive, the female as consumer is an identity often glamorized and idealized. However, *Madame Freedom,* set in impoverished, war-stricken South Korea, associates the female consumer with decadence in spite of inevitable fetishism thereof.[16] The film thus exhibits an imagined realm of commodity desire that exists in stark contrast to any possibilities for its realization or fulfillment.

As noted above, the tension exhibited in Golden Age films between representations of a generic woman and culturally specific significations that emphasized differences among women were manifested in class-marked narrative frictions and divisions among them. However, these tensions were most dramatically realized within another relationship. The recurrent subject positions of leading female characters—fallen housewife, widow, and maid—created a striking contrast with the married women (*ajumma*) of the target audience.

Woman Filmmaker and Comfort Women

The colonial past under the Japanese occupation is the most under-represented subject in postcolonial South Korean cinema. Evading the layers of modernity the Japanese colonial force introduced, South Korean cinema has focused on the precolonial past and the postcolonial present. Rather than confronting the legacy of Japanese colonialism, South Korean cinema instead offers scenes of underdeveloped or inadequate American modernity such as It'aewŏn, the U.S. military base and surroundings, or representations of the forlorn countryside that escaped the attention of state-governed modernization. Decolonization is displaced by nationalistic narratives, which feature "Korean hyper-masculinity and vigilance about female chastity."[17] The absence of representations of the legacies of

195

Japanese colonization can be attributed to the perception within the South Korean cinema industry that this subject is not marketable. Further, the South Korean military government's complicity with Japan contributed to the silencing of the comfort women issue, one of the most painful legacies of Japanese colonization. Therefore it is not surprising that the comfort women issue had not been represented on screen from a woman's perspective until 1991 when three former comfort women came forward to speak of their experiences in public. In spite of the political silence, the subjects of feminine sexuality and women's bodies in postcolonial South Korea have been associated with the repressed shame attached to comfort women, which in turn demanded a reconstruction of the nationalistic narrative. As You-Me Park poignantly states:

> I do not remember the exact plot. It was one of the numerous stories in Korea in the 1970s that used the metaphor of women's bodies being violated and raped to narrate the story of Japanese occupation and the U.S. presence after the Korean War. Korea as a nation was compared to a virginal body that was trampled upon and violated by aggressive outsiders. Again and again, these (almost exclusively male-authored) texts deplored the lost virginity and the shame inflicted upon their mother country by foreign forces.[18]

In addition to this kind of literary imagination, the history of comfort women was appropriated either as a backdrop of gang-rape fantasies in sex-exploitation films or as leverage to promote a nationalistic rescue fantasy in television documentary. Indeed, these two kinds of representational practices fluctuate between over-sexualization and de-sexualization of comfort women. Pyŏn Yŏng-ju, a feminist independent filmmaker, made an alternative approach to comfort women possible. Pyŏn launched her filmmaking career in the late 1980s when the independent film movement finally joined the populist *minjung* movement. The trajectory of her filmmaking is quite revealing. Pyŏn's first documentary *Living as Women in Asia* traced sex tourism from the Cheju Island in South Korea to Thailand. During production, a sex worker for Japanese tourists in Cheju Island confessed that her mother was a comfort woman. This resulted in the production of the films *The Murmuring* and its sequel *Habitual Sadness*.

Unlike the *Ch'ungmuro* "woman's film" that tends to bypass the shared history of women, *The Murmuring* and *Habitual Sadness* recognize that the postcolonial genealogy of womanhood stemmed from a colonial history that has not been reconciled or incorporated historically. The two films disclose how the present notion of feminine sexuality is deeply entangled with the comfort women as if it were a tacit historical transference. As such, the comfort women provide a way in which an identity known as woman can be historicized during the postcolonial period. When the comfort women speak in *The Murmuring*, shattering fifty years of silence, the female spectator is invited to partake in their grief and also to understand her own involvement in this history. The film-maker explicitly declared that her films were made to address female spectators who in turn responded to the films with enthusiasm. Many of them left their words of support on the board after the screening. Some of them related their own experiences of sexual violence to that of the comfort women's.

The re-vision of women's bodies is most clearly present in the final scene of *The Murmuring* when the camera dwells on a naked body of one of the comfort women who was forced to remain in China after having been released from the "Blood-Sucking House (the comfort women station)." The camera gently reveals her sapped and wrinkled body that seems to ridicule the inadequacy of Japanese monetary reparation. In general, *The Murmuring* is quite removed from the emasculated narrative of nationalism, which has subjugated the comfort women to the fossilized realm of nationalist tropes. In fact, this new *yŏsŏng* film is a collaborative product of the women's movement (in particular with the Korean Council for the Women Drafted for Military Sexual Slavery by Japan) and the independent film movement.

Whereas *The Murmuring* depends on a confessional mode of utterance to process overdue mourning through the film, *Habitual Sadness* mobilizes songs and jokes as vehicles to articulate the comfort women's long-repressed desires and needs. *Habitual Sadness* focuses on a group of comfort women who live together in a shelter (*Nanum ŭi chip*, The Sharing House) at the outskirts of Seoul. Growing vegetables on a small farm and sharing everyday life, these women slowly move in the direction of self-healing by exchanging their painful memories. The fact that the making of *Habitual Sadness* was actually requested by one of the former comfort women also indicates the move toward healing. After having been diagnosed with terminal cancer, Kang Tŏk-kyŏng asked Pyŏn to film her while she was alive. The other members of the Sharing House also agreed to participate. Instead of remaining passive informants, they actively involved themselves in the filming process. Kim Sun-dŏk wants to be remembered as a hard-working person and requests that the director film her working in the pumpkin patch. Sim Mi-ja and Yun Tu-ri take this occasion to reveal their wishes. Pak Tu-ri, who was reluctant to be filmed in *The Murmuring,* directs jokes and songs to the film crew. Since it was initially Kang Tŏk-kyŏng who asked Pyŏn to film her and her friends, the members of the Sharing House articulate their own experience voluntarily instead of remaining passive victims caught between exploitive nationalistic tropes and inadequate Japanese economic reparation.

Although the two films failed to reach a large audience, the discursive effect they created was far from negligible. The films toured college campuses across the nation and the story of the films and the filmmaker were covered by the mass media, including the major newspapers, television, and women's magazines. For women, the two films served to inscribe the issues of sexual violence in the popular consciousness. In addition, the filmmaker put her efforts toward linking the case of the comfort women to the ever-increasing sexual violence in the present. In the very last scene in *Habitual Sadness,* Pyŏn compares the statistics of contemporary rape cases with those of the comfort women. Although it is uncertain if the filmmaker's last-minute attempt to make a connection is effective and persuasive, it clearly points out the historical burden imposed on today's women. In many ways, *The Murmuring* and *Habitual Sadness* distinguish themselves from the preceding *Ch'ungmuro* "woman's film" not only in terms of their mode of production, distribution, and exhibition but also in their approaches to women as historical subjects.

Ch'ungmuro yŏsŏng films have provided a limited scope on women's roles as wives, widows, or maids—that is, of women positioned only in relation to their male counterparts or masters. In contrast, *The Murmuring* and *Habitual Sadness* focus on women's collective life and their discontentment with a history that remains to be reconciled. The exceptional and simultaneously marginal status of these two films in both *Ch'ungmuro* and the independent film contexts demonstrates that the *yŏsŏng* film has yet to tell narratives about women's experiences outside of the problematic representations of the maid, widow, or Madame Freedom.

Notes

1. In *The Gender of Modernity* (Cambridge: Harvard University Press, 1955), Rita Felski re-traces the trajectory of modern "through the lens of feminist theory." On one hand, she criticizes the male-centeredness implicated in the

notion of modernity in Marshall Benjamin's influential book, *All That Is Solid Melts into Air.* On the other hand, she mobilizes works that have already problematized the phallocentric theorization of modernity by Elizabeth Wilson, Christine Buci-Glucksmann, Rachel Bowlby, Nancy Armstrong, Andreas Huyssen, and Patrice Petro, for example. I use the expression of gendered modernity in order to give particular attention to the gender politics operating both in the theory of modernity and the formation thereof.

2. Supervisors routinely raped young female workers in order to intimidate them so they would not leave for other factories and sex industries. As the sex industry prospered in the 1970s, it was not uncommon for female workers to prefer it to factory work, because they could make more money and avoid intense labor. Female factory workers and sex workers were largely rural immigrants who sent most of their earnings back to the countryside to support their family. Under these circumstances the chastity ideology was reinforced in order to stop the female workers from shifting to the sex industry. This ideology was particularly apparent in the hostess genre film, which centered on a room salon hostess (or bar girl). The hostess film narrates and visualizes the tribulations of a female factory worker-turned-hostess who committed suicide toward the end of the film. While the real cause of the female protagonist's shift to the sex industry lies in financial need, the hostess film displaces it with her sexual desire.

3. In 1973, Claudia von Aleman organized the first Women's Film Festival in Berlin.

4. Claudia von Aleman expressed a similar view, replacing American film feminism with the West German variant.

5. I thank Chris Berry for suggesting Tani Barlow's article, "Theorizing Woman," in *Body, Subject, and Power in China,* ed. Angela Zito and Tani Barlow (Chicago: University of Chicago Press, 1994), when I pointed out the problem of translating the word "she" into Korean. I was also greatly indebted to his keen insight and suggestions on South Korean cinema in relation to gender and sexuality while we jointly taught a class on the issues at South Korean National University of Arts during the fall semester of 1997.

6. For instance, *yŏja* is often used to refer to situations in which a woman is suspected of violating the patriarchal codes of conduct.

7. Mary Ann Doane, "The Woman's Film," in *Re-Vision: Essays in Feminist Film Criticism,* ed. Mary Ann Doane, Patricia Mellencamp, and Linda Williams (Los Angeles: AFI, 1984), 69.

8. One department store coined the term *Missy* to lure housewives in their twenties and thirties, who surfaced as new consumers in the 1990s, into the store.

9. *Ch'ungmuro* is the name of the South Korean Film Industry. Analogous to the term Hollywood, it comes from the name of a district in downtown Seoul where film companies are located.

10. Rubber shoes, a form of inexpensive footwear, is a signifier of working-class or common women.

11. In Anglophone cine-feminism, the term "woman's film" refers to films produced from the 1930s to the 1950s starring a female heroine, often adapted

from women's literature and made for and consumed by a female audience. Typically the "woman's film" focused on women's issues, such as domesticity and motherhood.

12. A derogatory term for married women.

13. The modern term *singmo* replaced *hanyŏ,* the feudal term for female servant.

14. An interview with Kim Ki-yŏng by Kim Soyoung for the *PIFF Daily News,* The 2nd Pusan International Film Festival, October 13, 1997.

15. In relation to the issue of women's bodies and U.S. neocolonial domination, see Chungmoo Choi, "Nationalism and Construction of Gender in Korea," in *Dangerous Women: Gender and Korean Nationalism,* ed. Elaine H. Kim and Chungmoo Choi (New York: Routledge, 1998), 9–33.

16. In South Korea of this period, goods were hard to find even in department store display windows. In this context, the film screen might have served as a window to Western commodities.

17. Kim and Choi, eds., *Dangerous Women,* 4.

18. You-Me Park, "Against Metaphor: Gender, Violence, and Decolonization in Korean Nationalist Literature," in *In Pursuit of Contemporary East Asian Culture,* ed. Xiaobing Tang and Stephen Snyder (Boulder, CO: Westview Press, 1996), 34.

8

Lethal Work: Domestic Space and Gender Troubles in *Happy End* and *The Housemaid*

KYUNG HYUN KIM

Toward the end of *Happy End* (*Haep'i endŭ*, Chŏng Chi-u, 1999), Min-gi, the male protagonist, is seen riding on a train. Wearing a black suit and a tie, he is traveling to Taegu, a city about 150 miles away from Seoul, where the funeral of one of his former schoolteachers is being held. He nervously smokes in the moving train, his hands trembling. It is not the death of his teacher that is making him shake, but the death of Po-ra, his wife, whom he has just killed. Before departing Seoul, he had executed the meticulously planned murder, a bloody scene where he stabbed Po-ra repeatedly with a long jagged knife. He has an alibi because he was taken to the train station by his friend, and made sure he was seen on a train that departed earlier that day. He has also left no evidence, having carefully removed his fingerprints, the murder weapon and his blood-stained clothes from the scene. Leaving traces of Po-ra's blood in another apartment, he has instead framed Il-bŏm, Po-ra's secret lover. Min-gi, after having his cigarette, takes his seat and begins to toy with an elastic band. Across from him sits a young boy who curiously watches Min-gi's game, the band constantly twisting and evolving into different shapes. The boy's puzzled and naive expression offers Min-gi a moment of relief, and he smiles for the first time in the sequence.

It is here that any spectator who is knowledgeable of South Korean film history feels an eerie sense of familiarity and intimacy. The train, the funeral, the guilty man, the adulterous affair, the violent murder and, topping it all, the twisting and twirling elastic band evoke the memory of a legendary South Korean film, *The Housemaid* (*Hanyŏ*, Kim Ki-yŏng, 1960), that features a man, Tong-sik, whose affair with his maid ends up killing them both. The pumping engine and the blowing whistle of a train are vivid sights and sounds in *The Housemaid* when Tong-sik, the guilt-stricken protagonist, departs to attend a funeral to mourn the death of a

201

woman whose suicide he had indirectly caused.[1] The elastic band also recalls *The Housemaid*'s opening where the two children play "cat's cradle" with a cotton ball, taking turns to string different shapes. The film then turns to a textile factory where the real narrative unfolds.

Happy End's prominent cinematic references to *The Housemaid* are significant on many grounds. First, they signal the arrival of a new generation of South Korean filmmakers who are profoundly influenced by their national cinema, anchoring a historical continuity between the Golden Age of South Korean cinema of the 1960s to early 1970s, and the present-day renaissance of South Korean cinema.[2] South Korean cinema has only recently come out of its slump, after enduring the embarrassing period of the 1970s and 1980s in which government propaganda, B-grade quota quickies, and quasi-porn flicks were quickly churned out. Forgotten by the public at this time was the glorious and glamorous heyday of cinema in the 1960s, when even the most trivial activities of movie stars were closely monitored, national pathos was popularly expressed, and the cinema earned the respect of artists working in other mediums. *Happy End* amply demonstrates how South Korea's Golden Age has inspired the popular and artistic cinema thriving today. First, in the contemporary period, global impulses have forced the local cinema to compete with Hollywood and art-house films of the West, in part the result of the elimination of import quota restrictions during the 1980s.[3]

Second, the themes that thread through the two films allow us to reflect upon the transformative figurations of gender and family within each distinct historical period. In other words, the tropes of domesticity, masculinity, and motherhood are similarly juxtaposed against the severe financial and social crises that formed the backdrop for each film. *The Housemaid* was made in 1960, a chaotic year that brought down the corrupt Syngman Rhee [Yi Sŭng-man] regime only to have the subsequent democratic government overthrown by Park Chung Hee's [Pak Chŏng-hŭi] coup d'état a year later. Thirty-nine years later, *Happy End* was made in the midst of the catastrophic national bankruptcy of the late 1990s that required an IMF bailout of the South Korean economy. In this essay, I pay close attention to the domestic spaces of these two films to closely monitor representations of gender within them. I propose that both films re-conceptualize the question of gender, unconsciously or consciously constructing filmic tensions by tactically reassigning the sociosexual division of domestic space. The social uncertainties in the public realm inform the films' restructuring of gender, which displaces social anxiety onto the bourgeois family and its fragility. Both films intriguingly envision masculinity as vulnerable and repressed, thereby (falsely) invoking the need to awaken its violent nature. The intensity of each film's plot derives from the man's inability to maneuver the separate demands of public and private spheres. The pressure to master the new working environment and the familial responsibilities of newborn children leads the male protagonist to destroy his female partner, who is misidentified as the root of the man's problem.

I am most interested in how gender becomes the flashpoint for the staggering social changes that take place in South Korea over the span of the four decades between these two films. Much has changed as the society has moved from a poverty-stricken, postwar economy to a postmodern center of hi-tech industry where 15.3 million people (out of a population of 45 million) have an Internet connection at home.[4] There is no question that South Korea has economically caught up with even the First World, but whether this frenzied drive has significantly changed gender roles is an issue that cannot be answered easily. Although gender relations provide a focal point for the trauma of change in cultural texts, the most remarkable insight that emerges from comparing these two films, released at either end of these transformational decades, is actually *not* the changes that take place in terms of the gender representation, but *their fixity.*

South Korean society is one in which the economic structure rests on sexist principles. These are evidenced by statistics that consistently gauge the percentage of women in the upper echelon of public and corporate sectors as among the lowest in any industrialized or industrializing nation. In such a culture, bias dictates that only men can be agents of change. Yet the significant stresses placed on South Korean men by dramatic changes in ideology, ethics, and lifestyle has led to men's demands for more attention at home and a greater surveillance on women's proper domestic role. Thus, the pace of change has exaggerated gender inequities and led to a masculine policing of the home. We can perhaps begin to make sense of the connection between gender conservatism in media and radical social change by looking at other considerations of gender arrangements in the twentieth century in societies undergoing intense modernization. Lynn Spigel, in her book about the role of television in shifting domestic gender relations during 1950s America, writes, "faced with their shrinking authority in the new corporate world of white-collar jobs, the middle-class men of the early 1900s turned inward to the home where their increased participation in and control over the family served to compensate for feelings of powerlessness in the public sphere."[5] A similar ethos informs the representation of masculinity in *The Housemaid* and *Happy End*.

What also binds the two films is their assembly of desire, illicit love, and murder. Interestingly, extramarital affairs were a popular topic not only recently but also during the Golden Age of South Korean cinema. Some of the most controversial films in the history of South Korean cinema—including Kim Ki-yŏng's *The Housemaid*—have challenged the ethical conventions of the period by focusing on the tension between faithfulness and desire, and between conformity and passion. In the often-discussed film *Madame Freedom* (*Chayu puin,* Han Hyŏng-mo, 1956), a professor's wife changes from a modest mother to a promiscuous businesswoman, making her a scandalous representation of an otherwise ordinary middle-class housewife.[6] As South Korean feminist film critic Soyoung Kim [Kim So-yŏng] has argued, Madame Freedom's sexual identity is inseparable from the increasingly consumerist culture. Her new disposable income, which she earns independently of her husband's control, gives her access to a consumerist freedom and sexual desire pursued outside the domain of her home.[7] Although the productions of *The Housemaid* and *Happy End* are thirty-nine years apart, in each film the women's pursuit of work outside the home seriously threatens domestic life within it and is deemed as sufficient cause for punishment. The representations of working women are surely unpropitious; not only do they leave their domestic duties unattended, they also eventually end up involved with men other than their husbands.

South Korean society's economic need for women to be active in the workforce conflicted with social biases that condemned women's active agency in the public sphere during the early stage of industrialization. The angst generated by clashes between women's desire for social agency and conservative social mores, though still persistent, has been refigured in more recent images of promiscuous women and extramarital affairs that better correspond to a more recent phase of South Korea's anxiety during another economic phase: de-industrialization.[8] What marks off recent films such as *The Day a Pig Fell into the Well* (*Twaeji ka umul e ppajin nal,* Hong Sang-su, 1996), *No. 3* (*Nŏmbŏ 3,* Song Nŭng-han, 1997), and *An Affair* (*Chŏngsa,* Yi Chae-yong, 1998) from those in the 1950s and 1960s that dealt with extramarital affairs, is what motivates these affairs in the contemporary films—anomie or boredom are the dominant reasons for adultery. No longer do the narratives suggest that illicit sex is caused solely by women's public work. If it was the desire for social mobility that led to the hiring of the seductive maid in *The House-*

maid, and the desire to experience new Western consumerist culture that captured the curiosity of the professor's wife in *Madame Freedom*, now middle-class conformity and anomie push characters like Po-gyŏng in *The Day a Pig Fell into the Well* and So-hyŏn in *An Affair*, two housewives, onto the path of adultery.

The recent proliferation of extramarital affairs on screen prompts a very simple question that begets a not-so-simple response: Why aren't these women asking for divorces? Wouldn't Po-gyŏng in *The Day a Pig Fell into the Well*, a housewife who falls in love with a writer, or Po-ra in *Happy End* be better off with their lovers than their dreary husbands? Both characters do not truly indulge in "cheap thrills," nor are they severely bound by the obligations of motherhood. (Po-gyŏng's only child is presumably dead and Il-bŏm is willing to adopt Po-ra's child.) Yet, they are unable to leave their husbands, leaving themselves susceptible to vengeance and murder. The difficulty these women have leaving their husbands, even though their marriages are clearly failures, illustrates that the family in South Korea today is both a very resilient and very repressive institution, despite rising divorce figures every year. Many popular images of middle-class women having affairs effectively demonize women's desires to escape from the obligations of family, maternity, and housekeeping. The society's reluctance to completely embrace a break from orthodox perspectives on marriages leaves many of these characters dangling between tradition and modernity. This occurs even though South Korea has entered a condition of postmodernity, in which such tensions putatively had been resolved many decades earlier.

Could This Be a Happy End?

Made during the height of the 1998–99 financial crisis that destroyed South Korea's miraculous postwar industrialization drive, *Happy End* features a married couple in their thirties, Min-gi and Po-ra, and their baby daughter, Sŏ-yŏn, born around the time when South Korea signed the humiliating IMF Loan Treaty (December 3, 1997).[9] The resulting massive layoffs, which caused the unemployment rate to jump dramatically from 2.3 to 8.2 in a period of less than a year, have severely disrupted this family. Min-gi, a former bank employee, is jobless and spends his days reading in bookstores and parks.[10] He is also the primary childcare giver, as well as the principal domestic worker in his home; he picks up Sŏ-yŏn from the daycare center, feeds her, cooks, vacuums the house, does laundry, and cleans the car. Despite the fact that he is out of a job and employment prospects are not auspicious given an economy that is radically downsizing, his middle-class life is well sustained because Po-ra is a successful businesswoman. She runs a popular, modern after-school English institution for little children. South Korea's struggle against the global tide of recession has not discouraged it from opening up further to the West; on the contrary, the desire to learn from the West is clearly manifested by the crowded classroom at Po-ra's institution that employs American teachers. Po-ra and Min-gi are able to keep their spacious apartment, drive their sedan, and occasionally dine out because Po-ra provides opportunities for economically privileged children to "learn English as if it's their first language."

Po-ra's success reverses the conventional gender roles and power dynamics such that she, now the breadwinner, does not feel guilty for demanding that Min-gi become much more active in childcare and housework. Moreover, while Min-gi retreats to his sofa at night to watch television soaps and to the park bench during the day to read pulp fiction novels, Po-ra is publicly visible, referred to as the "President" by her clients and staff. These troubled gender arrangements endanger their marriage, a danger both signaled and compounded by Po-ra's extramarital affair with her former college classmate, Il-bŏm. The obsessive and mad nature of this lustful relationship cannot be safely contained in Il-bŏm's small apartment. Il-bŏm visits her in the office, takes her out to the beach, and even loiters around Po-ra and Min-gi's apartment, pressuring Po-ra to move in with him. Po-ra enjoys the pleasures and thrills offered by illicit sex, but she is unwilling to leave the security provided by her marriage and the family. Although she is financially independent, Po-ra, ambitious and driven, cannot risk the stigma that permanently compromises a divorced woman's reputation.

Min-gi grows suspicious of Po-ra's late return from work, the excessive mileage on the car, and an unidentified key he finds underneath the car carpet. Suspecting Il-bŏm, to whom he was once introduced, Min-gi waits for him to leave his home and, using the key, enters his apartment. There, Min-gi finds pictures of his wife, half-naked. Although initially so shaken that he is unable to confront Po-ra, Min-gi finally decides to kill her when he finds out that she has put their daughter's life at risk by feeding her a sleeping pill and leaving her unattended in order to meet Il-bŏm. Thus, Po-ra has failed to not only be a "good wife and housewife" but most importantly "a good mother," and it is the latter failure that drives Min-gi to murder. Significantly, the film visually conveys Po-ra's failure, her evil, by what she feeds her child. Good mothering is often precisely signified through themes and motifs of eating and food.[11] By feeding her child a toxic substance that threatens its life, Po-ra completely transgresses her maternal function in the most fundamental way, thereby committing an unforgivable sin. In this way, the film equates Po-ra's poisoning her child with her prioritizing sexuality over maternity, thereby utterly condemning the latter. The film condemnation of Po-ra rests in its conviction that "women's mothering . . . [is] a natural fact."[12]

After saving the baby in an emergency room and accidentally witnessing Po-ra in a heated moment with her lover (without them even recognizing him), Min-gi plots to kill Po-ra. Having first established an alibi to leave for the funeral in Taegu, he stays in Seoul and breaks into his own apartment. He holds Po-ra's body down on the same bed where they sleep together every night. Red blood spots soon become a smudge, and before too long Po-ra's white shirt is drenched in blood. As Min-gi repeatedly stabs her, her shudders and her muted cries for help cease. The only person in the house who is in a position to help her is unfortunately the very person delivering the fatal blows. If Min-gi had failed to sexually impress Po-ra (as instanced by an earlier sex scene between them where she blankly stared at the ceiling without a blink of her eye), he surely has her attention now by entering their bedroom as a criminal, ready to strike her. Without saying a word, Min-gi dials Il-bŏm's cell phone so that he can hear Po-ra's desperate moans. Il-bŏm rushes to the apartment where he finds her dead, thus falling into Min-gi's trap by leaving his fingerprints all over the scene of the crime. Po-ra's extramarital affair, the cause of the familial tension, is now over, but it required her death to put it to an end. Unlike *The Eel* (*Unagi*, Shohei Imamura, 1998) where the murder of the adulterous wife is spontaneously performed in the middle of an actual intercourse between her and her lover, Min-gi's murder is premeditated and meticulously planned so that Il-bŏm will be arrested and executed in his place. The unfaithful wife and the jealous lover will both die, leaving only the murderous husband alive. In the last shot of the film, however, Min-gi wakes up from a nap in his living room, leaving us in doubt about whether the murder truly occurred or not.

Thou Shall Not Cheat on *The Housemaid*

The same question was posed at the end of the film made thirty-nine years earlier: *The Housemaid,* as is well known, also frames an extramarital affair and consequent murder in the fantastic structure of a dream. This film, directed by Kim Ki-yŏng, catapulted the director to global arthouse stardom when it was rediscovered in the late 1990s.[13] After the film was showcased in a retrospective at the 1997 Pusan International Film

Festival, it—along with several other Kim Ki-yŏng films—was immediately screened at the Berlin, London, Belgrade, San Francisco, and Hong Kong film festivals, among others. An elaborate Web site has been created in tribute called "The House of Kim Ki-young."[14] More retrospectives are being planned, especially since his sudden death in 1998. Kim was an exceptional filmmaker, making hybrid genre films well before they became fashionable not only in South Korea but also in global cinema. If the national cinema aesthetics of South Korea are characterized by the thematic motifs of *han* (pent-up grief), mise-en-scènes of rural mountainous landscapes and understated emotions evident in the works of Sin Sang-ok and Im Kwŏn-t'aek, Kim Ki-yŏng is a filmmaker who falls completely outside this framework.[15] Instead of sublimating *han,* his characters plot revenge; instead of featuring mountainous rural landscapes and thatched roofs, his films display overpopulated asphalt boardwalks, neon lights, and Western mansions; and instead of understated emotions, he prefers stylistic excesses.[16] Freely mixing absurd fantasy with bizarre plots and exaggerated sexuality and violence, his films—including *Insect Woman* (*Ch'ungnyŏ,* 1972) and *Killer Butterfly* (*Sarin nabi rŭl tchonnŭn yŏja,* 1978)—act out the psychological angst and anxiety behind the nation's rapid pace of industrialization. Central to this paranoid pathos and grotesque visual style are the unconventional and absurdist props such as dead rats and out-of-control rice-cake poppers that whet the sexual appetites of his characters.

Compared to the cinematic excesses of his films from the 1970s, the earlier *The Housemaid* shows both stylistic and narrative restraints. Yet Kim's proclivity to belie narrative expectations and conventions are already well at work in this film. The film presents a crisis—a staple in family melodrama—provoked when a housemaid is employed in a middle-class home. The maid is hired to help manage domestic affairs after the woman of the house falls ill from overwork. Pregnant, she has been taking in sewing to augment the family's meager income. With her earnings, the family has acquired a new two-story Western-style house that now is simply too big for the ailing *patrona* to maintain. But, Myŏng-ja, the maid, soon turns out to be a wicked nightmare for the family.[17] Her sexual seduction and nagging of the father, Tong-sik, distract him from his employment: teaching music to young female factory workers.

Despite the casting of a maid as the central character whose psychological complications add depth to the story, *The Housemaid* is undoubtedly a masculine drama where the film's crisis revolves around Tong-sik's failure as a teacher in the public sphere and as a husband in the private one. In the film's beginning, Tong-sik suffers from a guilt complex after one of his students in his choral class commits suicide. The student was suspended from work after he exposed to his authorities her naive love letter to him. Following the student's funeral, the maid manipulates Tong-sik's guilt and seduces him. Already feeling responsible for the death of his student, Tong-sik cannot possibly refuse this other woman's pass at him.

Their subsequent and bizarre sex transforms the maid from a helping hand to a dangerous threat, who must be eliminated in order for familial stability to be restored. Yet matters are not so easily resolved, especially since Myŏng-ja is now pregnant with Tong-sik's child. Tong-sik is psychologically torn, and his downfall is soon tellingly signaled by a taxicab ride. Attempting to run away, Tong-sik hails a cab and tells the driver to go "anywhere very fast. Let's run away from the earth or crash into something." Thus, Tong-sik is like Ch'ŏr-ho in *The Stray Bullet* (*Obalt'an,* Yu Hyŏn-mok, 1960), the film voted by the critics as the best South Korean film of the last century that ends with the protagonist, half-conscious, riding through Seoul in a taxicab.[18] If Ch'ŏr-ho in Yu Hyŏn-mok's film was sedated by anesthetics given to him by a dentist, here Tong-sik drinks a bottle of gin to forget his troubles. The display of fearlessness and dynamism in this scene suggests a potential for masculine rejuvenation, but it also points to that rejuvenation as a "self-deluded state."[19] A drunk Tong-sik aimlessly swaggering to a taxicab that then lumbers through the neon lights in Seoul captures the very contradiction of masculinity that can only be asserted in a delusional or fantasy state.

Unfortunately, Tong-sik cannot hide from his domestic troubles, cannot forever remain drunk. He ignores the advice offered to him by a friend and ends up telling his pregnant wife that he has committed adultery with the maid. Surprising her even more, Tong-sik tells her that Myŏng-ja, too, is pregnant with his child. The once happy family—instanced by earlier scenes of a meal prepared by the father and the delivery of the television set that prompted the small son, Ch'ang-sun, to declare that they are the richest family in the neighborhood—now faces total collapse. Tong-sik's wife will not tolerate the scandalous births of two children in same house, and persuades the maid to abort her child. Opting for the most primitive and violent method, Myŏng-ja reluctantly throws her body down the staircase.

After the doctor's confirmation of the maid's abortion and the wife's safe delivery of her baby, this albeit excessive family melodrama becomes a horror film where the crazed maid takes revenge upon the family. She literally invades the married couple's bedroom, and demands that Tong-sik sleep with her in order to make up for the grief she has suffered. She protests, "Why did you kill only my child? Where is justice when one woman can keep her child while the other woman has to get rid of hers? Do you think my body is a toy for others? Since the two babies are fathered by the same man, they either live together or die together." As Tong-sik and his wife watch in horror, the maid then picks up the newborn and fakes throwing it on the ground.

Although the maid's rage is not completely incomprehensible, the film's slippage from melodrama to horror plot evidences a decidedly masculinist bias, one that renders the maid a monster while totally excusing Tong-sik of all responsibility for the calamity he has brought on his family. This bias raises interesting questions in terms of audience identification. Soyoung Kim reports that when the film was first released in 1960, female audience members reportedly responded to the seduction scene by screaming, "Kill the bitch!"[20] Suffering economic deprivation at this historical moment and therefore presumably more socially aligned with the maid rather than the bourgeois couple living in a two-story mansion, female spectators nevertheless identified and sympathized with the husband rather than the maid who, rationally speaking, had very good reason to be angry with Tong-sik. But the female spectators' display of anger locates a certain potential for rupture that transgresses the boundary of normalized identification with the abject subjects (the husband, the wife) onscreen. Confronted by the maid who refuses to remain a victim of circumstances, female audiences perhaps manage an unconscious over-identification with this woman who, acting on her own interests, plays out many of their own desires and fantasies. In other words, the "bitch" that they were so enraged about pointed to none other than their own desires to break out of and freely transgress a masculinist social structure very repressive to women.

As the plot turns, the piano that had previously produced harmonic choral music begins to produce dissonant sounds at night. Myŏng-ja's untutored fingers randomly strike the piano keys, awakening the family with its unbearably disruptive, yet eerily familiar sound to those audience members accustomed to the cacophonous, modernist soundtracks of horror films. The adorable son, Ch'ang-sun, ultimately is killed by Myŏng-ja; she arranges his fall from the top of the staircase. Despite witnessing this murder of their child, Tong-sik and his wife cannot turn the maid

210

over to the police because the necessary exposure of the affair between Tong-sik and the maid would irreparably damage Tong-sik's reputation and his job. The maid, who had no authority in the house before the affair, now emerges suddenly as its master, giving orders to her employers and instilling fear in them. The power dynamics between the mother and the maid reverse completely: the maid openly sleeps with Tong-sik and has her meals served to her by his wife.

This subverted familial structure cannot last. One fatal night, Miss Cho, another student of Tong-sik who has a crush on him, visits his home for her piano lessons. Cho initially introduced Myŏng-ja to the family. When she visits, Myŏng-ja cannot conceal her jealousy, and takes out a knife from the kitchen. The maid climbs up the staircase and, in a fit of uncontrollable rage, strikes Cho in the piano room.[21] Once Cho is driven away from the house in pain, blood dripping from her shoulder, Myŏng-ja proposes a double suicide with Tong-sik. He accepts her proposal in the same piano room where she first seduced him, and together they drink rat poison. Significantly, Tong-sik rejects the maid at the moment of death, and crawls down the staircase to share his last breath with his wife.

The film is extraordinary in many regards. The constant movement of the camera and exquisitely composed close-ups evoke both the expressionist cinematic styles of Weimar Germany and of Alfred Hitchcock, while the innovative soundtrack, use of shadows, and special lighting effects all showcase the cinematic talent of Kim Ki-yŏng who had independently produced the film while also serving as the film's screenwriter, music supervisor, and editor. The film's structure is particularly noteworthy in that its final scene returns to its opening wherein the family (Tong-sik, his wife, and two kids) discuss a newspaper article about a man who committed suicide with his maid, a woman with whom he was having an affair. Tong-sik defends the man in the newspaper story while his wife complains that all men are no different from "beasts." Just as the debate between the two heats up, the sliding door opens, and in enters the character who has terrorized the family. The maid, not unlike Dr. Caligari in the final scene of the classic film from the Weimar period, is now a changed character.[22] We see nothing of a killer or temptress—her hair is neatly pulled back and her manners are obedient when serving tea to her employers.

Yet, having a young woman in the house, according to the mother, is like "offering raw meat to a beast." After the maid leaves the room, Tong-sik looks directly into the camera and addresses the audience, saying: "Dear sirs and madams, When men age, they spend more time thinking about younger women. This is why us men become easy prey to women and also end up embarrassing the whole family." Humorously pointing his finger at the camera, Tong-sik continues, "That's right, you are no different . . . and there, shaking your head, Sir, this concerns you too."

Writing on this film, Jinsoo An [An Chin-su] writes that "[Tong-sik's] death signifies the symbolic reunion with the mother/wife and a regression to an infantile stage. The distant and brief sound of a baby's cry after his death affirms this point."[23] The signification of the infantile stage and the desire to return to the mother's womb had also been registered in *Happy End* when a fantasy sequence involving Po-ra and a balloon was inserted immediately before the last scene where Min-gi wakes up in the living room with his baby by his side. The strong death motif—present in both films—points to male anxieties about the self and their frustrated effort to claim an autonomous male domain. This search for autonomy was doomed to fail since Tong-sik had too many roles to fulfill: as an object of desire to his female student, a perfect husband to his wife, a nurturing father to his daughter, and a sex machine to the promiscuous maid. What finally precipitates *stable* and ideal manhood for Tong-sik concerns his mastering his interactions with the *instability* and dysfunction depicted as *the* feminine condition by the film: the wife is a distressed, overworked woman who must rest in bed; the female students are workers in an urban factory whose ties to their rural homes and families have been severed by economic necessity; the daughter is physically handicapped from the waist down; and, of course, the sexually deprived maid is threatening to kill all of them. Responsible for taking care of these "feminine symptoms"—neurosis, paranoia, and hysteria, all symptoms stemming from the economic malaise that references the demoralized, war-stricken nation—Tong-sik is doomed to fail in each category: teacher, husband, father, and lover.

The frame utilized in both narratives serves to assure viewers that the stories of adultery and sex are only fictions and also to hint at the forces that lurk beneath the veneer of the bourgeois family. Tong-sik's last statement is addressed largely to *male* viewers and is important because it implies that every man—including those in the audience—is susceptible to lust and desire, drives that are incompatible with the paternal function and that lead to death. Here, sex and death become intricately connected as an irrepressible force, eventually thwarting and contradicting the male subject's aspiration to disavow the crisis, to cure the "female" ailments and to reestablish familial sufficiency and authority.

Staircases and Elevators

The Housemaid and *Happy End* are visually suffocating because the domestic confinement of the male protagonists is meticulously depicted. The filmmakers, visualizing the home as the place where male agency becomes threatened, materialize this psychological issue through their rendering of space and other aspects of the mise-en-scène. From the staircase and the piano in *The Housemaid* to the special attention paid to everyday machines such as the elevator and the television in *Happy End*, the films use these modern appliances, instruments, and utilities to trouble gender and power dynamics. Throughout the remainder of this essay, I will discuss the spatializing of these relations and the household appliances used to crucially refigure family ones. For instance, the transformation of the kitchen from a space segregated from the rest of the communal living spaces in *The Housemaid* to the "open plan" featured in the modern apartment of *Happy End* renders not only different patterns of domesticity but also a new crisis of gender and familial relations. Perhaps this comes as no surprise since kitchens, televisions, and pianos already signify gender in complex ways. In these two films, they operate as agents of change, often disrupting and threatening the preexisting order of things. The simple placement of men inside the kitchen or in front of televisions or pianos symbolizes deepening gender crises.

The staircase in *The Housemaid* is where the desire for class mobility is both imagined and thwarted, becoming the ultimate setting for despair and death. The first time we are introduced to the Western-style house, the family has yet to move in. The house is still under construction, with plywood, ladders, and construction materials scattered all over, similar to war-stricken South Korea at the time. The first space the camera captures is the staircase where Ch'ang-sun, the younger child, taunts his handicapped sister on crutches and dares her to walk up the stairs to take a bag of cookies from him. She slowly struggles up the stairs, step by step, before collapsing halfway. The audience is led to wonder: Why would any family move into a two-story house with a long staircase if the daughter is handicapped by polio and her mobility is severely restricted? And, what is the significance of the young, disabled child desperately climbing up the stairs to get a bag of cookies from her brother, while her father observes them from a dark corner?

Her restricted body movements, the sweat dripping from her face, and the bag of cookies waved in front of her as a fetishistic reward for her desperate labor crystallize the ambition and inhumanity such a simple housing structure can elicit. The father's statement, whispered to Miss Cho who is sympathetic to the child, "Let her go up by herself. Exercise is good for her leg muscles," further confirms the cruelty and pain that one must face in any desire for physical rehabilitation or national redevelopment to occur. This staircase scene effectively spatializes the film's central themes: the fetishistic desire for an unattainable object, struggle to succeed against odds, and the cruelty and humiliation one must face before, during, and after the climb. In other words, the handicapped girl climbing up the stairs elicits sympathy from others, who face the difficult choice of leaving her on her own or helping her at the risk of humiliating her. And all hopes of moving up—either the staircase or the social hierarchy—will require discipline, sacrifice, and even the risk of death.

In *Happy End,* however, the story takes place in a modern high-rise apartment. Min-gi and Po-ra's residential high rise is just one of many mass urbanization projects built over the last thirty years. Its crammed parking lots, tiny mandatory playgrounds, and narrow driveways allude to the overwhelming quality of South Korea's industrialization. The metallic elevators allegorize ascent and descent somewhat differently than does the staircase in *The Housemaid.* Because elevators, unlike a private domestic staircase, are public and communal, many people randomly enter and exit. In the film, they become a venue where meetings—both cheerful and dangerous—happen. The up-and-down function of the elevator invokes the utility of the staircase that signified both the hope and the failure of class mobility in *The Housemaid,* but its compressed and automated condition removes the struggle involved during the industrialization process. Better suited as a machinery that symbolizes the postmodern condition of South Korea, the elevator dramatizes the society's unpredictability as it moves quickly up and down and radically shifts from an open public facility that gives people access to their destinations, to suddenly closed, cramped confinement. The openings and closings of the elevator door are dramatic and instantaneous, often demanding two strangers share standing-room-only space. In Seoul, one of the most densely populated cities in the world, elevators are ubiquitous in everyday activities, serving as a crucial mode of transportation at home, at work, and at leisure.

In the elevator featured in *Happy End,* time and space are structured through gender typologies. This particular elevator serves a residential route. Yet even in this residential apartment elevator, work is performed. In the film's beginning, Min-gi picks up his child from the day-care center and enters his apartment elevator. His body is laden with the baby, his bag, and the baby-care bag, and he fumbles awkwardly to press the elevator button. Accompanying him is a thirty-something woman who runs into the elevator balancing countless grocery bags in her arms. Here, a visual and social affinity is forged between the two, based on the domestic iconography of burden: baby and groceries. The gender of the two adults may be different, but they are affiliated by the accoutrements of what is conventionally conceived as feminine domestic labor. At the narrative level, they recognize each other as friends from college. The woman, Mi-yŏng, will soon become Min-gi's buddy, and they will bond as same-sex ("feminine") friends, shopping together, helping each other with child care, and gossiping on the telephone about television soap programs. The meeting between Mi-yŏng and Min-gi in the elevator is not coincidental as their days are bound by their gendered routine. It is near sunset, but for the two of them, the workday is far from over; only a couple of hours remain before their spouses, working in the public sphere, return home for dinner.

In *Happy End*, like *The Housemaid*, the waning of male authority is visually captured by infusing the home and its environs with ambiguity. Provident meetings in the elevator are not only pleasant but also dangerous. After the scene where Min-gi finds out that Po-ra risked the life of their child to rendezvous with Il-bŏm, he returns exhausted from the hospital emergency room where the baby was treated. Clutching the baby in his arms, Min-gi enters the elevator he rides every day. It is late and no one else is in sight. The camera follows Min-gi from the parking lot to the elevator and finally to the apartment corridor. Here in the corridor Min-gi witnesses Po-ra—who has rejected the role of "mother"—embracing Il-bŏm. Min-gi already knows that they are seeing each other, but seeing them at this moment is devastating to his self-esteem. The two lovebirds are both very drunk and indiscreet. The depiction of Po-ra as a lascivious drunk further enhances the gender reversal depicted in the film. Stunned, Min-gi takes a few steps back to the elevator, and hides in a stairwell. When Il-bŏm finally staggers into the elevator, Min-gi comes out of his hideout and checks to confirm the man's descent before "safely" returning to his own home. It is difficult for the audience not to be sympathetic with Min-gi at this point. Holding his baby in his arms, he has lost not only his wife and the mother of his child but also access to his home. He has also lost all claim to his status as "man" of the house.

Rather than in an elevator, in *The Housemaid,* power struggles are fought and resolved on the house staircase. The maid vies for authority there, and murders as well as significant plot reversals are staged on it. The drama, however, remains within the confines of domestic space. This contrasts with *Happy End,* in which dramatic reversals take place in the public/private spaces of the elevator, corridor, and even in the exemplarily liminal space of the doorway.

When the coast is clear, Min-gi lurches across the corridor and opens the door to his apartment. The camera remains static and does not reveal exactly what he sees. But from his reaction, we know that he is witnessing his wife having sex with Il-bŏm, who had rushed up the stairs on the other side of the building after descending in the elevator only one floor. Their intercourse is so passionate that even the presence of Min-gi goes unnoticed. Min-gi's humiliation is complete when he doesn't—and can't—intervene. The illicit sex between Po-ra and Il-bŏm drives Min-gi and his sick baby out onto the dark, damp concrete fire escape.

Rats in the Kitchen

While more pronounced in *Happy End,* the sharp differentiation between gendered public and private spheres is diminished in both of these films. Both films emphasize the gender confusion at their core in two ways: by visualizing that confusion in terms of domestic and public space; and by means of the work performed by both men and women in these spaces.[24] In the earlier film, Tong-sik cooks and teaches piano while his wife sews, her earnings allowing the family to pay for their new house. Four decades later, Min-gi cares for the baby, cooks, shops, and watches soap operas while his wife runs a company from her high-rise office. Thus *The Housemaid* and *Happy End* foreground vivid representations of domestic labor, especially, though not exclusively, performed by men. In both films, the kitchen receives critical attention as a space where domesticity is performed and also where social tensions, upward class mobility, and middle-class conformity are perhaps most effectively expressed. Both films startle their viewers by frequently placing men inside the kitchen, a spatial arrangement that is extremely rare elsewhere in South Korean cinema. Perhaps it is this rarity that makes the family relations in the two films both exceptional and unstable.

The function of "work" and the spatialization of the kitchen where this work is performed are clearly important to the themes of these films. The kitchen in the 1960 film, *The Housemaid,* is a clean Western-style one, installed with a bright electric lamp, wooden cupboards, a sink with two faucets, and a gas stove, all extremely scarce in South Korea at the time.[25] The wife tries to organize the kitchen after moving into the new house, opening up the cupboards and stacking things in them. These are happy days for her; the sound of a beginning student at the piano indicates that her husband is generating income, and the sound of children playing signifies successful childrearing. The fruit of her hard labor as a seamstress in the last ten years has finally paid off. All of a sudden, a rat appears in front of her. Letting out a sharp scream, she falls, as everyone in the house runs to her side. The rat is gone, but the shock lingers on, as she cannot easily recover from her fall. In order to prevent rats from invading the house, the family sets mousetraps by pouring rat poison over food. The poison purchased to get rid of the rats ironically ends up killing the people themselves.

The appearance of the rat destroys the mother's happiness, the kitchen's sanitation, and eventually the family's lives. Despite the family's effort to exterminate them, the rats are not easily removed. When the new maid first visits the house, she walks into the kitchen alone, a space segregated from the rest of the house. Myŏng-ja surveys the room, sampling food and opening the cupboards, familiarizing herself with the only facility that she will now rule. The rat again appears in the cupboard. Unlike her employer, who had screamed and fainted at the sight of the rat, Myŏng-ja curiously picks it up by its tail, and wiggling her tongue, sets it down on the floor as if it is her pet. However, as soon as she finds a small wooden bat used for cooking, she strikes and kills it. Surprised by the sound coming from the kitchen, the family congregates as the maid holds out the dead rat in front of them. Differences in class, region (rural versus urban), and delicacy are clearly established in the maid and the wife's different reactions to the rat. Further, the maid is able to catch and overcome the rat, and is, in her appearance and demeanor, visually aligned with it. She soon becomes the one who is dangerous and threatening to the family, her rabid sexuality seemingly invited into the home by the family's aspirations to social mobility.

Tong-sik, in an indifferent voice, tells her that rats should be trapped with rat poison and gives her the bottle that will later seal both of their fates. Both the intimacy and the cruelty she displayed in her relationship with a rat presage the complicated nature of passion and jealousy that she will soon exhibit in her relationship with Tong-sik. Her action installs her as fully in command of the kitchen, a critical space that contains and serves both food and poison, not unlike South Korea's domestic industrialization that will soon bring prosperity but will also simultaneously produce environmental pollution and contamination, economic dependence on the West, and class contradiction.

Just as important as the staircase where power is constantly contested, the kitchen, a part of the house where convention locates women and denigrating work, is refigured as the place in which the maid assumes power. The hiring of the maid allows the mother to recover and concentrate on her work with the sewing machine and also releases the father from the kitchen. The father had been cooking for the family just prior to Myŏng-ja's arrival. Wearing a checkered shirt with the sleeves rolled up and an apron around his waist in a Western-style kitchen, Tong-sik is a "modern man" who is capable of providing for the family both outside and inside his home. The availability of a stove, cabinets, china, and Western recipes aligns the unconventionality of Tong-sik in the kitchen with the Western influences that now permeate this private domestic space.

Even as Tong-sik and the maid are now installed in this space, so the wife is depicted as alienated from it, her "proper" place. Is it a matter of trivial coincidence or crucial significance that the wife collapses the first time she enters the kitchen, requiring Tong-sik to perform "woman's work" before he finds a housemaid? The film visually depicts his wife, dressed in traditional South Korean clothing, as out of place in this very Western, modern kitchen. Built to expedite housework, the kitchen instead is the site of the wife's collapse. Out of necessity, Tong-sik takes over housekeeping duties. Even though he is a "better cook than mom," this equation of domesticity with masculinity in South Korea in the 1960s simply seems out of place and even threatening to dominant perceptions of gender. Yet the time and its turmoil led precisely to these conflicts: between war-stricken poverty and massive industrialization; between tradition and modernity—these tensions and conflicts infusing gender relations and the domestic sphere. Thus, the film warns its viewers that a destructive element insinuates itself, destroying a family that gets caught in the liminal space between tradition and modernity and between male and female.

The other domestic space highlighted in *The Housemaid* is the piano room that also functions as a family room. In South Korean culture, no other material object is as highly prized or fetishized as the piano, an instrument that for this family signifies not only the character of their class ambitions but also provides the means for attaining them. Although South Korea is now one of the world's leading manufacturers and exporters of pianos, and they are common there to many middle-class homes, pianos were not easily accessible to the public in 1960.[26]

Tong-sik's occupation as a music teacher, with complete command of this elegant instrument, renders him an object of romantic interest and the romantic gaze to all the women around him. To be in control of such a graceful Western machine requires sensitivity, confidence, and cultural sophistication that none of the women working in the factory possess. The moment Tong-sik walks into the baroque-style room where he teaches music to the female factory workers, he is the center of amorous attention. He has the expertise and talent that these women desire and wish to acquire to enhance their social mobility. Women must be able to convey a type of femininity associated with material comfort and (Western bourgeois) taste, which they can really only attain through an auspicious marriage. The image of ideal femininity projected through the famous Dutch or French paintings during the nineteenth century that explicitly identify the keyboard instrument as a site of seduction appealed to many young women in the war-stricken environment of South Korea.[27] As if to aid the translation of their dreams into reality, Tong-sik makes an announcement in his class, expressing his intent to recruit piano students.

Critically, Tong-sik's offer to help these women learn the piano also works in the service of his own dreams. He states, "I purchased a piano in installments, and would like to get some return on my investment," acknowledging the piano is not only a machine that produces dreams, but also an expensive material investment that makes other dreams possible as well. The act of learning the piano packages the dream of upward mobility for both teacher and student in the cultural logic and aesthetic imagination of the European bourgeoisie. Thus, the piano—like many other props in the film—serves a dual function. It is an object of desire, generating fetishistic impulses by virtue of its rarity and delicacy. But, because it is so expensive, it also fosters the distinctions and class barriers that usher in the tragic plot of the film. When the maid curiously strikes a few keys, he warns her, "Whatever you do, never touch the piano." Even after they make love, the rules that ban Myŏng-ja from the piano still apply, signifying that the instrument is more sacred than her body. And, because it is so expensive, the piano ushers in the tragic plot: after the maid becomes hysterical and stabs Miss Cho, Tong-sik regrets having ever purchased the piano and blames it for all his family's misfortunes. Just as the staircase is a metaphor for the family's economic ascendance and demise, the piano, a fetishized symbol of the Western bourgeoisie and the primary source of income for the family, will turn out to be Tong-sik's "enemy."

Happy End's Open-Space Plan

Unlike the partitioned and distinct rooms that make up the domestic space in *The Housemaid,* the residential apartments in *Happy End* make the kitchen, living room, dining room, and hallways into one open area. This apartment's resulting spaciousness is contrasted with the confined and crammed public spaces such as the elevator, the bookstore, and even Po-ra's office. Not only is Min-gi associated with domesticity through various housekeeping chores but also through his ties to the television. Leslie Regan Shade writes that the television set is an "electronic hearth that replaced the fireplace and the piano as the center of family attention."[28] Television may have replaced *The Housemaid*'s piano at the center stage of domestic space, but the family is no longer there to give it much attention. Only Min-gi sits in front of it. Upon entering his apartment, he cannot turn his eyes from the television screen, even though the baby cries profusely, demanding to be fed. Min-gi's focus shifts between the soccer game on television in the living room, the baby lying on the sofa, and the powdered formula he's preparing in the kitchen. While he prepares this food for the baby, he realizes that there are small black worms in the powder, making its consumption impossible. The black worms—like the rats in *The Housemaid*—will continue to infest the house, especially the kitchen cabinet, symptomatically rendering once again the anxieties blending sexual promiscuity and financial aspirations and problems for the family.

Min-gi's relationships with kitchen and television are both conventional and extraordinary; conventional because domesticity has had a special relationship to the kitchen and television during the modern era, but also extraordinary given Min-gi is a "masculine" man with few "feminine" qualities. The actor cast as Min-gi, Ch'oe Min-sik, is a well-known "tough guy" in South Korean cinema, making the character's association with stereotypical images of femininity even more anomalous.[29] *Happy End*'s disaffiliation of femininity and domesticity departs from contemporaneous Hollywood films such as *Tootsie* (Sydney Pollack, 1982), *Mr. Mom* (Stan Dragoti, 1983), or *Mrs. Doubtfire* (Chris Columbus, 1993) that allow men in the kitchen only by masking their masculinity. In these films, Dustin Hoffman and Robin Williams had to literally dress up as women in order to perform feminine tasks and roles. In *Happy End,* these realigned gender roles constitute a profound threat to the family.

In one particular sequence, Min-gi performs various housework functions. Sequentially structured, Min-gi prepares a meal, organizes and loads empty cans and milk cartons into recycling boxes, and flips and pegs laundered sheets along the laundry line out in the balcony. This sequence of static shots—without music—that cuts between each task is sensual and effective, rendering beauty in simple everyday domestic labor without mocking or sentimentalizing it, and thereby defying the conventions of Hollywood comedies on gender-bending.

In the subsequent sequence, Min-gi reclines on the sofa, a glass of beer in his hand, watching a nighttime soap drama where two famous television actors in South Korea, Kim Hye-su and Pae Yong-jun, engage in highly melodramatic dialogue. In tears, Kim Hye-su, the woman, states: "I know it's wrong for me to do what I have been doing. There's no time for me to complain about it. I was a fool . . ." Unable to control her emotions, the famous television actress with heavy makeup bursts into tears, smudging her dark mascara. After having captured the television in full frame, the camera then cuts 180 degrees to Min-gi, who is intently watching the soap. Having had a full and tiring day, which we have seen, he is taking a break from work. Yet, he is distracted when Po-ra yells from her room, asking him to lower the television volume. Almost at the same time, the phone rings and the baby starts to cry. Min-gi gets not even a moment of peace when Po-ra—after several pleas to turn the television down go ignored—agitatedly rushes out to the living room. The phone keeps ringing, the baby continues to cry, and the kettle on the stove begins to whistle, intensifying the tension between the husband and the wife whose roles have been reversed.

Only Po-ra's work brought home from the office counts as "labor," while the domestic labor performed by Min-gi earlier in the day remains invisible to his wife. She only sees Min-gi watching television and sipping his beer; she is unaware that he, too, had a full day of work. In the ensuing family conference, Min-gi sits in the dining chair closest to the kitchen, symbolizing his closer proximity to the kitchen than his wife. Po-ra, seated on the other side, tells him that he must be responsible for all of the housework unless he is serious about looking for a job. She continues to chastise him: "Do you care to know which store has the cheapest juice price or which store has the best bread, or the time the freshly baked bread comes out? Would you like to care to know? You don't want to care, do you? Then, you must start 'work' (*il*) again. Why do you simply sit there, ugly, like someone who has just lost a war?" Min-gi feels humiliated not only because he is incapable of finding employment, but also because she is denigrating specific tasks of domestic labor, distinguishing it from the "masculine" work she is engaged in. His labor in the house does not qualify as *il*. Her ability to earn money is far more sacred and profound than "saving" it through "best buy" juice and bread.

This is precisely the moment where the terms of domesticity and gender relations shift and become troubled, laying out a foundation for which the merciless killing of Po-ra will be emotionally and subconsciously legitimized by the viewers. In other words, Po-ra has to die because she has all the qualities of a "bad husband" who ignores the difficulty of domestic labor, refuses to share childcare duties, and does not value television viewing as leisure integrated within the rubric of domesticity and communal social activity. (Indeed, as soon as the program is over, Min-gi receives a phone call from Mi-yŏng who asks him what he thought of the soap's new development.)

Masculinist/Feminist

The alignment of men with domestic spaces, imperiled masculinity, and an emphasis on illicit sexuality and desire in *The Housemaid* and *Happy End* all manifest the complexities of gender trouble in moments of financial crisis in South Korea. The punishments meted out to the women, Myŏng-ja in *The Housemaid* and Po-ra in *Happy End,* can be considered as rupturing instances distinct from the Mulvey-ian critique of misogynist structures of mainstream cinema. The stylistic excesses in *The Housemaid* cast not only women as monstrous but also men as hapless and terrible creatures. In addition, the attention paid to domesticity and the placement of Min-gi inside a kitchen allow readings of these films outside of the conventional gendered framework. Yet it is precisely Po-ra's masculine characteristics that transgress the conventional boundaries of gender that necessitate her punishment at the end of *Happy End*. And even though the housemaid is an "active sexual agent" (according to Chris Berry) that disassociates her from the conventional roles of femininity assigned by South Korean cinema, she is still only a "whore" or a "bitch" to the film's spectators in the early 1960s. For them, the film enacts the mother-whore dyad of patriarchal representation of women that South Korean cinema has patented throughout the postwar decades.[30] Further disqualifying these films as "feminist" is their refusal to question the conventional roles of gender, placing gender differentiation as the integral component of filmic tensions that ultimately usher in the respective narrative movements. In other words, the phallus in these films is *not* used in the Lacanian sense that has its realness stripped, but rather where power remains very much condensed.

The threats issued against male potency during both stages of nascent industrialization and de-industrialization have ways of re-directing themselves so that the gender relations are, on one hand, de-stabilized momentarily, but on the other, re-stabilized and re-organized through "normative" functions of gender. Gender roles have remained remarkably consistent where the representation of the woman is still caught between the mother and the whore, and the crisis belongs in the domain of men, who must resort to violence in order to recuperate from the trauma. But, this hardly accomplishes anything other than once again affirming gender essences. For instance, despite his dedication to housework and command of the domestic space, Min-gi can never be capable of withdrawing from his phallocentric universe. On a similar note, it is extremely difficult to imagine the mother in *The Housemaid* assuming the paternal role for her children, even after her husband kills himself. Gender essentialism in these films, where stylistic excesses and refigurations of domestic spaces potentially complicate the conventional notions of gender, cannot and will not easily be dismantled or deconstructed. Through such regressive social foundations, any masculinity threatened by social crisis will again be recuperated.

Notes

1. Trains have been commonly conceived as gigantic, metallic phalluses. From Sigmund Freud to Alfred Hitchcock, the use of trains as a sexual metaphor has been frequent and pervasive. Lynne Kirby in her study of the relationship between trains and cinema, *Parallel Tracks: The Railroad and the Silent Cinema*, states, "[f]ilms like Alfred Hitchcock's *North by Northwest* (1959), in which a train entering a tunnel is meant to signify and parody sexual intercourse, epitomize this popular notion . . . train as a specifically male object" (Durham, NC: Duke University Press, 1997), 77.

2. Kim Ki-yŏng hardly affected the New South Korean Cinema filmmakers who made their directorial debuts in the 1980s. Pak Kwang-su and Chang Sŏn-u, the most famous filmmakers who represent the New South Korean Cinema movement, were unfamiliar with South Korean film history and failed to recognize its importance. Although they were the first generation of filmmakers who learned the trade of filmmaking through film collectives, they were not formally trained in filmmaking, and the history of South Korean cinema was at that time rarely taught in colleges. However, Chŏng Chi-u, Pak Ki-hyŏng (best known for *Whispering Corridor* [*Yŏgo koedam*], 1998), and Pak Ch'an-uk (best known for *Joint Security Area* [*Kongdong kyŏngbi kuyŏk*], 2000), who made their first feature films in the 1990s, had made contact with South Korean film history through various formal filmmaking programs and film appreciation clubs. Retrospective screenings and South Korean film history classes featuring Kim Ki-yŏng films had also given them the opportunity to be profoundly affected by the man known as "Mr. Monster."

3. In 2000, there are three film weeklies, four monthlies, innumerable Internet sites, and a handful of entertainment dailies that cover cinema.

4. South Korea is now second only to the United States in the number of domain names registered each year and leads the world in online stock trading. See Mark Magnier, "'PC Bang' Helps S. South Koreans Embrace Net," *Los Angeles Times,* July 19, 2000, A-12.

5. Lynn Spigel, *Make Room for TV: Television and the Family Ideal in Postwar America* (Chicago: University of Chicago Press, 1992), 97.

6. Along with *The Housemaid* and *The Stray Bullet* (Yu Hyŏn-mok, 1960), *Madame Freedom* is one of the most popular films programmed in South Korean retrospectives in the film festivals abroad. In the 1990s, when South Korean films were showcased in various retrospectives around the world, *Madame Freedom* was regularly included. It also remains one of the most hotly debated films in South Korean film scholarship.

7. Soyoung Kim, chapter 7 in this volume. Also see chapter 1 in this volume for Kathleen McHugh's discussion of women's economic labor as it functions in this film.

8. Even in South Korean War films, women's promiscuity is highlighted as one of the most prominent cultural phenomena, provoking the male characters to violently react. See my article "Is This How the War Is Remembered? Deceptive Sex and the Re-Masculinized Nation in *The T'aebaek Mountains,*" in *Im Kwon-Taek: The Makings of a South Korean National Cinema,* ed. David E. James and Kyung Hyun Kim (Detroit: Wayne State University Press, 2001).

9. The economic situation in South Korea was quite dire in 1998, plunging millions of people into poverty. The "Miracle on the Han" economy that continued its phenomenal growth rate of close to 10 percent during the 1990s collapsed to negative growth in 1998, virtually stalemating the economy for the first time since the 1950s. "Middle Class Is Casualty of Asian Crisis," *Los Angeles Times,* December 27, 1998, A-9.

10. A fired bank employee is a recent phenomenon, since employment in a bank is one of the more socially stable and respected jobs in South Korea. That Min-gi is a former bank employee indicates that he is an educated man. Another hit film from the period, *The Foul King* (*Panch'ik wang,* Kim Chi-un, 2000), also places the central protagonist in the role of a banker as he tries to find relief from the work pressures in a depression where the bank demands its employees play by old and corrupt rules.

11. Anne Allison asserts that motherhood in Japan is explicitly elaborated by handsome and scrumptious children's lunchboxes that symbolize and fetishize full-time, stay-at-home mothers. See Anne Allison, "Japanese Mothers and *Obentos:* The Lunch Box as Ideological State Apparatus," in *Permitted and Prohibited Desires: Mothers, Comics, and Censorship in Japan* (Boulder, CO: Westview Press, 1996), 81–104. In one of the best-selling collections of short stories in South Korea during the 1990s, *P'unggŭm i ittŏn chari* (*The Place Where an Organ Used to Be*), Sin Kyŏng-suk creates a narrator—a woman who is having an affair with a married man—who recalls the childhood memory of her father's girlfriend. In this story, the father's

lover replaces the mother and tries to defer the initially credulous gaze of her brothers by generously packing their lunchboxes (*tosirak*) that "resemble flowerbed." This new "mother" impresses the narrator with her cooking skills, earning the respect of an ideal mother that the "real" mother never garnered. It is not coincidental that Sin Kyŏng-suk also centrally figures as a woman who is having an affair. Many female writers who emerged in the literary scene during the 1990s such as Ŭn Hŭi-gyŏng and Chŏn kyŏng-nin also frequently depict women having extramarital affairs. Sin Kyŏng-suk, *P'unggŭm i ittŏn chari* (Seoul: Munhak kwa chisŏngsa, 1993), 26.

12. Nancy Chodorow, *The Reproduction of Mothering* (Berkeley: University of California Press, 1999), 14. On the same page, Chodorow critiques this questionable assumption that refuses to take into consideration that human behavior, including mothering, is "not instinctually determined but culturally mediated." In addition, Mary Ann Doane writes, "In Western culture, there is something obvious about the maternal which has no counterpart in the paternal." Mary Ann Doane, *The Desire to Desire: The Woman's Film of the 1940s* (Bloomington: Indiana University Press, 1987), 70.

13. *The Housemaid*, with its bold representation of sexuality and eroticism, was a huge hit when it first came out in 1960. But, because of the South Korean cinema's slump during the 1970s and 1980s, as well as Kim Ki-yŏng's fall to relative obscurity during this period, *The Housemaid* was largely forgotten until its resurgence through retrospective screenings in film festivals during the 1990s.

14. The Web site can be found at http://www.knua.ac.kr/cinema/KKY/Open-Home/home%202.htm (accessed August 2004). The Web site, "The House of Kim Ki-young," is created by Kim So-yŏng and Chris Berry, and was co-authored with graduate students in the film studies program at the South Korean National University of the Arts.

15. See my article "South Korean Cinema and Im Kwon-Taek," in *Im Kwon-Taek: The Makings of a South Korean National Cinema*.

16. Controversial when it first came out, *The Housemaid* continues to irk present-day audiences. After its screening at the 1998 Post-Colonial Classics of South Korean Cinema Festival at Irvine, California, a couple of South Korean American spectators furiously complained to me and one of the festival programmers for showcasing the film. They protested that *The Housemaid* does not accurately represent South Korean society and should not have been programmed.

17. Kim Ki-yŏng's maid hardly has any of the qualities of Douglas Sirk's Annie Johnson in the contemporaneous *Imitation of Life* (1959), whose immaculate and sacrificial execution of domestic duties allows her employer, Lora, to concentrate on her public role and become a star.

18. Kim Chin-gyu, the actor who plays the father in *The Housemaid*, also plays Ch'ŏr-ho in *The Stray Bullet*.

19. Heavy drinking, argues Yuejin Wang, "can be a transgression of decorum, an act of defying convention, a route to visionary intensity for transcendental possibilities and poetic ecstasy, or a way of achieving autonomy." But it is also an embodiment of "spiritual degradation, over-indulgence, moral corruption

and social irresponsibility." Yuejin Wang, "Red Sorghum: Mixing Memory and Desire," in *Perspectives on Chinese Cinema*, ed. Chris Berry (London: BFI, 1991), 86–87.

20. Soyoung Kim, chapter 7 in this volume. Also, see "Interview with Kim Ki-young," in *Kim Ki-young: Cinema of Diabolical Desire and Death* (Pusan International Film Festival, 1997), 53.

21. The scene that features Myŏng-ja's stabbing of Cho is remarkably constructed, worthy of scrupulous analysis here. Accompanied by a modernist music orchestra soundtrack and the diegetic sound effects of a thunderstorm in the background, the film creates the ambience of a film noir. Shot from a side angle, the camera follows Myŏng-ja in her usual dark attire, clenching a knife in the kitchen and walking up the staircase. Even though the same staircase has been photographed many times prior to this scene, this is the first time it is shot from this camera position. Rather than the conventional long shot that had the staircase pictured either from the top or from below, the camera is placed on the side, with the handrail obstructing much of the view. We soon understand why: following Myŏng-ja as she moves with the camera in a full shot, we see her shadow reflected on the wall and prominently featured through the banister, visually escalating the drama. The sequence resumes in the piano room where Myŏng-ja, in a slightly crouched position, enters and points her knife at Cho. Captured from the outside balcony in a swift tracking movement, the maid enters the room quickly from the right, bypasses Tong-sik who stands in the front of the frame, and threatens Cho. Myŏng-ja tells Miss Cho, who is shuddering with fear, to get off the piano. "You are the real bitch," announces Myŏng-ja, and warns her that the next time she calls Tong-sik, *sŏnsaengnim* ("mister"), she will not stand pat. The camera settles briefly to a medium shot, showing Tong-sik pull away Myŏng-ja from Cho and framing Tong-sik and Myŏng-ja together, separately from Cho. When Cho ignores Myŏng-ja's warning, the camera moves into a close-up of Myŏng-ja's face that transforms from expressing anguish to rage. The next shot cuts to Cho's upper body in another close-up—neck to waist—with the knife thrusting from the lower part of the frame to the upper part. Once it strikes the target in the shoulder, the camera cuts to Cho's face. She screams and then slowly fades from the frame. During the crucial moment when the knife strikes, the drama is aurally enhanced by both Cho's scream and the sound of thunder. Visually, the shot of the knife piercing through Cho's shoulder is coordinated by the artificial lighting to heighten the effect of lightning, suddenly turning white followed by several frames of pitch black.

22. Kim Ki-yŏng's long involvement in theater before his filmmaking career (he was also a dentist and had trained at medical school) gave him access to the conventions of avant-garde theater where the boundary between fiction and reality is deliberately obfuscated through the rejection of the imaginary border between performers and spectators. Such stylistic codes including the actor's method acting and expressionist mise-en-scène and décor all remind us of Ufa's *The Cabinet of Dr. Caligari* (Robert Wiene, 1919). I raise this film as a point of reference for *The Housemaid* because they similarly insert

not only a narrative frame to attain a dreamlike quality but also the projection of madness that cannot be clearly and safely confined to a gated space. *Dr. Caligari* ends with a statement by the director of the mental asylum: "At last now I can understand the nature of his madness. He thinks I am that mystic Caligari. Now I see how he can be brought back to sanity again." The ambiguities of truth, the difficulty of determining who is the madman between Francis, the young student, and the director, as well as the subsequent historical emergence of Adolf Hitler in Germany who reminded the world of the evil somnambulist, have rendered the film legendary. Of course, in the South Korean film it may be an overstatement, not unlike the one Siegfried Kracauer made many decades ago, that the film's projection of ambiguity as to whether or not the father, who appears in the beginning and in the end, actually has an affair with the maid, is symbolic of a real dictator in South Korea: Park Chung Hee. Nevertheless, the ambiguity between truth and fiction and between madness and reason all symptomize the historical reign of terror and intense modernization pursued by the Park Administration (1961–79).

23. Jinsoo An, "Chungsanch'ŭng kajŏng ŭl yujihanŭn kŏt ŭn ŏlmana" (How much it takes to maintain a middle-class family), *Cine 21* (April 20, 1998).

24. In *American Domesticity*, Kathleen McHugh argues that staple narratives of American melodrama like *Imitation of Life, Stella Dallas,* and *Mildred Pierce* "engage modern cultural beliefs concerning gender and labor by bringing women and their love into explicit relation with what are characterized as public and masculine concerns: work, money, ambition, and success." Kathleen McHugh, *American Domesticity: From How-to Manual to Hollywood Melodrama* (New York: Oxford University Press, 1999), 131–32.

25. When I was living in South Korea as a child in a middle-class home, not until the late 1970s were we able to move into a house that had a kitchen fully equipped with a sink with two faucets.

26. In 1985, South Korea was the third largest piano manufacturing nation in the world behind Japan and the United States, that year yielding 129,000 pianos. See Cyril Ehrlich, *The Piano: A History* (Oxford: Clarendon, 1990), 222.

27. James Parakilas in his book, *Piano Roles* (New Haven: Yale University Press, 1999), states that many of the famous impressionists, such as Paul Cézanne, Edouard Manet, Edgar Degas, Gustave Caillebotte, and Auguste Renoir, used the image of "the woman at the piano" as a theme. He writes, "[T]hese illustrations attest to the centrality of piano lessons in feminine education, as well as to the cultural currency of the 'woman at the piano' motif" (216). During my adolescence in South Korea, one of the images that stuck with me is a Van Gogh painting of a well-proportioned woman seated in front of an upright piano in a rural bourgeois home. Images as such were pervasive in South Korea, and emblematized ideal femininity.

28. Leslie Regan Shade, "Women and Television," *Postmodern Culture* 3, no. 3 (May 1993).

29. Ch'oe Min-sik plays a villainous North Korean terrorist who conspires against his own president in order to force a war between the North and the South

in *Shiri* (*Swiri*, Kang Che-gyu, 1999), the most successful film of the decade.

30. Chris Berry, "Introducing 'Mr. Monster': Kim Ki-young and the Critical Economy of the Globalized Art-House Cinema," in *Post-Colonial Classics of South Korean Cinema,* ed. Choi, 42.

9

Morae sigye: "Social Melodrama" and the Politics of Memory in Contemporary South Korea

KEEHYEUNG LEE

Memory, even and especially in its belatedness, is itself based on representation.
    Andreas Huyssen

[Melodrama comes into being] in a world where the traditional imperatives of truth and ethics have been thrown violently into question . . . [melodrama] becomes the principal mode for uncovering, demonstrating and making operative the essential moral universe in a post-sacred era.
    Peter Brooks

Introduction

The SBS (Seoul Broadcasting System) originally aired the prime-time television serial, *Morae sigye* (*Hour Glass*), in the spring of 1995 for six weeks. *Morae sigye* became one of the most popular South Korean television dramas of all time. According to SBS News, it generated an average viewer rating of 45.3 percent, garnering a phenomenal 61.5 percent rating at its peak (January 14, 1998). As a high-budget *t'ŭkchipkŭk* (special drama) and a social melodrama, *Morae sigye* was produced to commemorate the fiftieth anniversary of Korea's independence from Japan.[1] My use of the term "social melodrama" refers to a subgenre that selectively uses actual sociopolitical histories, events, and figures in its narrative and visual economy. In this essay I approach this enormously popular television drama by examining the interconnected workings of key textual and visual codes and the representation of the popular memory in the radically altered sociopolitical terrain of 1990s South Korea. In doing so, I delve into the cultural politics of memory and history in the age of electronically produced historical images, signs, and plural media flows.

On the Brief History of Melodramas in the Korean Televisual Field

By the 1980s, nearly every household in South Korea had more than one television set. Posing a serious threat to the country's film industry, the new medium began producing its own televisual melodramas, churning out a number of highly successful "melos" (*mellomul*).[2] Yet in the context of television's association with the domestic sphere and the strict regulation of the industry, the majority of television melodramas contain formulaic thematic structures and predictable narratives. Over the past decade, there have been a series of highly successful melodramas on South Korean television that not only generated high ratings but also created a broad, loyal, and heterogeneous fan base, thereby generating socially charged debates on the themes explored in these popular television shows. Targeted to a predominantly female audience, television melodrama has long been shaped by ideologies of heterosexual romantic love, motherhood, monogamy, and intimacy in the private sector.

Above all, the social world captured and represented by television melodrama is centered around women's suffering, sacrifice, and the predicaments that emerge from the cracks in the institutions of marriage and family. Some well-known television melodramas embrace the following themes: the morally tuned interpersonal battles and (personified) conflicts between virtuous heroines and Machiavellian villainesses (*The Sand Castle* [*Morae sŏng*, 1989], *The Lover* [*Aein*, 1998], *Lies* [*kŏjinmal*, 1999], *The Trap of the Youth* [*Ch'ŏngch'un ŭi tŏt*, 1999]); the adaptation of the Cinderella myth in a modern setting (*To Have Love in Your Heart* [*Sarang ŭl kŭdae p'uman e*, 1994], *To Have Stars in My Heart* [*Pyŏl ŭn nae kasŭm e*, 1997]); the female protagonist's sacrifice of her own dream for the sake of her family (*Kukhŭi*, 1999); women's unfulfilled desires, fantasies, and sufferings, their own awareness of women's repressed agency (*How Do Women Live?* [*Yŏja nŭn muŏt ŭro sanŭn'ga*, 1993]).[3]

Although they have been despised and devalued for a long time as a "cheap," "excessive," "syrupy," "formulaic," and "over-sentimentalized" genre, television melodramas have nonetheless demonstrated steady popularity due largely to their protean nature and enormous affective power. In recent decades, South Korean melodrama has been shown by feminist scholars to be composed of polysemic cultural texts.[4] Cultural theorists have explored the cultural and ideological contradictions contained within television melodrama and have used semiotic, interpretive, discursive, and

230

ethnographic analysis to identify a wide range of audience responses to these texts.[5]

One reason behind the phenomenal success of South Korea's television melodrama arises from the fact that viewers can insert their own histories into the shows by identifying or dis-identifying with characters and their situations, bringing their own memories to bear on the narratives.[6] To simplify greatly, popular melodrama tends to generate a wide range of critical, ambiguous, and negotiated responses, including comments, gossip, and debates, initiated and engaged in by audiences who bear significant cultural knowledge about the genealogy of melodramatic plots and characters.

From a different angle, television melodrama also reflects on the radically changed material success of South Korea. The shows sometimes recreate the past, which is characterized as a poor, but simpler and more harmonious time before modernization eroded and reshaped family and communal structures. Often in these nostalgic family melodramas, such as *Sons and Daughters* (*Adŭl kwa ttal*, 1995) or *Kannani* (1994), the reinvented images of poverty and struggle are packaged and consumed as entertainment.[7] David Thorburn argues that U.S. television melodrama provides an "intimate, therapeutic, and yet potentially reactionary site/forum in which traditional ways of feeling and thinking are brought into continuous, strained relation with powerful intuitions of change and contingency."[8] Such an observation can be applied to Korean melodrama as well.

Another interesting feature of Korean television melodrama is that over the years it has evolved into a relatively malleable popular form that has undergone significant variations within established generic conventions. For instance, what is fascinating in *Morae sigye* is that it presents a new kind of melodramatic mode that extensively reconstructs into its diegetic world actual sociopolitical events of great historical significance. In other words, unlike the dominant South Korean melodramas that do not deal with historical issues and events seriously, to a significant degree, *Morae sigye* successfully incorporates political and historical themes, recollecting traumatic events of the 1980s.

The Eye of the Dawn (*Yŏmyŏng ŭi nundongja,* 1995), another hugely successful character-driven social melodrama, focuses on the plight of three characters who live through the turbulence of the Japanese colonial era, World War II, and the Korean War. In this drama, an epic quality is layered on a romance-driven melodramatic format that centers on the intertwined destinies of three characters. The selective adoption of specific historical events distinguishes *The Eye of the Dawn* from typical costume dramas that employ calculated mise-en-scène and decorative period music to evoke a vague suggestion of history.[9]

Morae sigye as a Social Melodrama and a Shared Media Event

Morae sigye is both distinctive and effective as a social melodrama because it uses historical events, moods, and figures far more extensively than, and in part against the grain of, received melodramatic norms. In conventional South Korean melodrama, history is often shaped by comforting nostalgia or shallow historical nominalism. The shows' representations of the past are often aided by the limited use of period set pieces, location, soundtracks, costume, and other audio-visual cues that correspond to the perceived notions of authenticity. Instead, in *Morae sigye,* the discursive representation and refiguring of extraordinary historical events are shot through with pronounced signs of cinematic realism.[10] Furthermore, the central characters in *Morae sigye* are allegorical or composite types resembling the "social personalities" found in the socially conscious popular fiction and in serious nonfiction that characterized South Korean literature in the 1980s. These context-specific ideal characters include the dedicated student-activist, the authoritative and rigid bureaucrat, the crooked and cunning politician, and so forth.

On the surface, *Morae sigye*'s storyline is rather simple. It deals primarily with three main characters—U-sŏk, T'ae-su, and Hye-rin—and their friendship, love, and tangled lives during the turbulent 1980s, a decade of "negotiated revolutions" and the collective struggle to achieve a constitutional democracy in South Korea. U-sŏk and T'ae-su meet in high school in the mid-1970s. It is their intertwined destinies that ultimately drive the narrative flow. U-sŏk is a smart student who becomes a tutor to T'ae-su, a tough rebel and outsider. After high school, T'ae-su applies for the military academy, but his admission is denied because his father was a communist sympathizer during the Korean War. Unable to pursue a normal life, T'ae-su steps on the wrong side of the tracks and ends up joining the tough underworld of gangs. By contrast, U-sŏk is drafted into an elite unit of paratroopers sent to Kwangju to suppress a popular uprising in the city. Coincidentally, T'ae-su visits friends in Kwangju during the uprising and joins the fight against government troops. After the uprising is brutally crushed, T'ae-su escapes the city and U-sŏk becomes a prosecutor. U-sŏk is assigned to the role of investigating organized crime. A third protagonist, Hye-rin, crosses paths with both T'ae-su and U-sŏk. The daughter of a wealthy casino owner, Hye-rin joins an underground student group involved in the pro-democracy movement. She joins female laborers who are staging a sit-in in the opposition party building. Hye-rin is arrested and tortured by the police. She succumbs to torture, revealing the names of her fellow rebels, before her father, who has government connections, finally secures her release. After his sudden death, Hye-rin runs the casino, but she is under relentless pressure from high-ranking officials who demand bribes. Hye-rin resists and becomes a key witness in the trial of an official who collected slush funds from her father and other businessmen.

Meanwhile, T'ae-su gradually rises in the underworld of organized crime and is approached by a shadowy figure in the government who wants to recruit gangs to support the corrupt government. Upon learning of Hye-rin's dire situation, T'ae-su secretly helps her. U-sŏk successfully prosecutes a high-ranking official and sends him to prison. T'ae-su is soon involved in a fierce gang war and kills the boss of a rival faction. He is arrested and encounters U-sŏk in court. Eventually, T'ae-su is sentenced to death for his crime. After his execution, U-sŏk and Hye-rin go to a mountaintop and scatter T'ae-su's ashes. In situating the complexity of the narrative structure of *Morae sigye*, let me elaborate on the workings of genre-specific codes, conventions, and the functioning of character-centered causality as the key textual devices through which meaning is produced.

The Inter-Workings of Codes and Other Textual Devices in *Morae sigye*

According to Richard Allen, the term "codes" is "used in a loose sense to indicate the interpretive mechanism linking signifier to referent."[11] Using his definition, let me discuss several distinctive codes in *Morae sigye:*

(1) Codes of the Melodramatic Form (*Generic/Stylistic Codes*). A number of South Korean melodramas tend to adopt a "distilled" Classical Hollywood narrative style in which "elements of style [and narrative] function in support of diegetic illusion" and the seeming "reality" of the narrative world is maintained through diverse audio-visual and other non-discursive strategies.[12] Although *Morae sigye* is a highly complex narrative with a number of microconflicts, closures, and plural subplots, its narrative coherence is maintained through continuity editing and a linear chronology. The narrative ultimately converges around two ends: first, the resolution of the main conflict in the form of punishing of the

crooked government official as an allegorical figure who represents the "evils" of the authoritarian regime; second, the affirmation of virtue on the part of the main characters and the elevation of their selfless support of one another in the face of various hardships.

There are also genre-specific audio-visual codes at work. In terms of the visual code, one of the most memorable scenes in *Morae sigye* is its re-creation of the clash between citizen armies and government troops in front of the Kwangju City Hall. In particular, the massacre is depicted through an extended montage. It is generated through a detailed "realist" visual scheme that brings out a high degree of verisimilitude, which is produced through the careful re-creation of historical settings. In particular, the show uses detailed mise-en-scène and authentic locations, strategically inserting several fragments of "real" newsreels intermittently into the main text. Among other things, these visual devices collectively produce a series of powerful and highly emotional reality effects that go far beyond conventional melodrama's limited visual scale and its established visual codes. In addition, there is a nondiegetic musical code at work; a Russian folk song with a sweeping epic tone accentuates the show's tragedy.

(2) In *Morae sigye, textual codes* are often manifested through a tight causal link between characters and their actions. As the much simplified summary above suggests, its narrative structure follows the familiar literary tradition of the bildungsroman. The first half of *Morae sigye* especially includes the highly gendered male bonding between T'ae-su and U-sŏk. Such scenes evoke nostalgic memories of school days with which especially the male audience can easily identify. These main characters literally grow old and mature against the backdrop of familiar historical events and locations in 1980s South Korea. They are constructed as eyewitnesses to historical events and participants in well-publicized political scandals of the 1980s. As a key device of identification for viewers, they are endowed with idealistic traits. T'ae-su is a victim of the deep-running anticommunist sentiment that permeates South Korean society, but he is a gangster with a conscience whose essential goodness is restored at the end. U-sŏk is a hard-working, rule-bound, and conscientious prosecutor who is not swayed by political pressure. Hye-rin is a beautiful, politically savvy, and strong-willed woman who redeems herself by making the right political choices.[13]

In terms of character motivation, *Morae sigye* relies on somewhat two-dimensional melodramatic character types. Moreover, the psychology of these characters is in part shaped by masculinist ideologies of home, male bonding, and romance. But with the narrative's progression, the main characters convey a sense of courage, righteousness, fortitude, and compassion that becomes an effective tool in driving the narrative action. For one thing, unlike characters in more conventional television melodramas, these three characters don't go through sudden transformations or drastic emotional ups and downs. Unlike the television melodramas that include excessive emotional, musical, and narrative accompaniments to the characters' romantic entanglement, the initial "love triangle" between the main characters in *Morae sigye* is rather quickly resolved to sustain the moral seriousness and heroism of the principal characters. U-sŏk and Hye-rin form a camaraderie and deep mutual understanding through their struggle to expose the crimes and injustices committed by the military government.

Nonetheless, the principle characters in *Morae sigye* are still close to what Thomas Elsaesser calls "dramatis personae." They are characters who "figure less as autonomous individuals than to transmit the action and link the various locales within a total constellation."[14] *Morae sigye* also relies on polarized morals, a number of typically engineered coincidences, and medium close-ups that accentuate the principal characters' agonies, self-sacrifice, and pathos. In this way the show tends to reiterate a classic Manichean moral scheme that polarizes good and evil. This problematic narrative strategy is based on a calculated liberal-humanist historical correctness rather than on more informed, radical or multi-perspectival views of the social struggles of the 1980s.

(3) In terms of the workings of *intertextual codes*, what is most striking about *Morae sigye* is that, to local viewers, it has a number of narrative and visual elements that can be readily associated with a vast network of preexisting and complementary popular genres. Historical novels and films, documentaries, reportage, and epic poems are examples of such genres that contain various narratives on the social repression and struggles of 1980s South Korea.

Yet, above all, the strength of *Morae sigye* as a highly popular and multi-accented text lies in its hybridity and shrewd genre-bending aesthetics framed by intertextual codes. For instance, in its many memorable and exciting fight scenes, *Morae sigye* skillfully appropriates the fast-paced aesthetics of violence and the display of well-orchestrated kinetic energy and flying bodies that characterize Hong Kong cinema. Such a skillful and inventive mixture of various narrative styles and visual grammars extends the received formulas of traditional melodrama. Moreover, *Morae sigye*'s skillful appropriation of the stylistic conventions of masculine genres—gangster films and buddy movies—has successfully created a loyal following of male viewers who usually shun the genre. In addition, well-known actors play the three main characters and much of the supporting cast. Ch'oe Min-su, a local actor who plays the role of "tough guy" T'ae-su, was already familiar to South Korean audiences through a number of gangster roles in television and film.

(4) *Ideological Codes. Morae sigye*'s stance on the highly traumatic events of the 1980s is shaped by a kind of progressive historical revisionism that could not be expressed in popular media until the rise of civilian rule in South Korea. Even in the 1990s, mainstream television only minimally dealt with the Kwangju Uprising and other sociopolitical repressions perpetrated by the military dictatorship in the 1980s. Almost all the topics mentioned above, up until the Roh Tae Woo regime (No T'ae-u, 1988–93), were considered untouchable. The South Korean broadcast media throughout the 1980s were tightly controlled by the state, and even in the early 1990s there existed the legacy of state censorship and informal intervention in media institutions. Television networks rarely attempted to adapt the popular struggles of the 1980s into television texts. Only in the early 1990s, after the investigative committee on the Kwangju Uprising (*Kwangju chinsang kyumyŏng wiwŏnhoe*) was held in the National Assembly, did South Korean television begin to address the country's recent political history with a documentary entitled *A Mother's Song.* This documentary—which covers the incidents in Kwangju mainly through survivors' interviews—marked the first time this incident was represented on network television.

Although *Morae sigye* is purely fictional, it nonetheless touches on several highly traumatic historical events of the 1980s, which most viewers can vividly recall. *Morae sigye* contains a number of powerful, epic sequences that closely reassemble painful historical narratives of the contentious 1980s: the Kwangju Uprising of 1980, the massacre of civilians by the South Korean army in the City of Kwangju, political terror staged by members of organized crime who acted as hired guns, the strong and dedicated student movements, the human rights abuses in the state-run "correctional" camps where the "undesirables" (the homeless, mentally retarded, and gangsters) were harshly disciplined, and so forth. In *Morae sigye,* the main characters are inserted strategically into actual or composite historical sites of the late 1970s and 1980s—whether the torture chamber in the state security building, a sit-in staged by female workers in the New Democratic Party headquarters, or a gang's raid on political

236

rallies. They are portrayed as both witnesses and participants in the memorable historical events of the 1980s. In doing so, *Morae sigye* brought to life memories of the formative events of the 1980s that were hitherto frozen into newspaper headlines and newspaper photos of key players and locations.[15]

By flexibly merging a stylized melodramatic format and a dose of visual and rhetorical realism, *Morae sigye* presents a highly entertaining and engrossing drama to local audiences. No wonder "the streets of South Korean cities were almost emptied during the evening hours when *Morae sigye* was telecast on the SBS channel because people were glued to TV sets in their homes or even in taverns."[16] After the phenomenal success of *Morae sigye*, SBS produced an abridged—more fast-paced and visually stunning—version composed of four episodes rather than original twenty-four for individual purchase. Meanwhile *Morae sigye*'s producer, Kim Chong-hak, and writer, Song Chi-na, who together created *The Eye of the Dawn* founded a new production company in 1998, later launching a joint venture with Steven Spielberg's DreamWorks. The local success certainly invited a global interest. The show was exported to China, Taiwan, Indonesia, Thailand, Vietnam, and Hong Kong.[17] *Morae sigye* was also re-aired on network television by popular demand in the spring of 1998. It was one of the most well-packaged cultural products that the South Korean culture industry produced in the 1990s.

Morae sigye as a Vehicle of the Politics of Memory in South Korea

Significantly, *Morae sigye* not only garnered phenomenal ratings but also rekindled debates about the nature and role of the Kwangju Uprising. To a considerable extent, it awoke viewers from their collective amnesia regarding the Kwangju massacre and the social oppression suffered under the authoritarian regime of Chun Doo Hwan (Chŏn Tu-hwan) in the 1980s. *Morae sigye* captured popular attention by "not only divulging the saga of the notorious South Korean military dictatorship but also bringing the *unsayables* during the dictatorial era to the public domain, thereby turning them into the *sayables*."[18] A number of cultural critics would agree that *Morae sigye* has provided a welcome opportunity for exploring—albeit momentarily—the larger question of the politics of popular memory. By tackling the still thorny and once unrepresentable historical events on otherwise generally conservative and commercially motivated television, *Morae sigye* created what Horace Newcombe calls a kind of charged "cultural forum" through which contemporary South Koreans came to remember and discuss the horrors of Kwangju and other contentious events of the 1980s.[19]

Yet this does not mean that *Morae sigye* is a radically historicized text. After all, it hardly takes a radical antimelodramatic stance, nor a more extensive and self-reflexive documentary turn. With all the aforementioned rich visual and textual realism and sense of historical accuracy, *Morae sigye* still is a schizophrenic text. For instance, the strong melodramatic elements and clichés create havoc for the show's realist elements. The romance between T'ae-su and Hye-rin is deployed as a crucial and effective motor in the first half of the show. However, this works as a double-edged sword. It helps maintain the quintessential melodramatic flow, generating both pleasure and easy points of identification to the viewers. Yet at times this formulaic narrative structure tends to destabilize the drama's *progressive historical codes*, which may anchor more politicized or subversive readings of the dramatic social events that occurred under the military dictatorship.

That *Morae sigye* could even address these traumatic historical events and repressed histories signals the loosening of state regulation during the 1990s. Under the Kim Young Sam regime (Kim Yŏng-sam, 1992–97), the clearing of colonialist history became an official mantra. Under these circumstances television producers found some room to maneuver in representing the once-repressed histories of the 1980s and translating them into a range of media forms. Also the generation of the 1980s—the so-called 386 generation of people who were born in the 1960s, grew up and went to college in the turbulent 1980s, and who are now in their middle and late thirties—has moved into the mainstream of cultural translating, albeit unevenly, their collective experiences into various popular forms. At the same time, they have capitalized on people's desire to experience past events through accessible popular genres and a diverse array of cultural texts. In doing so, the cultural producers in 1990s South Korea became accidental historians in the field of popular memory.

Conclusion: Television and the Representation of History in the Era of Prosthetic Memory

Morae sigye is a remarkable landmark text, yet a series of unanswered questions about its representation of history still lingers: Is this the right way to narrate and construct traumatic historical events? Is not narrative an incomplete medium for representing history? Does not the spectacularization of history through a mass-produced medium actually efface sociohistorical struggles staged by anonymous people?

Although I do not have definitive answers to these questions, let me respond to them. First, *Morae sigye* is in a limited sense a "progressive" text that brought the memory of the Kwangju Uprising and the social struggles of the 1980s to life more vividly than any public (state-endorsed) commemorative works, ceremonies, or exhibitions did. *Morae sigye* should be placed in the larger context of South Korean television, located unevenly at the intersection between the European public service tradition and American commercialism. In that sense, I find it fair to say that it was what John Hartley calls a "useful" program for the public—especially for the younger generation of South Koreans who only remember the Kwangju massacre and the horrors of state-run correctional camps as collections of still photos or through limited literary works.[20] In this respect, *Morae sigye* displays both enormous commercial and pedagogical potential.

However, the South Korean media environment has undergone radical changes since *Morae sigye* was first aired in the mid-1990s. Cable and satellite television have become new areas of rapidly growing media markets in South Korea where local culture industries freely appropriate transnational images. In the midst of this explosion of hi-tech media and electronic images, one must be acutely aware that although television can function occasionally as a useful repository of cultural memories, television is an awkward medium to enact historical documentation and trigger public reactivation of historically repressed memories. Television, engrossed in live coverage and signifiers of immediacy—which is its ideology—lives in the present. As Mary Ann Doane puts it, television "thrives on its own forgettability" and the recycling of disembodied historical signs and signifiers.[21] In doing so, it has a tendency to privatize historical time into the pool of floating historical images as "hyper-realist historiogemes," which are ultimately to be consumed. As Anton Kaes aptly puts it, "A memory preserved in filmed images does not vanish, but the sheer mass of historical images transmitted by today's media weakens the link between public memory and personal experience. The past is in danger of becoming a rapidly expanding collection of images easily retrievable but isolated from time and space, available in an eternal present by pushing a button on the remote control."[22] If one can accept a general proposition that the representation of history in the current context of the rapid-fire succession of television images presents both pedagogical possibilities and cultural anxieties, *Morae sigye* has provided a rare opportunity to ponder seriously the elusive place of popular memory at the dawn of an increasingly media-saturated world.

CODA: Pleasurable Negotiations and the Construction of the Past in Televisual Texts

> History is what hurts.
> Fredric Jameson

In the mid-1990s, in a Midwestern college town in the United States, I, with my friend, ran a film club whose members were mostly South Korean graduate students and their spouses. The group met once a month and watched mostly European "art films," contemporary South Korean films, and occasionally South Korean television dramas. After the viewing, the members would engage in discussions regarding the themes, narrative and textual devices in, and the social effects of the films the club members viewed. On one occasion, the group chose to watch *Morae sigye*, a hugely popular television serial that almost every South Korean in that town was talking about.

Since I was asked to lead the discussion, in preparing for my presentation, I watched *Morae sigye* several times. My gut feeling was that though I thought *Morae sigye* was an exceptionally well-made television text with high production values and brilliant visual representation that clearly exceeded the received norms and scales of conventional South Korean television melodrama, from the beginning, I didn't like its schizophrenic structure: strong "realist" and historical elements that dealt with the traumatic social wounds of 1980s South Korea were constantly interlaced and interrupted by excessive and typical melodramatic elements—in particular the heightened and personalized narratives on love, devotion, and camaraderie between the main characters as well as the Manichean conflicts between good and evil. I felt the extensive use of historical events and situations in *Morae sigye* was to promote the program's status and credibility as a "serious" melodrama on the 1980s and to target the older audiences who still vividly remembered this decade of social suffering and popular struggles against the dictatorship.

After the group viewed *Morae sigye*, I argued that the program should be regarded as a new breed of televisual text that attempted to commodify the memories of emotionally charged past historical events in calculated ways. I emphasized that I would prefer a "serious" documentary or a self-reflexive docudrama if the text was to tackle charged historical events—such as the Kwangju Uprising—and to narrativize the mem-

240

ories of the painful past. I added that *Morae sigye*'s mixing and blurring of fictional and nonfictional elements as well as the use of a sentimentalized mode of address troubled me. I said that in order to create reality effects, the drama shamelessly recycled images, cultural signifiers and signs of the 1980s, and that it might signal a new trend in the South Korean television industry in the postauthoritarian period to package history as visual signs for popular consumption.

Upon finishing my presentation, I immediately met "resistance" from other members. The majority of them said they truly enjoyed *Morae sigye*. Others seemed to be impressed with the kind of "hybrid" representational strategy *Morae sigye* took in grafting public history and private stories. Some members told me that the drama reminded them of many wrongdoings and the political repression of the 1980s, thereby giving them moments for reflecting on the past. One member, during the discussion, told me that I seemed to regard the memories of 1980s social struggles as "something that should be consecrated," and that I seemed to resist any kind of textualization of historical events into the "lowly" melodramatic form. Another member, much younger than I, told me that I demonstrated an "elitist" approach to popular films and dramas. He added that, as I was a college student in the 1980s, I had generation-specific memories and an intellectual "bias" that led to my rather harsh judgment of *Morae sigye*.

I was both frustrated and intrigued by these unexpected responses of the film club members. Such a mix of frustration and surprise left a lasting impression on me. Weeks later, when I researched South Korean daily newspapers and weeklies that covered *Morae sigye*'s phenomenal success and the debates and social commentaries it initiated in South Korea, I came to realize that I definitely missed something. I realized that by focusing on *Morae sigye*'s textual form and narrative strategies through an academic lens, I did not pay due attention to the textual effects and subsequent social dialogues *Morae sigye* engendered. Years later when I finally decided to write a paper on *Morae sigye* and the kind of the politics of memory it mediated, I saw the drama several times. And this time I found myself becoming more appreciative of the text. Although still there were moments of uneasiness in me when I was viewing the segments in it that were heavily framed by the generic conventions of South Korean melodrama and Hong Kong action films, I realized that the program could stir emotions, pathos, and affects. It demonstrated an uncommon ability to awaken once-submerged memories of the turbulent and brutal realities of the 1980s.

I came to realize that even with all its "defects"—the glorification of male bonding, moral schematization, and the short-circuiting of social issues into personal ones, *Morae sigye*, within its ideological and institutional confines, did an admirable job in combining elements of realism and romance, passion and action, suffering and pathos, fictional narrative and historicized memory that could emotionally and affectively appeal to the wider audiences. It was only recently that I came across Linda Williams's writing that attempted to restore the "importance of melodramatic pathos [and affects]" against a dominant view in critical television studies that privileged the "realist" text over the melodramatic one regarding the "right" style of historical representation in visual genres. I have gradually realized that what was lacking in my initial reading of *Morae sigye* was not to look at its potential and power to move the viewers—what Linda Williams aptly calls "[the affective process] of being moved by a moving picture [image]."[23]

Currently I teach classes on the politics and poetics of televisual texts in which I use *Morae sigye* with other well-known filmic texts—such as *Battleship Potempkin*, *JFK*, *Shoah*, *Saving Private Ryan*, *Hiroshima Mon Amor*, *Schindler's List*, and *Petal* (*Kkonnip*), a South Korean film that dealt with the massacre in Kwangju and the lingering violence of the 1980s in a politically nuanced and aesthetically experimental fashion. A number of my students consider *Morae sigye* as an engrossing text that can bring out not only the pleasures of viewing but also a charged emotional experience in which to think about the 1980s and the lived experiences of people under dictatorship. They are impressed with *Morae sigye*'s special ability to evoke the particular historical events and milieu, while, against my expectation, they seem to be intimidated and occasionally bored by the aforementioned canonic texts that attempt to reconstruct historical events and moods in a more serious tone and through more complex narrative strategies. My intended aim of using and cross-viewing these well-known texts in the classroom is to make the students aware of the various modes—documentary realism, cinematic modernism, postmodern hyperrealism, televisual melodrama, and such—of representing history in visual media. At the same time, I want them to begin to understand critically the role of melodrama's complicated relations to history, historical storytelling, and memory culture. By juxtaposing more politically and aesthetically experimental visual texts and *Morae sigye*, I have intended to present a forum for my students to come to terms with multiple viewpoints on, and ways of representing, history.

Looking back, *Morae sigye* turns out to be a more useful and performative television drama than I initially expected in that it invites a range of questions on the various modes of historical storytelling, as well as on affective responses in the classroom. Given that the current generation of youth live in a media-saturated world where all kinds of "reality-based" programs, twenty-four-hour news flows, and docudramas now compete and lay claim for a piece of history, *Morae sigye* becomes a useful tool for discussing how fact, fiction, and memories are crucial elements in visualizing history through popular genres and existing televisual conventions. Furthermore, I came to recognize that well-crafted melodramas equipped with serious or reflective historical sensibility, pathos, and imagination can, every once in a while, provide not only "pleasurable negotiations" between the text and its readers but also offer new possibilities for historical representation and reconstruction. In the age of omnipresent yet elusive memory culture, shaped by various forms of reality-based programs and televisual texts, I believe social melodrama can re-articulate historical issues to a significant degree while it cannot necessarily resolve the question of how televisual texts should represent history.

Notes

1. "Special Dramas" in South Korea are made to air on exceptional occasions and are thereby invested with more resources and preparation than average television dramas. In the South Korean television scene, for economic reasons, daytime soaps do not exist, though some foreign-made and homemade mini-series are run on cable channels. Although such American melodramas as *Dallas, Dynasty,* and *Beverly Hills 90210* were aired on South Korean TV in the 1990s, the reception of these foreign products was a mixed one. They have never been more popular than homegrown dramas. In fact domestic prime-time melodramas dominate South Korean television programming. This certainly warrants nuanced and historicized studies of the formation of drama viewership as well as the differentiated reception of foreign and local television dramas in South Korea. For detailed studies of various types of melodramas and soap operas, see Richard Allen, *Channels of Discourse, Reassembled: Television and Contemporary Criticism* (Chapel Hill: University of North Carolina Press, 1992); Manuel Alvarado and John Thompson, eds., *The Media Reader* (London: BFI, 1990); Ien Ang, *Living Room Wars: Rethinking Media Audience for a Postmodern World* (New York: Routledge, 1996); John Fiske, *Television Culture* (London: Methuen, 1987); Christine Gledhill, ed., *Home Is Where the Heart Is: Studies in Melodrama and the Woman's Film* (London: BFI, 1990); and Marcia Landy, ed., *Imitations of Life: A Reader on Film and Television Melodrama* (Detroit: Wayne State University Press, 1990).
2. Chae-ch'ŏl Chŏng, "An Analysis of Research on Korean Television Drama

(Han'guk t'ellebijyŏn tŭrama yŏn'gu kyŏnghyang puksŏk)," in *The Lover: Television Drama, Culture, and Society (Aein: TV tŭrama, munhwa, kŭrigo sahoe)*, ed. Hwang In-sŏng and Wŏn Yong-jin (Seoul: Hannarae, 1997).

3. As most of the titles of these melodramas suggest, they are concerned with love stories often couched in fairy-tale endings, excessive emotional invest-ment, and a moral polarity. Yet in recent times there have also emerged less formulaic forms of melodrama that deal with more serious family and women's issues on matrimonial and sexual problems. Min-u Lee and Chong Heup Cho, "Women Watching Together: An Ethnographic Study of Korean Soap Opera Fans in the U.S.," *Cultural Studies* 4 (1991): 30–45.

4. In-sŏng and Yong-jin, eds., *The Lover.*

5. The semiotic or narratological approach to popular media forms tends to "neaten up" the texts under interrogation and often fails to tackle the histor-ically specific features of the texts and the different social context of viewing. Nonetheless, semiotic analysis carries potent explanatory power for decoding a number of textual devices and signifying mechanisms.

6. Nancy Abelmann, "The Melodramatic Imagination in Contemporary South Korea: Preliminary Thoughts on Television Dramas," (Urbana-Champaign: University of Illinois, unpublished manuscript, 1996); Minu Lee and Chong Heup Cho, "Women Watching Together"; Sŏk-kyŏng Hong, "Television Drama and Social Communication," in In-sŏng and Yong-jin, eds., *The Lover.*

7. Chin-song Kim, "Aestheticizing Poverty in Television Drama: The Sons and Daughters," in *TV: Looking Closely, Reading from a Distance,* ed. Hyŏnsil munhwa yŏn'gu (Seoul: Hyŏnsil munhwa yŏn'gu, 1993).

8. David Thorburn, "Television Melodrama," in *Television: The Critical View,* ed. Horace Newcomb (Oxford: Oxford University Press, 1976).

9. It should be pointed out that television melodramas are different from docu-dramas in that the former do not deal with historical events in any serious sense or demonstrate any desire to grapple with the burdens of representing the past in a serious manner. In addition, in "serious" docudrama, such as "The First Republic," "The Second Republic," and "The Third Republic," the melodramatic imagination and conventions appear only minimally. South Korean docudramas tend to depict a man's world and a monumental-ized history accompanied by excessive veneration of the great men and their heroics. Melodramas, on the other hand, are often charged with heightened emotional realism, sensationalism, and fantasy solutions. Jacky Bratton et al., *Melodrama: Stage, Picture, Screen* (London: BFI, 1994); Lynne Joyrich, "All That Television Allows: TV Melodrama, Postmodernism, and Consumer Culture," *Camera Obscura* 16 (1988): 129–54.

10. Regarding the multiple definitions of cinematic realism, see Julia Hallem and Margaret Marshment, *Realism and Popular Cinema* (Manchester: Man-chester University Press, 2000).

11. Richard Allen, "A Reader-Oriented Poetics of the Soap Opera," in *Imita-tions of Life: A Reader on Film and Television Melodrama,* ed. Marcia Landy (Detroit: Wayne State University Press, 1991), 513.

12. Allen, *Channels of Discourse, Reassembled,* 502.

13. Actually there is another notable character, Chae-hŭi, who is Hye-rin's body-guard. Chae-hŭi secretly loves Hye-rin and protects her. Chae-hŭi dies while trying to save Hye-rin when she is kidnapped by a gang. Chae-hŭi is a romantic figure who is used to boost the tragic structure of feeling and romanticism in *Morae sigye*.

14. Thomas Elsaesser, "Tales of Sound and Fury: Observations on the Family Melodrama," in Gledhill, *Home Is Where the Heart Is*, 44.

15. Kyong Liong Kim (Kim Kyŏng-yong), "A Semiotic Analysis of *Morae sigye (Morae sigye ŭi kihohakchŏk punsŏk)*," *Contemporary Thought (Hyŏndae sasang)* 5 (1998): 185–216.

16. Kyong Liong Kim, "A Semiotic Analysis of a Korean TV Drama: *Morae sigye*," paper presented at the 83rd Annual Meeting of the National Communication Association (1997).

17. *Daily Sports*, February 11, 2000.

18. Kyong Liong Kim, "A Semiotic Analysis of a Korean TV Drama: *Morae sigye*," 1. (Italics mine.)

19. Horace Newcomb, *Television: The Critical View* (New York: Oxford University Press, 2000).

20. John Hartley, *Uses of Television* (New York: Routledge, 1999).

21. Mary Ann Doane, "Information, Crisis, Catastrophe," in *The Historical Film: History and Memory in Media,* ed. Marcia Landy (New Brunswick, NJ: Rutgers University Press, 2001), 272.

22. Anton Kaes, *From Hitler to Heimat: The Return of History as Film* (Cambridge: Harvard University Press, 1989), 198.

23. Linda Williams, "Melodrama Revised," in *Refiguring American Film Genres,* ed. Nick Browne (Berkeley: University of California Press, 1998), 47.

Contributors

Nancy Abelmann teaches in the Departments of Anthropology, East Asian Languages, and Women's Studies at the University of Illinois at Urbana-Champaign. She is the author of *The Melodrama of Mobility: Women, Class, and Talk in Contemporary South Korea* (University of Hawai'i Press, 2003) and *Echoes of the Past, Epics of Dissent: A South Korean Social Movement* (University of California Press, 1996).

Jinsoo An is a PhD candidate in the Department of Film, Television, and Digital Media at the University of California–Los Angeles. His essay "*The Killer:* Cult Film and Transcultural (Mis-)Reading" appeared in *At Full Speed: Hong Kong Cinema in a Borderless World* (edited by Esther C. M. Yau). He is currently working on the question of "Japan" in South Korean cinema of the 1960s.

Eunsun Cho is a doctoral candidate at the School of Cinema-Television, University of Southern California. Her publications include "The Female Body and Enunciation in *Adada* and *Surrogate Mother*," in David E. James and Kyung Hyun Kim's *Im Kwon-Taek: The Making of A Korean Cinema* (Wayne State University Press, 2002).

Hye Seung Chung is a postdoctoral fellow in the Department of Asian Languages and Cultures at the University of Michigan. She has contributed to *Asian Cinema, Film Quarterly,* and *Film and Philosophy,* with additional essays to appear in the forthcoming anthologies *East Main Street: Asian Pacific American Popular Culture, New Korean Cinema,* and *Contemporary Korean Cinema and Society.*

David Scott Diffrient is a PhD candidate in the Department of Film, Television, and Digital Media at the University of California–Los Angeles. He has written articles on contemporary South Korean cinema for such journals as *Asian Cinema, CineAction,* and *Film Quarterly,* and

247

contributed co-written essays to the forthcoming anthologies *Contemporary Korean Cinema and Society* and *New Korean Cinema*.

Kyung Hyun Kim teaches in the Department of East Asian Languages and Literatures and serves as the director of the Film and Video Center at the University of California–Irvine. His latest book is *The Remasculinization of Korean Cinema* (Duke University Press, 2004).

Soyoung Kim teaches in the School of Film and Multimedia at the Korean National University of the Arts. She has published extensively on Golden Age Korean film, women's cinema in South Korea, and on contemporary Korean cinema and media.

Keehyeung Lee is an assistant professor in the Department of Journalism and Mass Communication at Kyunghee University. He specializes in cultural and media studies and has published articles and book chapters on the genealogy of television, TV fandom, and the emergence of cultural studies in South Korea.

Kathleen McHugh teaches in the Department of English and the Department of Film, Television, and Digital Media at the University of California–Los Angeles. She specializes in film feminism and melodrama, topics she explores in *American Domesticity: From How-To Manual to Hollywood Melodrama* (Oxford University Press, 1999) and in a forthcoming book on Jane Campion.

Index

Page numbers in italics refer to figures.

CPSIA information can be obtained
at www.ICGtesting.com
Printed in the USA
LVHW082306300119
605889LV00024B/944/P

9 780814 332535